MW00777870

ROBERT RUARK'S
AFRICA

ROBERT RUARK'S
AFRICA

by
Robert C. Ruark

Collected and Annotated
by
Michael McIntosh

Illustrated with Original Etchings
by
Bruce Langton

COUNTRYSPORT PRESS
TRAVERSE CITY, MICHIGAN

To the hunters, past and present,
Who have met their souls in Africa ...

ILLUSTRATIONS

ROBERT RUARK'S

AFRICA

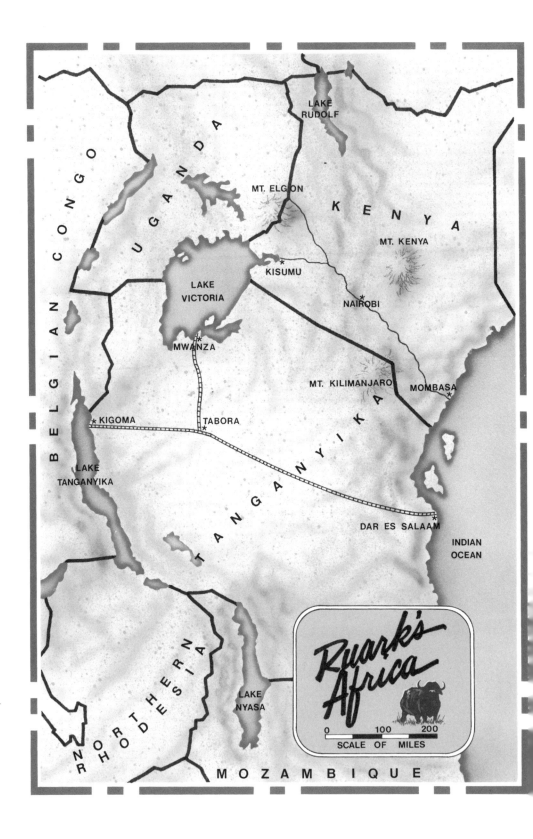

INTRODUCTION

A WRITER IN SEARCH OF A SOUL

I n June 1951, Robert Chester Ruark, Jr., fled from New York City to Nairobi, Kenya, pursued by demons. He was thirty-five years old. He owned a mustache and a receding hairline and an enormous reputation as a writer of acerbic social commentary. He brought with him a wife, luggage that weighed 278 pounds over airline allowance, and a liver already suffering the ravages of too much alcohol. He would die, largely at the behest of that same organ, almost precisely fourteen years later. He described waking in the African bush for the first time as a feeling of having, for the moment at least, outdistanced his soul.

Which was not an unfamiliar problem, because Robert Ruark and his soul never were constant companions.

His was a life, both personal and professional, largely governed by polarity and contradictions. He was a poor boy who made a fortune and never really knew what to do about it. He was an extremely skillful reporter who gained his first flush of fame writing wise-guy opinions. He was a serious novelist without any great talent for purely imaginative fiction. He was an enormously gifted writer who left behind a body of work remarkable for the unevenness of its quality. He was one of the best-known and most controversial writers in America, willing to tackle any subject but best remembered as a sporting writer. He was both a celebrity and a mystery.

Even now, twenty-six years dead, he is revered by some as an iconoclast, dismissed by others as a bombast and a boozebat.

He was all those things. Most of all, he was a writer and a man in search of his soul, a connection that broke and re-established more than once in his lifetime. Though it never was a permanent bond, Robert Ruark and his soul found their closest harmony in Africa, and out of that, he created some of the twentieth century's finest African hunting literature.

Now, Ruark's reputation rests largely upon one non-fiction book and two novels – *Horn of the Hunter, Something of Value,* and *Uhuru.* To a lesser extent, it also rests upon *Use Enough Gun,* a slapdash collection of excerpts from his earlier work, put together and published shortly after his death.

What laid the foundation of that reputation during his own lifetime, however, were magazine articles. Although he wrote more than four thousand pieces during the nearly twenty years he served as a syndicated columnist for the Scripps-Howard newspaper chain, Ruark's best genre was the magazine feature, a form that offered just enough space for him to develop his themes without losing control of them, as he tended to do in his later novels.

No one has ever compiled Ruark's complete magazine bibliography, but the total certainly would exceed one thousand articles, most of them written in the last fifteen years of his life. During one period in the early 1950s, he turned out sixty-five magazine stories in eighteen months, an effort that earned roughly $100,000. Others have been equally prolific, but few have accomplished that volume of work at a level of quality equal to Ruark's.

Between 1951 and 1965, his love-affair with Africa produced more than thirty magazine pieces, twenty of which are presented here, collected for the first time in book form. Together, they make up a fascinating, surprisingly coherent narrative of a man discovering himself.

Which brings us back to the matter of Robert Ruark and his unruly soul.

They seem to have started out together well enough. He was born December 29, 1915, is Southport, North Carolina, on the mainland across from Smith Island and Cape Fear. His father was a bookkeeper, his mother a teacher. Judging upon the evidence of his writing, the greatest influence in Ruark's early life was his maternal grandfather, Captain Edward Hall Adkins, whom he later made famous as the Old Man of "The Old Man and the Boy" stories.

From these we get an image of idyllic childhood, as if Robert Ruark were created from a montage of Tom Sawyer, Huck Finn, and young King Arthur, shaped by the pervasive presence of the archetypal mentor, who represents infinite wisdom in a slightly seedy package. From the Old Man, the Boy learns the lore of the outdoors, of hunting, of sportsmanship. He learns a philosophy built upon the ethic of hard work and self-sufficiency and personal honor. He learns first-hand the cycle of life and death and the handing-down from one generation to another the lessons necessary for the ancient rituals of passage.

In the truest sense, the "Old Man and the Boy" stories are the stuff of myth and archetype, built upon a theme that exists in the art and folklore of every human culture since human cultures began. Taken strictly upon their own merits, they are splendid pieces of literature. Whether they also are reliable autobiography is highly questionable.

Using art as a means of understanding the artist is seldom truly productive. What seems so temptingly real is usually, by the very nature of art, a fabrication. While Ruark certainly based the Old Man stories on his own childhood relationship with his grandfather, we cannot simply substitute Ruark for the Boy and take the stories as literal reports of fact – although Ruark himself certainly invites us to do so, as his Author's Note to *The Old Man and the Boy* in book form simply says: "Anybody who reads this book is bound to realize that I had a real fine time as a kid."

Perhaps. But these are stories, after all, and Ruark was a writer, and a writer's job is to manipulate literal reality into images of deeper, broader truth. At a figurative level, the stories ring with unmistakably authentic feeling and thought, and to that extent they explain something of the foundation upon which Ruark wished his life were built.

But are they literal fact? I doubt it. And even if they are, they leave something glaringly incomplete.

Almost without exception, the few people who in recent years have attempted any serious understanding of the man and his writing seem to accept "The Old Man and the Boy" stories as autobiography and therefore find themselves at a loss to explain why Ruark bore so little semblance to the man the Boy should have become.

Ruark may have wondered as much himself. The central characters of his later novels are all men who struggle with similar questions. In the cases of Peter McKenzie and Craig Price and Brian Dermott and Alec Barr, Ruark's best answer is that circumstance is the ultimate victimizer. And as he commented early in 1953, announcing that he was moving to Europe and radically changing his approach as a syndicated columnist: "I have a yen to be what I was [a reporter] before public demand perverted me into a wise guy."

His obvious sense of powerlessness, of being unable to chart the course of his own life in the face of circumstance, is both a contradiction and a key. In the fall of 1930, shortly after Captain Adkins died, Ruark entered the University of North Carolina as a fifteen-year-old freshman, and over the following years made his way in the world quite by his own devices, apparently fueled by sheer determination.

Young, unsophisticated, and as penniless as many another boy during the Great Depression, Ruark nonetheless worked his way through college; graduated in 1935 with a degree in journalism; landed a reporting job with the *News-Messenger* in Hamlet, North Carolina; worked aboard the merchant ship *Sundance* as an ordinary seaman, for the Works Progress Administration as an accountant, and for the Washington *Daily News* as a copyboy and then a sportswriter; married Virginia Webb on August 12, 1938; and was assistant city editor at the *Daily News* by the beginning of World War II.

Following wartime service with the U.S. Navy, he hired on with the Scripps-Howard Newspaper Alliance and in less than a year was the most controversial, and therefore most noticed, columnist in America. Further exercising a truly prodigious talent for satire, he wrote four novels: *Grenadine Etching: Her Life and Loves* (1947), *I Didn't Know It Was Loaded* (1948), *One For the Road* (1949), and *Grenadine's Spawn* (1953). Although the approach might seem a bit hokey by current standards, all four are as fresh, funny, witty, and sparkling as some of his later novels – especially *Poor No More* and *The Honey Badger* – are ponderous and plodding.

By 1950, Ruark was a celebrity, the toast of New York's boulevard-ier society, crony of Toots Shor and Bernard Baruch and Frank Costello and everyone else who was anybody. His income, about $50,000 a year, was sufficient to provide a Midtown penthouse apartment, mink coats for Virginia, all the amenities of an urban society going through its first serious change since the 1920s.

By any definition, it was a long way for a rural North Carolina boy to have traveled, and Ruark accomplished it all by exercising the hard work and self-sufficiency central to the Old Man's legacy. But for Ruark himself, success was an empty room, insubstantial as a theatre set, a flimsy bulwark against a reality that might come crashing down at any moment to sweep everything away.

By early 1951, his indulgence in what he later called "saloon society" had brought him literally to collapse. Surveying the wreckage of what once had been a fully functional liver, his physician suggested that in return for a radical change of living habits he might manage to survive a year. A few months later, he and Virginia landed in Kenya.

As I said earlier, an inability to gain control over his own life goes a long way toward explaining the contradictory nature of Robert Ruark. His success was entirely of his own making, and yet he never believed it could last. At the core, he was a deeply fearful man, lacking all but the merest shreds of confidence in his own ability, perpetually afraid that the hard-won acclaim and success could be snatched away in an instant. If he didn't literally consider himself a fraud, he certainly didn't feel that his ability could justify what he had accomplished.

Like Macbeth, Ruark lacked a vital element of character, and although in Ruark's case it could hardly be called a tragic flaw, it was a destructive one nonetheless. What was missing in Ruark was the ability to be himself in the face of success.

In April 1953, he and Virginia left the United States to take up residence in Spain, and in November *Reader's Digest* published a Ruark essay titled "Good-bye, New York!" in which he outlines his reasons for cutting back his career as a columnist and becoming an expatriate. "My day," he writes, "was telephones, appointments, and invitations I couldn't duck... I never seemed to have time to write until everybody else was in bed." He is happy in Spain, he says, because there he is "fettered by no chains not of my own making."

One has to wonder who he thought made the chains that fettered him in New York. He blames the city and the demands of a lifestyle he apparently believed he was obliged to adopt, and through it all he seemed genuinely unaware that he had any choice in the matter. If the crucial question is why did Robert Ruark destroy himself in pursuit of an ultimately empty way of living, the most compelling answer is that he thought he had to.

Some have explained Ruark's excesses as attempts to compensate for the pleasures he believed he'd missed during his college years and later as a young man during the Depression. Perhaps Ruark himself even believed that; he did, after all, write a semi-autobiographical novel titled *Poor No More* in which the central character discovers little of substance in a wealthy life.

That view may hold some truth, but as an ultimate answer it smacks too much of sophomore psychology. It oversimplifies a complex and troubled man. More accurately, I believe, Ruark was unable to recognize himself as worthy of his own success. He seemed to believe that he must meet certain requirements, and the life he adopted was almost a caricature, a cliche of the successful writer as hard-drinking carouser whose lust for living transcends the need for sleep, peace, and rejuvenation of the spirit.

Had he not discovered Africa when he did, Ruark almost certainly would not have lived to see his fortieth birthday, and he would have left behind little of enduring worth. As it happened, however, Africa provided not only a reprieve from self-destruction but also engendered the full reach of his talent.

At first, even the decision to visit Kenya seems to have been motivated as much by Ruark's fatal flaw as by any serious interest in hunting big game. Ernest Hemingway was Ruark's hero, and it's hardly surprising that Hemingway's lifestyle was a blueprint for the one Ruark took on. He considered Hemingway "the best writer over the course who ever lived." Nearly twenty years before, Hemingway had written brilliantly of Africa and of hunting with Philip Percival, who by Ruark's time was retired as the dean of East African professional hunters. Ruark booked his first safari with the young Harry Selby, Percival's former apprentice and professional heir, and it isn't hard to imagine that he was looking for the same mysticism that Hemingway had found in big-game hunting.

What Ruark found apparently was not exactly what he'd expected. In a particularly revealing passage in *Horn of the Hunter*, he describes the sweat and exertion and gut-twisting fear of hunting Cape buffalo: "I got up on my feet. I had the gun with me. 'God *damn* Ernest Hemingway,' I said bitterly, and when the bull lurched up, crooked-kneed, I walloped him."

Hemingway and rude surprises notwithstanding, Africa laid firm claim to Robert Ruark, as the stories you'll find in Part I of this book clearly attest. The first safari showed him, finally, something more substantial than saloon society could hope to offer, and even if he didn't understand that saloon society was not to blame for what he had become, he at least got a clear view of a better future.

Horn of the Hunter, published in July 1953, was his finest extended work to date and still is one of the best African books of the latter twentieth century. But even before *Horn* came off the presses, Kenya itself provided an even greater opportunity.

In early October 1952, the secret society that called itself Mau Mau turned East Africa into a bloodbath. Under the leadership of Jomo Kenyatta, young men of the Kikuyu tribe determined to drive British settlers from Kenya through a campaign of terror. By October 20, forty-three whites had been slaughtered in ferocious attacks on isolated farms, livestock had been horribly mutilated in blood rituals, Britain had imposed martial law in the colony, and a batallion of Lancashire Fusiliers had landed in Nairobi.

In mid-December, Ruark also landed in Nairobi, all set for his second safari, only to find the country in turmoil. He eventually got to his hunting and wrote some splendid magazine pieces about it, but his journalistic instinct recognized in Mau Mau a tide of history about to break. His first story on the terror, which leads off Part II of this collection, is as solid a piece of reporting as he ever did. And it was not to be the last.

For all the tumult and misery it brought to its victims, black and white alike, Mau Mau ironically was a stroke of extraordinary good fortune for Robert Ruark. He had just discovered an immense personal fondness for Africa and had staked a small claim as an African writer. When Mau Mau made Kenya a source of international news, Ruark was in a perfect position to interpret what was happening for the rest of the world.

From early 1953 through mid-1955, Ruark continued to report on Mau Mau, either incidentally or as the main subject of magazine articles, but his major work of the period was a novel. About the time *Horn of the Hunter* was published, he had commented: "I knew someday I was going to put my guts on the table and write a real book, or a real try at a book. *Horn of the Hunter* gave me a chance for a practice swing – a straight book with no flashy phrases, no gags, just an honest piece of writing."

On November 24, 1954, Ruark delivered to his agent Harold Matson a 300,000-word typescript titled *Something of Value*. It was a novel about Kenya, about the British settlers who had struggled to establish farms in the Kenya Highlands, about hunting, about Mau Mau and the horrors it brought. It is big, bloody, and unquestionably Ruark's finest book.

Despite decidedly mixed reviews, *Something of Value* was a smashing success, a best-seller even before it appeared on bookstore shelves in April 1955. It was the Book-of-the-Month Club's main selection the following month; Metro-Goldwyn-Mayer paid more than $300,000 for movie rights and signed Ruark to write the film treatment. By the end of August, Book-of-the-Month Club had sold 200,000 copies, bookstores another 80,000. Eventually, sales in both hard and soft-cover, in English and at least ten other languages, went well past a million copies.

So now Robert Ruark was truly rich. He and Virginia owned a summer villa at Palamos in the Costa Brava region of Spain and a winter home in Barcelona, kept a townhouse and Rolls-Royce in London, and spent part of every year in Kenya, hunting with Harry Selby, whom he had made into an international celebrity. Since February 1953, when the first "Old Man and the Boy" column was published, he had appeared on the masthead of *Field & Stream* as an associate editor. He traveled the world, writing on the primitive peoples of New Guinea, on trout fishing in New Zealand, tiger hunting in India, on Lenny Bruce and heads of state. And he was the world's foremost writer on hunting African big game.

For a while, he and his soul kept company together.

That Ruark found Africa profoundly moving is clear in virtually every story he wrote. Africa afforded him an interest larger than himself, an opportunity to test codes of conduct and philosophies of living. In the process, he underwent the sort of transformation that many, though by no means all, hunters achieve – from exuberant shooter to passionate hunter to that curious state of grace in which hunting becomes an exercise of the mind and spirit.

Africa could not, however, ultimately change the nature of the man. A newspaperman who was a colleague of Ruark's around 1940 described him as "brash, ambitious, cocky, fast, and good." Not long after *Something of Value* was published, Ruark described himself by saying, "Look, I ain't humble, and I ain't played Uriah Heep lately." In 1962, a *Newsweek* writer observed: "He is, when the light is wrong, an arrogant, boastful bore." The old insecurities, the old self-doubts, and the old, abrasive, destructive ways of dealing with them plagued him still.

By 1960, his heavy drinking had once again reached a critical stage, and he was abusing every friendship, every relationship, every means of emotional support in his life. Only Africa itself seemed to offer any shred of salvation, but Africa was once again on the brink of change.

Colonialism was dying, suffocated by rising tides of African nationalism, and Robert Ruark deplored the future he saw. In mid-1962, he published *Uhuru*, his last great novel. Essentially a sequel to *Something of Value*, *Uhuru* (which is the Swahili word for "freedom") explores the coming of independence and black rule in Kenya.

The novel is blunt and powerful, filled with rage at the imminent destruction of a way of life not only for the soon-to-be-dispossessed British but for native Kenyans as well. In an NBC television news special aired June 1, 1962, under the title "Robert Ruark's Africa," Ruark sums up his view of the matter in comments that also capture the central theme of *Uhuru*: The Africans' way of life "wouldn't work if they had to live in America, and our way of life wouldn't work in Africa... We're not returning them to their own land or their own customs or their own culture. We've already superimposed our civilization with all its responsibilities and complexities, and now we're just waltzing out and dumping it in their untrained, uneducated laps." African independence, he concludes, is a matter of giving freedom "to people who haven't got a sneaking chance of benefitting from it."

Reviewing both the broadcast and the novel, most American critics, clearly ignorant of anything African other than what they'd gleaned from *Tarzan* and *King Solomon's Mines*, were content to castigate Ruark for his "Victorian, racist" opinions and thereby missed the point entirely. The governments of Britain and Kenya, however, did not, at least to the extent of recognizing the bedrock of truth in Ruark's argument. London, already under severe criticism for further dismantling a dwindling empire, objected strongly to the political implications of *Uhuru* and posed obstacles to Ruark's travel privileges in Kenya. Nairobi, where a hundred people had been arrested as recently as July 1960 on charges of aiding the Mau Mau, bided its time. Jomo Kenyatta, freed in August 1961 after nine years in prison for his role in Mau Mau, was elected Prime Minister in May 1963; Kenya gained independence within the British Commonwealth in December, and thereafter one Robert C. Ruark was officially considered an undesirable immigrant and barred from entering the country.

Ruark loved Kenya, and Kenya in turn nearly saved him from himself, but by then it scarcely mattered. He and Virginia had divorced early in 1963, and his persistent problems of health showed no signs of improving. He had given over his syndicated column and ended his ten-year staff position with *Field & Stream*. Perhaps he wished, as others have suggested, to create a "new Bob Ruark," and indeed he did establish a relationship with Marilyn Kator, the Food Editor at *Look*, that might have culminated in a second marriage.

But he was nearing fifty; Hemingway was dead; the world had a new set of heroes difficult for one of Ruark's generation to understand; and Viet Nam had supplanted Africa as a source of international interest. There simply wasn't time to start over, and besides, there was nothing left to create a new Bob Ruark *from*. Doing so from the reservoirs of his own character was out of the question.

He continued writing, of course, notably the clumsy, thinly autobiographical, almost unreadable novel *The Honey Badger*. But he wrote magazine stories, too, and even though some of them read with a weary and desperate tone, there are flashes of his old brilliance as well. The magazine article has yet to receive the distinction it deserves as a genre unique to itself, but when that time finally comes, Robert Ruark will be recognized as one of its finest practitioners.

Still, it was almost over. His health deteriorated even further during the summer of 1965, and late in June he flew from Spain to the London hospital room where he died on the first day of July.

Reports of his death circulated worldwide, Virginia Webb Ruark and Marilyn Kator engaged in a brief, fairly vitriolic court dispute over the disposal of his estate, and then the world slowly forgot about Robert Ruark. One by one, his books went out of print, even the paperback editions. Ten years later, when I first conceived and began assembling this anthology, no publisher in America had the slightest interest in the man who was one of the toughest, grittiest, and best journalists of his generation.

But times change – or perhaps the enduring magic of hunting simply survives. Robert Ruark has now joined the pantheon of African writers, the last great voice of an age gone forever. He was a sadly troubled man, an intensely difficult drunk, opinionated, prone to braggadocio, all the things that have contributed to the stuff of distasteful legend. Hang out in the right places long enough, and you'll hear any number of Ruark stories, nearly all second–hand and nearly all disgraceful. Those who truly knew him – Harry Selby, for instance, and his son, my friend Mark Selby, who is Ruark's godson – choose, admirably, not to practice petty gossip. No doubt Ruark treated them both less kindly than he should have, but he treated himself most unkindly of all.

Best we remember Robert Ruark as a writer and leave his tormented ghost to whatever measure of peace it's been able to find, for he was, after all, simply a man – a man, as he put it, "glad, sad, puzzled, and occasionally triumphant." As our perspective improves, the frailties diminish and the triumphs loom larger, as if pointing toward some wild place where a man might finally meet his soul.

Michael McIntosh

ACKNOWLEDGMENTS

T he idea for this book occurred to me sometime in the summer of 1974, while I was studying Shakespeare as a National Endowment for the Humanities Fellow at Princeton University. Princeton's Firestone library had a magnificent collection of sporting literature - with any luck, it still does - and it was the Sporting Room that inevitably drew me after long hours immersed in the Elizabethan Age.

The African section contained no Ruark, as I recall, but my own library did, from *Horn of the Hunter*, through the African novels, to *Use Enough Gun*. The more I read there in the Firestone basement, the more it seemed to me that Ruark deserved better than he had so far got. Remembering, in turn, the magazine stories I'd read with great appetite in the '50s and early '60s, I began to wonder if there wasn't yet one more Ruark book to be brought forth.

Months later, back at my teaching job in Missouri, I began browsing the periodicals section and *The Reader's Guide to Periodical Literature*, exploring the possibilities. Presently, I had a list of titles and began securing articles through that splendid institution called Interlibrary Loan.

Bill Chambliss, my old writing teacher at UCLA, once told me that a skilled and helpful reference librarian is worth more than an electric typewriter and a fatted calf, and he was right. The librarian who helped me put together the bulk of this book was the answer to a researcher's dream, and to Norma Lindensmith, formerly of the Hearnes Learning Resources Center, Missouri Western State College, my fond affection and my deepest thanks. I'm sure there were times when she, as I did, despaired of ever seeing her labors blossom in print.

And to that particular end, other thanks are also due: to Steve Smith and Bryan Bilinski of Countrysport Press, who helped bring to an end the publishing world's era of profound indifference toward Robert Ruark; to Carol McNally of Fair Chase Books, for providing additional material in support of a good text; to Lew Razek of Highwood Book Shop, for the same reason; to Marcia Terrones of *Playboy*, for help with "Far-Out Safari"; to Katherine Burns of *The Reader's Digest*, for permission to reprint the chapter titled "A Hunter and a Man"; to my good friend Bruce Langton for contributing his wonderful talent as an artist; to Ben Camardi of the Matson Agency, and to the Estate of Robert Ruark, without whose cooperation this book would literally be at a loss for words.

Michael McIntosh
Copper Creek Farm
Camdenton, Missouri
February 1991

ACKNOWLEDGMENTS

A special thanks to Michael McIntosh, and to Lon Deckard, Steve Smith, and Bryan Bilinski of Countrysport Press for giving me an opportunity to express my feelings about Africa through my cover painting and copper plate etchings found within this book.

An artist's creativity is often sparked by having outstanding photography to work from. With this in mind, I want to thank my good friends and photographers Stan Osolinski, Frank Davidson, Dr. Ron Grow, and John Jaffee for the magical images they created on film.

Most important is the thanks I owe to Rebecca, Brett, and Rory, my family, the ones who suffer the most, never complain, and understand the long hours required to produce artwork on cue when needed. Thank you for sharing with me the natural world and giving me loving support. I could never have as full a life as I enjoy today without you.

Bruce Langton
Granger, Indiana

PART I

DISCOVERY

T his is not the first article Ruark wrote after his fateful safari of 1951; he'd published nearly a dozen African pieces by the time "I've Got To Go Back" appeared in *Field & Stream* in July 1953, the same month Doubleday brought out *Horn of the Hunter*. Except for the first eleven and the last six paragraphs, "I've Got To Go Back" was in fact taken directly from the book.

Although the timing undoubtedly was contrived as a means of promoting book sales, this is more than simply a gussied-up excerpt. The paragraphs Ruark created to give the piece its shape and its frame articulate an idea only hinted at, albeit broadly, in earlier stories – that something had happened in Africa to change Ruark's view of the world around him, to change, actually, his entire life.

That idea, and the seventeen paragraphs that don't appear in *Horn of the Hunter*, seems to me the perfect place for this book to begin.

Michael McIntosh

CHAPTER ONE

I'VE GOT TO GO BACK

The man and the woman got off the plane and climbed into the car that the TWA people had thoughtfully sent to meet them. They drove in moody silence into the great city of New York, where a big, comfortable apartment, two grateful dogs, and all the niceties of modern living awaited them. They had been away for more than two months, and it is presumed they had friends and relatives who would be eager to see them and to listen to their tales of high adventure.

They came into town over the Triborough Bridge, and the big car passed through the upper East Side and headed toward home. The el roared on Third Avenue. Trucks and taxis honked and parked cars crowded both sides of the crosstown street. Children were playing stickball. Gas fumes filled the air. Pedestrians were dodging traffic. Everywhere they looked they saw a television mast, a corner bar-and-grill. Just as they reached their apartment the air-raid sirens loosed off in a practice drill, a horrifying, ear-shattering noise. The man looked at the woman and the woman looked back at the man. There was something akin to panic on the faces of both.

"Isn't this awful?" the woman said.

"Let's go back to the bush," the man answered. "Even with the snakes in the cook tent and the tsetse flies, Tanganyika was never like this."

"I'm lonesome," the woman told him. "I'm lonesome for the baboons and the ant-hills. I want to go back home."

"I miss Katunga," the man admitted. "Mad or not, he was a wonderful skinner. Must be about the time of the month for him to start howling his head off when the moon comes up."

"There are so many people in New York," the woman said. "I'm scared."

That is a rough approximation of the homecoming conversation between my wife and me as we returned sourly to the delights of civilization after a couple of carefree months in the backmost bush of Kenya and Tanganyika on safari. It was not a very grand safari – just Virginia, myself, the white hunter Harry Selby, and thirteen very fine dark gentlemen who gradually came to be our great good friends. We had some good luck and some bad luck. Nobody got sick and nobody got hurt. Parts of it were rough, and parts easy. But it worked a sea-change on both of us that will never rub off. It is entirely true that Africa does strange things to a man. It grabs hold of a piece of his heart, and never quite lets it go.

Months later, things still look strange to eyes accustomed only briefly to the broad vistas of what the British residents call "M.M.B.A. – miles and miles of bloody Africa." I think of size not in terms of moving vans, but of elephants. I am impatient of all the annoyance of contrived civilized living. I occasionally eat fancy vittles, but they don't measure up to a cold Tommy gazelle chop, and expertly fashioned drinks can't touch a warm martini in Tanganyika for taste. I suppose Africa spoils everybody for the routine excitement of the atom age.

I am thinking somewhat of the indirection of achievement in big business in American cities. A man wants to meet another man in order to effect a simple business transaction. He has his secretary call someone else's secretary to find out if the man knows Mr. X. The man says yes. So he has his secretary call Mr. X's secretary to ask if Mr. X will be free to lunch with Mr. Y on Tuesday, and Mr. X's secretary eventually calls back to say that Mr. X will be delighted to lunch with Mr. Y. Four old-fashioneds and a lot of small chatter finally lead to a masked presentation of the idea that Mr. Y has something Mr. X wants. Nineteen thousand light years later they consummate the deal, whatever it is, aided by public relations counsel, advertising agencies, legal advice, tax advice, financial ratings, bank endorsements, mortgages, insurance premiums, television, radio, newspaper editorials, stock-market quotations and the sound and fury from Capitol Hill.

It is simpler over there. You are driving slowly homeward to your permanent camp by the River Grummetti in Tanganyika, and you

Robert C. Ruark

are pretty happy, because the best waterbuck that ever came out of Tanganyika is tucked into the back of the hunting car, and a celebration is indicated. It is about 11 A.M., and already you are looking forward to a bottle of luke-warm beer and about four pounds of cold guinea-hen. Very simple.

Any man who has ever waited for a leopard to come to a kill finds little suspense in a radio soap opera, and I can no longer seem to care a great deal about who wins the boxing match. The elaborate machinations of my business acquaintances, to grab this account or swing that deal, seem fumbling when I recall Selby's mastery of all animals, from lions to over-bold rhino. Everything, somehow, seems cheaper than formerly, and less important, and more confused. I have developed a claustrophobia about New York that I never had before. The elaborate wardrobes and artificialities of American women seem slightly ridiculous when you recall the dignity of a half-naked African woman with a shaven skull and a baby on her back. We have lots of chairs in our house, but as often as not I find myself squatting on my hams on the floor. More comfortable that way.

I have not the same zest for toil I used to have. I didn't mind getting up before dawn in Africa, hunting hard and often fruitlessly and walking over mountains and crawling through ooze to return, dead beat, at eight with barely enough strength left to take the *bathi* and eat the *chacula*. Spending two weeks after kudu seems a praiseworthy effort. Pounding a typewriter seems a waste of time when I might even now be crawling after buffalo.

You find yourself looking at people through new eyes. I will see some elegant gentleman, clad in purple and fine linen, lounging against the bar in some fancy salon, recounting his triumphs of commerce or amour, and I wonder about him. I wonder if this bum would go into the bush after a wounded buffalo. I wonder if he'd shoot it out with a rhino. I wonder if the blacks would joke with him – or if the hunter would accept him as a friend.

I don't believe I've had the television on since I came back. I have not heard the radio. I have trouble reading newspapers. All I want to do is find somebody to listen to me talk about Africa. My wife and I have probably earned the title of the most outstanding Africa-bores now in captivity. We don't go to the movies on Sunday afternoon any more. We go to the zoo. I am buying no new clothes this year, either.

On the way home I stopped off in London and bought a .318 double that wrecked the budget for a year.

Everything looks very strange in New York. Too many people. Too many cabs. Too much confusion. Too many things – gadgets, gimmicks, gizmos, handy helpful aides to overcomplicated living. I am very short-tempered, I find. I don't want to go to night clubs. I want to go back to Swamp Kiteti and sit under the baobabs and think.

Africa has changed things for me, all right. Right now I'd rather be Katunga, grinning through filed teeth as he squats over a carcass, than Mickey Mantle or President Eisenhower or Elizabeth Taylor's next husband. I've got the bug. I've got it bad, and as soon as I can afford it I'm going home again to Africa. I'm not sleeping well in New York. There aren't any hyenas on 83rd Street, and I miss the comfort of their laughter outside the camp.

"The Truth About Safari," which appeared in the March 1952 issue of *Field & Stream*, is one of Ruark's first African magazine stories. "The First Time I Saw God," which you'll find a few chapters farther along, was published in *Esquire* the same month, and there's now no way of knowing which he wrote first.

Thematically, the piece suggests a fair measure of presumptiousness, considering that Ruark's claim on the "truth" about African hunting is based upon a single safari. He certainly wasn't the first to become an expert after only a month or two in the bush, but in this case Ruark the wise guy proved no match for Ruark the hunter. At the heart of it, this story rings true, and the final paragraph offers an early summary of what he discovered in the African experience – "prime adventure…astounding beauty…unimaginable peace."

Science Digest also published this story in condensed form in July 1952 under the title "The Truth About Big-Game Hunting." The text presented here is the original, full-length version.

Michael McIntosh

CHAPTER TWO

THE TRUTH ABOUT SAFARI

Tony Dyer laughed until his sides hurt. Tony is a professional hunter. He was sitting in a bar in Nairobi, Kenya Colony, British East Africa, and he was literally holding his sides as he read aloud a clipping from an American weekly magazine.

"Listen to this," he said, his face screwed up with the pain of his mirth. "I quote: 'Care to have your nine-year-old son shoot a rhino? Does your wife want to get her picture taken with her foot on a leopard's head? It's easy in modern Africa, this correspondent writes from Nairobi, where they hunt big game from taxicabs.' Ho! Ho! Ho!" said young Mr. Dyer. *"Ouch!"*

This occurred last summer in Nairobi, and the reason why young Mr. Dyer was holding his sides was actually to keep them from splitting at the seams. A week before he had experienced what he would call a rather nasty do with a buffalo, the big, cruel, ugly Cape buffalo that is generally accorded to be Africa's meanest game.

Tony was skippering a safari in the vicinity of Babati, Tanganyika, something more than a taxicab's run from Nairobi, since it takes two days of hard driving to get there. His client, a professed purist, was after something bigger and better in the way of buffalo. Tony found him one.

As I recall the story, the Buff absorbed some ten heavy slugs from the big double rifles that are used against dangerous game – .450 No. 2's and .470's, both of which eject a slug the size of a carrot. Buff took off for the bush. Tony and client – always, clients are nameless – went into the bush after the buff, which a *kamikaze* pilot would generally regard as a risky operation. The buff was down, and very sick. "Better wallop him again," Tony said to the client, who raised his big rifle and popped the buff twice behind the shoulder. Whereupon the buffalo, annoyed, arose and charged.

The client, shall we say, dropped his gun. And went away. Dyer knows about buffalo; that you can't outrun 'em, and you can't outdodge 'em, that you just have to stand firm and shoot it out with them. Tony hoisted his ugly double and whacked the buff twice, and the buff didn't quit. Since the last shot was at about four feet, Tony did a very sensible thing. He flopped down on his back, put his boots in the buffalo's face and grabbed for the evil sweeping horns.

"This did not particularly agree with the creature's mood," Dyer said. "He got one horn into me and tossed me about twenty feet, opening me up here. Then he came and collected me and tossed me another rod or so, and opened me up here. I expect we would have been playing ping-pong all day if somebody hadn't gotten brave and found the rifle and finished off the beast, who at the moment was testing his knees on my ribs.

"Ho! Ho! Ho!" Dyer said. "They hunt from taxicabs in Nairobi. If you will pardon the pun, this leaves me in stitches."

The young hunter with whom Dyer was having his elevenses laughed without much mirth. Most of them had horn wounds or leopard scratch marks. All, within the year, had been six feet away from unpleasant death. And all agreed solemnly on one thing: There has been more arrant nonsense written about big-game hunting in Africa than on any other single subject. Their contempt for the quick visitor who generalizes in print on the subject of their safari is only equaled by their amusement at the naive world that accepts these short-time verdicts as gospel. Both contempt and amusement are outweighed by their disgust at the average client – and they make a curse word of it – who comes to Africa coldly to amass a bag to impress his business associates over the week-end in the lodge in Connecticut. And who doesn't care who shoots it, so long as he gets it.

I would like, for once, to try to straighten the record on safaris. I had a fairly complete one – not as one Wolfgang Langewiesche shamelessly admits in his recent authoritative treatise: "Please don't judge by my experience. My safari was only a quickie…"

The only qualification I claim is that three professional hunters have invited me back to hunt as an equal, sharing the cost of the food, the petrol and the salaries of the native boys. And if I may brag heavily, the native-boys with whom I hunted used to joke with me. This is the greatest compliment a man who takes a safari can be paid.

The conception that a bona fide hunting safari is a cinch is the worst of the libels on a real sport. You do not hunt from taxicabs out of Nairobi, because Nairobi is on the edge of a game reserve. You go out and look at the animals, which have become tame from protection, yes. But you do not shoot. You can also go to the Bronx Zoo in a taxicab, and there, too, you do not shoot.

In order to shoot big game, you may drive a day and part of a night to achieve the Northern Frontier of Kenya, or a long day's drive into the southern Masai country. In the Masai the shooting of lions is forbidden, and under protection the lions have become as tame as the bears in Yellowstone. If you really want to hunt, it takes two mean, grueling days to get into Tanganyika, and if you went where I went first, across the Serengeti Plains, into the Ikoma country, it takes three days and a good portion of the night. No roads, either. Dust and mountains and streams and pig holes and muck that sticks your truck. On at least one occasion, when the rains came, it took a party two days to do two miles, and they hand-carried every last item on their lorry. Another party I know was marooned ten days.

The intrepid week-ender who is responsible for the latest piece of misinformation for national consumption writes of lions on the reserve outside Nairobi. He says, truthfully enough, that wild animals do not fear autos, and he's right. Then he says, "If the lion had singled out, in all the jumbled shape of the car, the human figure there, he would have been on us in an instant."

Merciful heavens! There is no beast more apt to flee at human presence than a lion, judging from the sixty-some I've dealt with, and there is no recorded instance – with the possible exception of the man-eaters of Tsavo – of a lion ever charging anybody unless he was wounded. In the case of lionesses, maybe, if she has cubs and you come too close; but a pussycat will claw you, too, if you monkey with her young.

Our man mentions that he wasn't real worried, because his hunter had "his pistol handy on the seat." Oh, boy! Saying that the lion was feeling nasty, a more apt weapon would be a .375 Winchester magnum, for not even Tarzan would tackle Simba with a hand-gun.

The point that has rarely been made about big-game hunting is that it is as safe or as dangerous as chance will make it. Safety comes from skill and good luck, and danger comes from lack of craft and bad luck. If there is a generalization, it is that no wild animal is mad at anybody, and he would rather run than fight – until you hurt him, startle him, or pester his progeny. And there are always exceptions. Many a native walks around with half a face, on account of sleeping drunkenly where the hyenas prowl, and old Fisi, the most cowardly of them all, snaps off a piece of his puss.

Given the preference, an unhurt animal will run away from a human. But the meekest will turn and rend when pressed. I recall one night, coming back to camp, when a tiny little bat-eared fox was running down the trail ahead of our hunting car's headlights. With the peculiar fascination of animals for pathways, he ran along at forty miles an hour until his strength gave out. Then this tiny, inoffensive little critter turned, snarled and *charged the car!* My friend Harry Selby, the professional hunter, nearly killed us all in order to avoid hitting the little bloke.

A Thomson's gazelle is one of the smallest and mildest and cutest of all African animals. He is also a favorite in the culinary department. Fred Poolman, a native East African and a fine professional hunter, shot one for the pot, and as he approached it the Tommy – not much bigger than a fox-terrier – riz up and charged Poolman, stabbing him completely through the hand.

Harry Selby has been a full-fledged professional hunter for seven years, and he was shooting elephant for their ivory when he was fifteen. He has had a dozen narrow escapes from death at the tusks and horns of elephant, rhino and buffalo. One recent buffalo absorbed all they could give him in the engine room, and still came on. Harry shot him over one eye, under the other eye, and finally killed him at four or five feet by shooting him *through* the right eye!

But Selby's narrowest escape from actual demolition occurred on my safari, and at the feet and teeth of a lowly, silly zebra. It was the last hour of the last day of the safari, and we needed one more zebra to fulfill a consignment of hides for friends. I whacked a big stallion in the rear end as he was going away at a couple of hundred yards. It is generally a deadly shot, since the bullet either breaks the back or plunges forward to pierce the vitals. The big old Punda took off in a dead run, always a sign that he is fatally hurt, and after a thousand yards or so dropped like a stone.

We climbed back in the car and drove up to collect his hide and tallow. Adam, the Mohammedan gun-bearer, jumped out to administer the *hallal*, the Moslem kosherizing operation of cutting the throat to make the meat edible. Adam slit the animal's throat, and all of a sudden old Punda came alive. Somebody had forgotten to tell him he was dead. He tossed Adam fifteen feet and came at Harry and me.

A zebra stallion has teeth that can take your head off. He has flailing forefeet that can cut you to bits. He came roaring at the pair of us, and trapped Selby against the side of the jeep. While Selby was fending off this maddened creature I ran round the front of the jeep, dived through the back, dipping up the gun in a sort of flying tackle, and more or less shoved it down the zebra's throat.

"My sainted aunt!" muttered Mr. Selby as the boys started to skin out the carcass. "Fancy the laughter in Nairobi when the word comes back that old Selby's been done in by a bloody zebra."

But the unsuspected is what gets you. The vitality of African game is astounding. Unless you kill it dead, which is difficult unless you hit it in the brain, it will run and hide and wait for you. I have known a buffalo, shot twice through the chest, to go three miles. A rhino takes a lot of killing, and a lion will soak up a power of lead before he quits. Once it is hurt, the African animal drops its meekness and concentrates on one thing: destroying the creature that is responsible for the hurt, which is you.

If you wish to have "your nine-year-old son shoot a rhino," you may reflect that Tommy Shevlin, an American sportsman, got trapped in a blind alley of bush with Philip Percival, the dean of all the white hunters, while three rhino came busting down the avenue. Shevlin shot one so close that it fell on Percival's legs and they had to pry the old boy loose from the dead critter. This is one of the rare instances of the client protecting the professional.

If your wife wishes "to get her picture taken with one foot on a leopard's head," it might be apt to mention that one particular sportsman has spent fourteen years and $100,000 trying to shoot a leopard, and hasn't got one yet.

There are all sorts of safaris, all sorts of hunters, and certainly there are all sorts of clients. Actually, there are only about thirty men in East Africa who are qualified to be called professional hunters, which means that they know game, know the untrammeled game areas and the grass situation, and can be counted on to get the client home alive.

A safari outfitter, such as Nairobi's Ker & Downey Safaris Ltd., or Safariland, provides the basic equipment for a safari. Anything under a month in the bush, a reputable firm will tell you, is largely a waste of time and money. Food, tents, camp equipment, vehicles, the necessary number of native boys, gasoline and the services of a professional white hunter are included in a lump price, which will average about $75 a day for two people.

The extras are considerable. The client provides his own guns, ammunition, transportation to Nairobi, his game licenses, whisky and cigarettes. He also pays for the curing and shipment of his trophies. Even if he owns his guns and cameras, he is a lucky man if he is not out of pocket about $10,000 by the time the postman finally brings him his heads and hides, a year later.

There is no real shortcut to a true hunting trip in Africa. The services of competent personnel and good equipment come high. Even by plane, you cannot do the long trip from New York to Nairobi in less than three full days, and you are dead beat at the end. It takes three or four days to outfit, and at least one, more often three or five, to get where you can find a catholic collection of shootable game.

Nor is it possible to pull it all out of one camp. After we shot lions, leopard, buffalo and minor game, we piled into the car and drove three more hot, miserable, dusty days, across steaming plains and chill mountains, before we reached the next camp site, which was Lake Manyara in Tanganyika. We hunted rhino and oryx abortively for ten days, and got in the car again. Another three days of hard driving got us into the greater kudu country, where we hunted another ten days. Back in the car again, back to Manyara, three days, hampered by a broken axle and two burned bearings. Two more days to Nairobi, and had we gone on to Tibora, as originally planned, it would have been two more days to get there, and four days home. Just driving. Not hunting. Driving hard and slow, stopping for accidents, always delayed by hauling the overladen truck out of sink-holes and sand-traps.

Vicious Angle - Black Rhino

One of the African axioms is that you must go where the game is, to get it. A comprehensive bag would take you on a driving trek of about 3,000 miles, and you would spend the best part of three weeks just driving. And to go where the game is, you must know grass. Grass depends on rain. When grass is high, because of heavy and lengthy rains, unless your man has tucked away an isolated spot or two where the grass is always short, you shoot very little and very seldom. When the land is wet and the grass long, not only is transportation terrible, but the game hides out in the hills, where water still exists in pockets, and does not come down to the plains.

Game on the plains means not only a profusion of shootable horned animals, but also a heavy incidence of the lions and other carnivores that follow big-game migrations. The animals on which the big cats prey – the antelope and zebra and wildebeest – shun the high grass with horror, since high grass makes things so much easier for the big carnivore to creep up on her dinner. So they cling to the foot-hills or make for isolated strips of short-grass country. Or, more important, refuse to leave the big preserves, like the Serengeti, so long as a smitch of moisture is to be found in the seepage spots and water-holes.

While on safari the living is pleasant, but not over-lush, even in the best-equipped outfit with the finest in safari personnel. You still sleep on cots in tents. Your Swahili cook still does the best he can over open fires with a cracker-tin oven, and you subsist mainly off tinned food and fresh meat, with a heavy incidence of starch in the diet. A diet of Thomson's gazelle, guinea-fowl, sand-grouse, buffalo tongue, spur-fowl, eland chops and impala cutlets is interesting and good, but wearing on the eater after the first novelty has worn off. When this diet is supplemented almost entirely by the canned food that one is able to stock or supplement at the nearest country store, or *ducca*, you are apt to grow just a touch bored with canned spaghetti, canned cheese, canned vegetables and potatoes for every meal.

In the best-ordered camp you will still shake the odd scorpion out of your shoe. We found a cobra in the cook tent once, and observed a rather wide variety of other reptiles. As for bugs, Africa is ruled by bugs. The mosquitos have four motors and a lance like a young Masai warrior. Tsetse flies have a sort of brace-and-bit arrangement that takes the *dudu's* drill through three layers of clothing. Safari ants bite like white-hot lancets, and there is a species of caterpillar that crawls up your pants and leaves angry, aching welts wherever his treads touch. The trees are full of bees, and the grasshoppers that hit you in the face as you drive along are as big as a bar of soap.

If you are a man to whom the white hunter is still speaking at the end of the trip, you will work harder than you ever worked in your life, and on at least half a dozen occasions you will be scared witless. Hunting is done from hunting cars – generally four-wheel-drive vehicles that will climb mountains, swim rivers and bulldoze trees. But you do not shoot from a car. The law wants that car at least 500 yards away from you when you pull the trigger. And I am here to say that an average 125 miles per day over rugged, volcanic-dust terrain, coupled with from ten to twenty miles of walking, struggling up and over mountains and through swamps, plus crawling on your belly, is neither child's play nor attractive to old gentlemen with big fat tummies and short breaths.

The car is fine up to a point, but you can't stalk a buffalo five miles away on a hillside, or across a swamp, in a car. You walk, run and crawl. You can't take a car into the bush after a wounded, dangerous animal. You walk a foot at a time, and crawl or hack your way with a *panga* through the thorns. You can't cross a tough swamp in a car. You stagger through it, falling, cutting your hands on sword-grass and sometimes falling flat in four feet of ooze and stinking water. And the car is never a protection from dangerous game, because even if you wanted to shoot from it the hunter would forbid it, if only to protect his own license.

Jorge Pasquel, the Mexican individualist, is the only man ever to be black-listed by the white hunters' association of Nairobi, largely for his persistence in shooting from the car. Three of the hunters in Pasquel's safari, and Pasquel himself, were injured grieviously by animals because of his flouting common rules of hunting behavior.

There is an unwritten law among big-game hunters that no animal be left wounded in the bush, basically to prevent undue suffering, but more practically to keep him from killing the first native to wander by. A wounded leopard, rhino, lion or buffalo, hurt, angry and vindictive in thick bush, is quite a different animal from the placid critter you banged at a moment before. A great many clients earn lasting contempt from the white hunter and the black entourage, even to the scullery boy, for either refusing to enter the bush or by panicking, throwing away his gun and running off when the critter comes boiling out from behind a bush with his mind set firmly on homicide.

If you say so, the hunter will go after your botched-up animal, and risk his own life to kill it for you while you sit outside in safety. But he won't look at you with much respect, nor will the blacks who carry your guns and build your fires and wash your clothes and pitch your tents. He will also shoot all your game for you, if you command him, but he will wonder, with a brave man's full contempt, why the devil you didn't stay home and order the stuff from Cain's Warehouse.

The hunter is always contemptuous of the killer, the man who just likes to shoot to slay things with no reason save blood lust. He will prevent it if he can, and if he can't he will leave your employ as soon as possible in high disgust. He tries to find you the best available specimen of game, hunts it seriously, tries to get you the best shot possible – which means the closest shot possible – and then passes on to a new species. Otherwise you kill only to feed your band of fifteen or twenty men, and you kill sparingly, because meat only keeps about three days unless it's thoroughly dried into biltong, or jerky.

On all dangerous game, closeness is the secret of staying alive. No intelligent hunter wants to shoot a lion at more than forty yards, because of the risk of maiming him and having to go after him. It was our general practice to stalk into the midst of a buffalo herd and to let fly at no more than twenty yards, if possible. The danger here is only stampede, during which some 200 animals, each weighing well over a long ton, might run you down by accident. At least when you shoot, you have a big target, close. I expect I looked at 2,000 buffalo at close range, and I shot only two. We stalked to within thirty yards of the lions, and I have looked at several at six feet when I wasn't shooting. We inspected twenty-eight rhino at ranges varying from a thousand yards to twenty feet, and have yet to shoot at one because the horn wasn't worth the killing of the animal.

But I have been in two buffalo stampedes during which I might easily have been killed, and we stood off a lioness' charge within stroking distance of the old girl. We didn't want to shoot her because she had cubs. Also, I have been three hours in the bush after a wounded buff, and the leopard was shot at some thirty yards. All such animals seem much larger when there are no bars between you and them, no trees to climb, no car to drive away in. Just you and the critter and whatever faith you have in your trigger finger. I trusted mine some, but I trusted Friend Selby's more. Which is why I am pleased to report that he shot only four times in two months, and never protectively. Missed once, too.

It is generally believed that Africa is still a paradise of game, especially big stuff like lions, leopard, buff, elephant and rhino. To some extent it is – especially where it is protected. But there are more shootable lions in your local zoo than in an average fifty square miles of lion country in Tanganyika, and the lion is becoming increasingly hard to collect as a trophy. So is the rhino, because it takes about forty years to build a worthy one. So is the elephant, because it takes a year for each pound of tusk, and nobody sportingly shoots ivory under seventy pounds per tusk.

The leopard is very elusive, entirely unpredictable and hard to bring to bait. The cheetah, the leopard's cousin, is almost impossible to see these days, and will probably become the first African animal to celebrate extinction. There are masses of common game, and will continue to be, but a man wearies of slaying Tommy and Grant's gazelle, topi and kongoni or zebra, since it is exactly like hog-killin' time down to the farm. But I reiterate that a fellow who gets a decent lion, a leopard of any sort, a fairish rhino and a good buffalo has had a successful trip for himself. Forty-three inches of spread on a buffalo is only medium good, but young Bob Maytag recently spent three months looking at seventy-odd bulls at close range without bettering his forty-three-inch job.

If you are taking pictures, and not shooting, it is still wondrous in exactly the same sense as shooting pictures in the local zoo. There is practically no danger, since most stuff is shot by the camera from the car. Close camera work is only dangerous on elephant, which mostly have to be approached on foot, and even then you have a skilled hunter standing behind you with a hefty double rifle. Of course, he could miss ....

The record of the white hunter in protecting his client has been excellent, but excellent mostly because a great many clients let the hunter do all the work and take all the debatable chances. As mentioned, most of the living ones have been clawed, bitten, pummeled and horned. If the average client took the average chances of the average hunter, the score would be considerably more impressive on mangled sportsmen.

But a true shooting safari still is not easy. It is not a cinch to get your lion, "or have your wife's picture taken with one foot on the neck of a leopard." You don't shoot from taxis, you don't shoot in the suburbs, and you can get yourself killed with practically no trouble at all, especially if you fancy elephant or buffalo as your quarry. You can catch malaria, and you can catch sleeping sickness from the tsetses, and you can break your neck falling off mountains. You can be bitten by snakes. It is expensive as all getout, and short–order safaris are almost entirely fraudulent, run by incompetents who figure their work is done when they take you through the park or up to a game preserve where the beasts are as tame as kittens.

But if honestly attempted, it is still a prime adventure, a staggering experience, and a daily recital of astounding beauty and unimaginable peace, accompanied by moments of almost unbearable excitement and drama. If I can just scratch up the dough and the time, I will be back in Tanganyika again. Soon.

I n Harry Selby, Ruark found a hero whose character and accomplishments he never tired of recounting. You'll find, for instance, the Duchess of Grafton incident and the story of Selby shooting a charging Cape buffalo through the eye in *Horn of the Hunter* and in several early magazine pieces.

Swashbuckling aside, however, Harry Selby clearly represented the sort of man that Ruark, in large part, wished to be.

The relationship proved fruitful to both. Selby still is regarded as one of the finest professional hunters of his generation, but Ruark's writing carried his reputation far outside the relatively small coterie of African hunters and made him, in fact, something of an international celebrity.

This brief piece was published in *Reader's Digest*, August 1954, as "The Most Unforgettable Character I've Met." The present title, "A Hunter And A Man," is my own invention; it seems to me precisely the idea Ruark had in mind.

Michael McIntosh

CHAPTER THREE

A HUNTER AND A MAN

Harry Selby, a professional hunter of Kenya, British East Africa, is the *most* man I ever met. It is a rare thing to find a man who can combine gentleness with toughness, bravery with timidity, recklessness with caution, sophistication with naïveté, kindness with harshness, mechanics with poetry, adult judgment with juvenile foolishness. And, all the while, making every woman he meets want to mother him or marry him, and every man he meets respect him. I forgot to mention honesty. He invented it.

I have seen Selby slap a lion in the face with his hat. I have seen him hide from a woman. I have seen him equally at home with Bernard Baruch and with a witch doctor in Tanganyika. His business is killing, yet he is gentler with animals than anybody I ever saw. He knows his way around New Orleans and New York and the remote bush of Northern Kenya. His retinue of black savages adores him.

When I first met him in Nairobi, what I saw was a young man with black curly hair, the kind of eyelashes ladies buy to stick onto their real ones and a voice like that of a cultivated schoolboy, soft and Englishy-precise. Within a few days I would have trusted him with my life – in fact, did.

Selby is the top hunter of Ker & Downey Safaris, Ltd. He knows more about firearms, animals, birds and weather than anybody I ever met, and in recent years he has brought in more outstanding trophies than any of his competitors. His skill at his profession is such that he is normally booked two years in advance. And he is not yet thirty years old.

Selby greets the world with calm assurance because on his own heath he is the social equal and the technical superior of anybody he meets. He is responsible for outfitting the client and arranging for all the needed equipment, and for his retinue of fifteen to fifty natives, mostly Wakamba and Swahili. What he runs is a small circus – tents, trucks, food, guns, water, repairs.

The moment the lorry with its black boys clinging to the top and the little British Land Rover with Selby at the wheel leave Nairobi, he is the boss of the prince or the zillionaire he is taking on safari. He is as much in command of the life or death of his client as the captain of a ship, and he accepts no argument.

His job is to get the client where the game is – either for photography or for trophy shooting. He arrives at his decision by a consideration of weather and grass. If the grass is too high because of recent rains he will know a secret pocket where the grass is short. If the grass is burnt by drought he will know a secret pocket where there is enough green to lure the animals.

I can remember two of Harry's safaris involving other people. One contained a client – and what contempt a white hunter can put in the word "client" – whom Harry considered unworthy of being in Africa at all. Harry bore down hard, collected the complete bag in twelve days, and sped the "client" on his way.

On another occasion Selby had a man and his son out. The man, rather an overweening sort, wanted it *all*. Selby set his down-turned lip and produced it. In one month's time he got them these trophies: two elephants, two rhino, two lions, two leopards, two Cape buffalo, two eland, two waterbuck, and all the common game – impala, gazelle, warthogs, zebras and the rest.

Considering that it usually takes a month to get a decent elephant, and that maned lions worth shooting are hard to come by these days, Selby's achievement is almost unmatchable. If a man just wanted to shoot, Harry will turn on the heat and get the job done in a hurry. He wouldn't work that hard for anybody he liked.

Selby is not a trick shot with a rifle, but he never misses what he *has* to hit –such as a wounded lion or leopard in thick bush, or a wounded charging buffalo at six feet. One buffalo took about sixteen shots from the big .470 rifle of his client and himself and still kept coming. They shot it over and under both eyes, and it still kept a-coming. I asked Selby what he did then. "I shot it through the pupil," he said, and showed me a photograph of the eyeless buffalo.

Another Day Out

If a wounded animal gets away, it is Harry's business to go into the bush after it and finish it – a business which, if it involves elephant, leopard, rhino, buffalo or lion, is a fair bet to get the hunter trampled or killed. I have known him to spend whole nights prowling around in the bush with a pressure lantern looking for a wounded leopard – *the* most dangerous of wounded game, in my book – that some client had mis-shot in the guts.

Selby can run as well as shoot. They tell a story about him, back in his younger days, when he had the Duchess of Grafton out on a picture-taking safari. While they were photographing antelope, the Duchess literally stumbled over a rhino. They were in a national park, and one hesitates to shoot there because the game warden takes such a misty view of it. Harry gave the Duchess a nudge and said: "You'd best make for yon tree, Your Grace." While she was climbing it, Harry diverted the rhino.

In an interview in Nairobi, the Duchess said:

"I was safely ensconced in my tree when I heard a small schoolboy's voice beneath me. Mr. Selby was running round the tree with the rhinoceros snorting behind him. Mr. Selby said: 'If you please, Your Grace, would you mind moving up another branch? I may need the one you're sitting on.'"

Selby in the bush is both cautious and reckless. He knows game as the game knows game. He will play with one lion, who seems to have a nice face, and drive a mile around another, who does not have a nice face. He will take calculated risks with buffalo that make my hair frizzle. He is probably the best procurer of leopard in the world, since he thinks precisely like a leopard. He will walk you right up to an elephant, and know what to do with you when the wind changes and the most evil-tempered of all African big game suddenly gets your scent.

Many times Selby showed his love of animals. One day he nearly overturned the jeep to keep from killing some baby birds on the ground in front of us. Another time, when a tiny fox, running ahead of us, turned and charged our oncoming jeep, Harry ran against a rock to avoid hitting the creature, and shook us up badly. On another occasion he let an ornery lioness come within a few feet of the three of us – Harry, my wife Virginia, and me – without shooting her. When I stopped quivering I asked him why he let her come so close.

"She has *cubs*, old boy," he said. "One doesn't go about shooting females anyhow, especially one with cubs."

Harry began shooting elephant when he was fifteen. He was a sergeant in the war. Afterward he apprenticed himself to Philip Percival, the hunter of Ernest Hemingway's first African experiences and the prototype of all the white hunters in Hemingway's stories. With Percival, Harry learned his trade; when Percival quit the business, Selby inherited his string of native bearers. They will follow him anywhere. He knows precisely when to joke, when to pitch in and help, when to punish, when to cajole.

To understand Selby you would have to see him on all fours, running like a dog on an animal's trail, his delicate nose following the spoor. You would have to see him carrying two rifles weighing about fourteen pounds each straight up the steep side of a mountain. You would have to see him fix a ruptured rear wheel-bearing assembly with a wrong-sized bearing, a piece of strap iron and a nail. When Selby came to New York and walked into my apartment, my antisocial boxer dog took one look at him and crawled into his lap.

His kindness to others is striking. There is no more jealous breed than professional hunters, yet Selby went to great effort over a period of two years to teach a young fellow named John Sutton his cherished professional tricks. This was like an oil prospector baring his secrets to a competitor. And Harry's tact is such that never has even a despised client been made to feel inadequate in Selby's special province.

Contact with Harry enabled me to define a sense of values in a mixed-up and highly hysterical world. It was through him that I quit a job in New York and a way of life I didn't like. It was through him that I was able to measure life in terms of control – controlled fear, controlled courage, controlled labor and, above all, controlled peace.

Harry's job is hunting. But his pleasure is to go out on the broad plains or into the high hills to look and to admire, not to kill. He remarked to me in Tanganyika: "You know, there's an awful lot of God loose around here." I asked him once what was the greatest day he had ever had in the African bush. He looked at me earnestly.

"You must know," he said. "It was that day in the southern Masai – the day we saw the antelope grazing on the plain, with the lions watching them. It was the same day we saw the cow rhino giving birth to her baby calf. That was also the day we saw the zebra stallions flat on the ground, wrestling. I'd never seen anything like that before."

On that day, and for some weeks before, we had not fired a serious shot. Except, of course, occasionally for food.

This was not a shooter talking, or a killer. This was a hunter – and a man.

D uring his first safari, Ruark developed what he describes as a "mania" for Cape buffalo, and fueled with that passion, he produced some of the best buffalo-hunting literature ever written. The fascination came to a crescendo in the second safari with a respectable though not spectacular trophy, and even though it wasn't his last buffalo, something in the experience conferred a symmetry sufficient to bring the mania to a close. "Suicide Made Easy," published in *Field & Stream*, January 1954, is a splendid example of Ruark at the peak of his enthusiasm.

It also is a good example of his skill at recasting essentially the same material in forms different enough to be welcomed by editors and readers alike. Such material wasn't easy to sell thirty-five years ago, and the intense competition among magazines nowadays has made it almost impossible. But Ruark was nothing if not the consummate professional, and it makes little difference that he described this particular hunt and this particular buffalo in *Horn of the Hunter* and in several excerpts published as magazine pieces– Ruark always seemed to find just the right way of making an old story seem new.

Michael McIntosh

CHAPTER FOUR

SUICIDE MADE EASY

S ome people are afraid of the dark. Other people fear airplanes, ghosts, their wives, death, illness, bosses, snakes or bugs. Each man has some private demon of fear that dwells within him. Sometimes he may spend a life without discovering that he is hagridden by fright – the kind that makes the hands sweat and the stomach writhe in real sickness. This fear numbs the brain and has a definite odor, easily detectable by dog and man alike. The odor of fear is the odor of the charnel house, and it cannot be hidden.

I love the dark. I am fond of airplanes. I have had a ghost for a friend. I am not henpecked by my wife. I was through a war and never fretted about getting killed. I pay small attention to illness, and have never feared an employer. I like snakes, and bugs don't bother me. But I have a fear, a constant, steady fear that still crowds into my dreams, a fear that makes me sweat and smell bad in my sleep. I am afraid of *mbogo*, the big, black Cape buffalo. Mbogo, or *Nyati*, as he is sometimes called, is the oversized ancestor of the Spanish fighting bull. I have killed Mbogo, and to date he has never got a horn into me, but the fear of him has never lessened with familiarity. He is just so damned big, and ugly, and ornery, and vicious, and surly, and cruel, and crafty. Especially when he's mad. And when he's hurt, he's always mad. And when he's mad, he wants to kill you. He is not satisfied with less. But such is his fascination that, once you've hunted him, you are dissatisfied with other game, up to and including elephant.

The Swahili language, which is the lingua franca of East Africa, is remarkably expressive in its naming of animals. No better word than *simba* for lion was ever constructed, not even by Edgar Rice Burroughs, Tarzan's daddy. You cannot beat *tembo* for elephant, nor can you improve on *chui* for leopard, *nugu* for baboon, *fisi* for hyena or *punda* for zebra. *Faro* is apt for rhinoceros, too, but none of the easy Swahili nomenclature packs the same descriptive punch as *mbogo* for a beast that will weigh over a ton, will take an 8.8 millimeter shell in his breadbasket and still toddle off, and that combines crafty guile with incredible speed, and vindictive anger with wide-eyed, skilled courage.

From a standpoint of senses, the African buffalo has no weak spot. He sees as well as he smells, and he hears as well as he sees, and he charges with his head up and his eyes unblinking. He is as fast as an express train, and he can haul up short and turn himself on a shilling. He has a tongue like a wood rasp and feet as big as knife-edged flat-irons. His skull is armor-plated and his horns are either razor-sharp or splintered into horrid javelins. The boss of horn that covers his brain can induce hemorrhage by a butt. His horns are ideally adapted for hooking, and one hook can unzip a man from crotch to throat. He delights to dance upon the prone carcass of a victim, and the man who provides the platform is generally collected with a trowel, for the buffalo's death-dance leaves little but shreds and bloody tatters.

But mostly Mbogo flatly refuses to die. He will soak up enough lead to sink a carrier and still keep coming. Leave him alone, and he is cattle and will mostly gallop off at a loud "Shoo!" Kill him dead with the first shot through the nose and up into the brain, or get his heart and break his shoulder, and he dies. But wound him, even mortally, and he engenders a certain glandular juice that makes him almost impossible to kill. I would not know the record for lead absorption by a buffalo; I do know of one that took sixteen .470 solids in the chest and still kept a-coming. I know another that took a couple through the heart and went more than two miles. Don't ask me how. He just did.

I expect I have looked at several thousand buffalo at close range. I have stalked several hundred. I have been mixed up in a stampede in high reeds. I have stalked into the precise middle of a herd of 200 or more, and stayed there quietly while the herd milled and fed around me. I have crawled after them, and dashed into their midst with a whoop and a holler, and looked at them from trees, and followed wounded bulls into the bush, and have killed a couple. But the terror never quit. The sweat never dried. The stench of abject fear never left me. And the fascination for him never left me. Toward the end of my first safari I was crawling more miles after Mbogo than I was walking after anything else – still scared stiff, but unable to quit. Most of the time I felt like a cowardly bullfighter with a hangover, but Mbogo beckoned to me like the sirens that seduced ships to founder on the rocks.

For this I blamed my friend Harry Selby, a young professional buffalo – I mean hunter – who will never marry unless he can talk a comely cow Mbogo into sharing his life. Selby is wedded to buffalo, and when he cheats he cheats only with elephants. Four times, at last count, his true loves have come within a whisker of killing him, but he keeps up the courtship. It has been said of Selby that he is uninterested in anything that can't kill him right back. What is worse, he has succeeded in infecting most of his innocent charges with the same madness.

Selby claims that the buffalo is only a big, innocent kind of he-cow, with all the attributes of bossy, and has repeatedly demonstrated how a madman can stalk into the midst of a browsing herd and commune with several hundred black tank cars equipped with radar and heavy artillery on their heads without coming to harm. His chief delight is the stalk that leads him into this idyllic communion. If there are not at least three mountains, one river, a trackless swamp and a cane-field between him and the quarry, he is sad for days. Harry does not believe that buffalo should be cheaply achieved.

Actually, if you just want to go out and shoot a buffalo, regardless of horn size, it is easy enough to get just any shot at close range. The only difficulty is in shooting straight enough, and/or often enough, to kill the animal swiftly, before it gets its second wind and runs off into the bush, there to become an almost impregnable killer. In Kenya and Tanganyika, in buffalo country, you may almost certainly run onto a sizable herd on any given day. I suppose by working at it I might have slain a couple of hundred in six weeks, game laws and inclination being equal.

As it was, I shot two – the second better than the first, and only for that reason. Before the first, and in between the first and the second, we must have crawled up to several hundred for close-hand inspection. The answer is that a forty-two or forty-three-inch bull today, while no candidate for Rowland Ward's records, is still a mighty scarce critter, and anything over forty-five inches is one hell of a good bull. A fellow I know stalked some sixty lone bulls and herd bulls in the Masai country recently, and never topped his forty-three-incher.

But whether or not you shoot, the thrill of the stalk never lessens. With your glasses you will spot the long, low black shape of Mbogo on a hillside or working out of a forest into a swamp. At long distance he looks exactly like a great black worm on the hill. He grazes slowly, head down, and your job is simply – simply! – to come up on him, spot the good bull, if there is one in the herd, and then get close enough to shoot him dead. Anything over thirty yards is not a good safe range, because a heavy double – a .450 No. 2 or a .470 – is not too accurate at more than one hundred yards. Stalking the herd is easier than stalking the old and wary lone bull, which has been expelled from the flock by the young bloods, or stalking an old bull with an *askari* – a young bull that serves as stooge and bodyguard to the oldster. The young punk is usually well alerted while his hero feeds, and you cannot close the range satisfactorily without spooking the watchman.

It is nearly impossible to describe the tension of a buffalo stalk. For one thing, you are nearly always out of breath. For another, you never know whether you will be shooting until you are literally in the middle of the herd or within a hundred yards or so of the single-o's or the small band. Buffalo have an annoying habit of always feeding with their heads behind another buffalo's rump, or of lying down in the mud and hiding their horns, or of straying off into eight-foot sword-grass or cane in which all you can see are the egrets that roost on their backs. A proper buffalo stalk is incomplete unless you wriggle on your belly through thorn-bushes, shoving your gun ahead of you, or stagger crazily through marsh in water up to your rear end, sloshing and slipping and falling full length into the muck. Or scrambling up the sides of mountains, or squeezing through forests so thick that you part the trees ahead with your gun barrel.

There is no danger to the stalk itself. Not really. Of course, an old cow with a new calf may charge you and kill you. Or the buffs that can't see you or smell you, if you come upwind in high cover or thick bush, might accidentally stampede and mash you into the muck only because they don't know you're there. Two or three hundred

Short Tempered

animals averaging 1,800 pounds apiece make a tidy stampede when they are running rump to rump and wither to wither. I was in one stampede that stopped short only because the grass thinned out, and in another that thoughtfully swerved a few feet and passed close aboard us. If the stampede doesn't swerve and doesn't stop, there is always an out. I asked Mr. Selby what the out was.

"Well," he replied, "the best thing to do is to shoot the nearest buffalo to you, and hope you kill it dead so that you can scramble up on top of it. The shots may split the stampede, and once they see you perched atop the dead buffalo they will sheer off and run around you."

I must confess I was thoroughly spooked on buffalo before I ever got to shoot one. I had heard a sufficiency of tall tales about the durability and viciousness of the beasts – tall tales, but all quite true. I had been indoctrinated in the buffalo hunter's fatalistic creed: Once you've wounded him, you must go after him. Once you're in the bush with him, he will wait and charge you. Once he's made his move, you cannot run, or hide, or climb a tree fast enough to get away from a red-eyed, rampaging monster with death in his heart and on his mind. You must stand and shoot it out with Mbogo, and unless you get him through the nose into the brain, or in the eye and into the brain, or break his neck and smash his shoulder and rupture his heart as he comes, Mbogo will get you. Most charging buffalo are shot at a range of from fifteen to three feet, and generally through the eye.

Also, we had stalked up to a lot of Mbogo before I ever found one good enough to shoot. We had broken in by stalking a herd that was feeding back into the forest in a marsh. Another herd, which had already fed into the bush and which we had not seen, had busted loose with an awful series of snorts and grunts and had passed within a few feet, making noises like a runaway regiment of heavy tanks. This spooked the herd we had in mind, and they took off in another direction, almost running us down. A mud-scabby buffalo at a few feet is a horrifying thing to see, I can assure you.

The next buff we stalked were a couple of old and wary loners, and we were practically riding them before we were able to discern that their horns were worn down and splintered from age and use and were worthless as trophies. This was the first time I stood up at a range of twenty-five yards and said, "Shoo!" in a quavery voice. I didn't like the way either old boy looked at me before they shooed.

The next we stalked showed nothing worth shooting, and the next we stalked turned out to be two half-grown rhino in high grass. I was getting to the point where I hated to hear one of the gun-bearers say, "Mbogo, Bwana," and point a knobby, lean finger at some flat black beetles on a mountainside nine miles away. I knew that Selby would say, "We'd best go and take a look-see," which meant three solid hours of fearful ducking behind bushes, crawling, cursing, sweating, stumbling, falling, getting up and staggering on to something I didn't want to play with in the first place. Or in the second place, or any place.

But one day we got a clear look at a couple of bulls – one big, heavily horned, prime old stud and a smaller askari, feeding on the lip of a thick thorn forest. They were feeding in the clear for a change, and they were nicely surrounded by high cane and a few scrub trees, which meant that we could make a fair crouching stalk by walking like question marks and dodging behind the odd bush. The going was miserable underfoot, with our legs sinking to the knees in ooze and our feet catching and tripping on the intertwined grasses, but the buff were only a few thousand yards away and the wind was right, so we kept plugging ahead.

"Let's go and collect him," said Mr. Selby, the mad gleam of the fanatic buff hunter coming into his mild brown eyes. "He looks like a nice one."

Off we zigged and zagged and blundered. My breath, from overexertion and sheer fright, was a sharp pain in my chest, and I was wheezing like an over-extended pipe organ when we finally reached the rim of the high grass. We ducked low and snaked over behind the last bush between us and Mbogo. I panted. My belly was tied in small, tight knots, and a family of rats seemed to inhabit my clothes. I couldn't see either buffalo, but I heard a gusty snort and a rustle.

Selby turned his head and whispered: "We're too far, but the askari is suspicious. He's trying to lead the old boy away. You'd best get up and wallop him, because we aren't going to get any closer. Take him in the chest."

I lurched up and looked at Mbogo, and Mbogo looked at me. He was fifty to sixty yards off, his head low, his eyes staring right down my soul. He looked at me as if he hated my guts. He looked as if I had despoiled his fianceé, murdered his mother, and burned down his house. He looked at me as if I owed him money. I never saw such malevolence in the eyes of any animal or human being, before or since. So I shot him.

I was using a big double, a Westley Richards .470. The gun went off. The buffalo went down. So did I. I had managed to loose off both barrels of this elephant gun, and the resulting concussion was roughly comparable to shooting a three-inch anti-aircraft gun off your shoulder. I was knocked as silly as a man can be knocked and still be semiconscious. I got up and stood there, stupidly, with an empty gun in my hands, shaking my head. Somewhere away in Uganda I heard a gun go off, and Mr. Selby's clear Oxonion tones came faintly.

"I do hope you don't mind," said he. "You knocked him over, but he got up again and took off for the bush. I thought I'd best break his back, although I'm certain you got his heart. It's just that it's dreadfully thick in there, and we'd no way of examining the wound to see whether you'd killed him. He's down over there at the edge of the wood."

Mbogo was down all right, his ugly head stretched out and twisting. Blood seeped from his nostrils, and from his throat came the most awful moaning, like the bellowing you hear in the knacker's room of the stockyards. He was lying sideways, a huge, mountainous hulk of muddy, tick-crawling scabby-hided monster. He was down, dying, bellowing, and there was a small hole just abaft his forequarters, about three inches from the top of his back – Mr. Selby's spine shot.

"You got him through the heart, all right," said Mr. Selby, cheerfully. "Spine shots don't kill 'em, and they don't bellow unless they're dying. Load that cannon and pop him behind the boss in the back of his head. Knew a dead buffalo once that got up and killed the hunter."

I sighted on his neck and fired, and the great head dropped into the mud. I looked at him and shuddered. If anything, he looked meaner and bigger and tougher dead than alive.

"Not too bad a buff," Selby said. "Go forty-three, forty-four. Not apt to see a bigger one unless we're very lucky. Buff been picked over too much. See now 'twasn't any use my shooting him. He'd have been dead twenty yards inside the bush, but we didn't know that, did we? I'll bet he's a mess inside. Kidogo! Adam! Taka head-skin!" he shouted to the gun-bearers and sat down on the buffalo to light a cigarette. I was still shaking. The boys made the correct cuts to strip off the cape and the head-skin, sliced through the vast neck and took a *panga* to the neck vertebrae, and dragged Mbogo's scalp to one side. Three of them, husky Africans, could barely lift it. Then with knife and *panga* they performed an autopsy.

As I said, I was shooting a double-barreled Express rifle that fires a bullet as big as a banana. It is a 500-grain bullet powered by seventy-five grains of cordite. It has a striking force of 5,000 foot-pounds of energy. It had taken Mbogo in the chest. Its impact knocked him flat – 2,500 pounds of muscle. It had cut his windpipe. It severed his jugular. It smashed the top of his heart, and completely destroyed the main arteries. It had continued on to wreck the lungs. There were no lungs – only a gallon or so of blackened blood. Yet Mbogo had not known he was dead. He had gotten up and had romped off as blithely as if I had fired an air-gun at his hawser-network of muscles, at his inch-thick hide that the natives use to make shields. What had stopped him was not the fatal shot at all, but Harry's back-breaker.

"Fantastic beast," Selby murmured. "Stone-dead and didn't know it."

We stalked innumerable buffalo after that. I did not really snap out of the buffalo-fog until we got back in Nairobi, to find that a friend, a professional hunter, had been badly gored twice and almost killed by a "dead" buffalo that soaked up a dozen slugs and then got up to catch another handful and still boil on to make a messy hash out of poor old Tony.

I am going back to Africa soon. I do not intend to shoot much. Certainly I will never kill another lion, nor do I intend to duplicate most of the trophies I acquired on the last one. But I will hunt Mbogo. In fear and trembling I will hunt Mbogo every time I see him, and I won't shoot him unless he is a mile bigger than the ones I've got. I will hate myself while I crawl and shake and tremble and sweat, but I will hunt him. Once you've got the buffalo fever, the rest of the stuff seems mighty small and awful tame. This is why the wife of my bosom considers her spouse to be a complete and utter damned fool, and she may very well be right.

A lthough he touches on it only briefly in *Horn of the Hunter*, Ruark discovered a great delight in African bird shooting, as evidenced by "Strictly For The Birds," published in the October 1952 issue of *Field & Stream*.

The voice here is not Ruark the big-game hunter, but rather the Old Man's Boy, who was nurtured as a bird-shooter and never lost the passion.

Michael McIntosh

CHAPTER FIVE

STRICTLY FOR THE BIRDS

The native boys who make up the personnel of an African safari are a perceptive lot. They can smell cowardice as a dog smells fear. And they have a way of ferreting out personal idiosyncrasies that mark a man for what he is – of selecting salient characteristics of character that the *Bwana wa safari*, the man who pays their freight, never even suspected he owned. They will call a client Bwana Blabbermouth if he talks overmuch, or Bwana Ginny-Bottle if he fancies the booze extremely, or Bwana Big Belly if he eats too much. Generally the subject of the permanent name is surprised when, at the end of his hunting trip, the boys gather round the cook fire to choose up a nickname for him. And generally he is not flattered.

In my case, this Bwana was neither surprised nor unflattered when they hung my handle on me at the end of a recent shooting trip I made to Tanganyika. They had two names, both rather scornful, but both to be expected. One was Bwana Ndege, which means Master Bird. The other was Bwana Kanga, which means Master Guinea Fowl. Both were to the point. They meant simply that here was a mad American who would waste his time and ammunition potting at little birds when there was a fat eland just over the next hill, or a topi behind every bush.

I didn't mind at all. Each man has his faults, and most of mine are compressed into a madness for bird shooting. And the parts of Africa I know best – Kenya Colony and Tanganyika – come closer to being a bird hunter's paradise than can possibly be contrived in heaven. If a man never saw a lion or a game herd, the long, expensive trip would still be a little more than worthwhile. It is the best real glut of game birds left in the world. With no limits, so that a hog could wear out his shootin' shoulder on almost any fowl he chose.

I had a difficult time shooting birds in Tanganyika, however. I was hunting with a crew of purists who went out each morning, with a dedicated gleam in their eyes, to shoot the lion or the buffalo or the kudu or whatever, with no nonsense about the "shotty-gun." Each day I would look longingly at the flight of sand grouse slanting in to the waterhole, or the massed array of spur fowl running down the path ahead of the hunting car, or the ducks crowding the banks of Lake Manyara, and each day I would get the same stern answer: *"Hapana shotty-gun. Kesho."* No shotgun. Wait until tomorrow.

Sometimes, if I was very good and punctured the eight-horned rhino or whatever we were after, they would relent, and allow me to take the little 16-gauge double out of the case. At the end of serious hunting at each permanent camp I was allowed one day to steep myself in bird shooting. Or sometimes, on the way home, when it was too dark to crawl after buffalo, Kidogo, the gun-bearer, would suffer an attack of conscience and inquire if Bwana wished him to *toa* the shotty-gun, as one indulges a silly child who has been pretty decent about eating his spinach that day. Even with these stern restrictions, I got in more shooting than the average passionate bird shot sees in a lifetime of luck.

The pet for sport was the imperial sand grouse and his little brother, the pintail. The pet for the pot was a toss-up between guinea fowl and francolin, or spur fowl. But the ducks were wonderful, and so were the geese, and so were the partridge, and so were the quail, and the lesser bustard was right tasty, too. I never bothered with the plover and the snipe and the doves. There was too much other stuff around. Didn't mess much with the quail, either. There were so many that it robbed the time-hallowed American bobwhite of his difficulty. After all, who wants to walk through a field and flush 5,000 quail from under his feet?

But I believe that, for sheer sport, shooting sand grouse is on a par with high pass-shooting of teal. A pintail coming downwind with his eye on a waterhole is logging about fifty knots or better, and he's no bigger than a billy dove. His long, back-swept wings are more waterfowl than anything else, save possibly hawk, and when he is passing high you lead him like a teal, or he goes away from there. He is no grouse, actually, but closer to the plover and pigeon family, and he is strictly stripped for speed. He's a plump little fellow of brown, buff and black with a thin pointed beak, and he's great in the pot, even though his meat is dark.

Essentially a desert bird, he comes to dip his beak in the waterhole about 8 A.M., and then he takes off to squat in the sand or among the rocks for the rest of the day. He flights in by the hundreds per flight, and if you wished, you could blow a hole in a mass of them as they flutter down to drink and carry off a bushel. The sport is not browning into the big mobs, but waiting for the twosomes and threesomes and foursomes, and exposing yourself by standing just as they come in range. The little devil takes off like a streak, flying some thirty yards up, and if you hit him it's because you know something about small ducks in a high gale.

On this past trip to East Africa I had phenomenal luck in the big-game field, acquiring a couple of fine lions, an eight-foot leopard, a cheetah, a good buff, a world's-record waterbuck and a gross of other record-book heads. But the day I remember as finest was a bright, clear morning on the plain near Ikoma, Tanganyika, standing under a scrub acacia at the only available water-hole and waiting for the grouse to flight in. The sky was that brilliant washed blue of a fine African morning, the sun just warm enough, and the breeze just breezy enough. I had completed the serious work, the hard work, and this day was just for me and the *shotty-gun kidoga*, which is what the boys called the old 16-gauge.

Presently the air was full of a throaty chuckle-chuckle and you could see the spots in the distance – 200 spots here, 500 there, twenty over yonder, twos and threes and fours. The whistle of wings sounded like pintails taking off, and in the little beggars came.

We shot blind into some of the big mobs, just to break them up, and then crouched to wait for the twosomes. It was such selective shooting that my white hunter, Harry Selby, and I decided to shoot only at doubles, and only at doubles in restricted areas, so that they would drop on clear ground within a few feet of the trees.

We had no blind, but merely crouched, one on each side of the tree. As the birds approached, one or the other of us would stand, and the grouse would step on the gas. We missed a lot, and we took no lengthy shots, because English shotgun shells, unlike English rifle ammunition, are pretty weak in the poop. I later found myself using

No. 2s on guineas, whereas they were easily killable with American 6s and 7s.

Harry and I created a young war. Twenty minutes and several boxes of shells later, I called a halt and we took a tally. We had shot forty, and had missed possibly fifty percent. We knocked off, but forty grouse in twenty minutes make something of a hot barrel. Also, we had grouse stew for two days, when we were not having grouse pot roast.

I never saw shooting like it, save on one other occasion, when my hardy bride stationed herself at one waterhole and placed me at another, and we chased a wiser and warier brand of the breed back and forth between us. I was behind a screen of trees that kept the birds high, and the only possible shots had to fall in a thirty-foot-square area to avid being lost in excessively high grass. This meant you shot at one out of a possible fifty, and I acquired another twenty in less than that many minutes – all tough, high, quartering shots. The old lady, who had never touched a shotgun until a couple of months before, had racked up a dozen on her own – and that was before she became the self-acknowledged expert of the camp.

Until you have seen African game in its various profusion, there is no adequate way to describe it. The best way I know is that a grown woman, who had to be shown how to slip a safety catch in May, had sufficient practice to become an accomplished wing-shot by August 1. Mama went out every other morning when she wasn't hunting with us and, while she burnt a lot of powder, she kept the bill of fare in good shape. Chege, her chauffeur, finally decided she was nuts too. When she began to brag about her prowess with the shotty-gun, we figured she was forever hooked.

We started Mama off on spur fowl, or francolin, for a double reason. The first was that they're a big, slow, even-flying fowl; the yellowneck's about the size of a hen pheasant, and the redneck's a little smaller, like a big grouse. They are speckled buff, brown and white partridge-looking critters, and are called "pheasant" in some parts of Africa. They are scratchers and runners, and they can hide under a blade of grass.

But mainly they are the finest-eating fowl in the world. They are clear white meat, clean down to the instep, and the second and first joints of the leg are as big and plump and white as the breast of a

After the Rain – Sand Grouse

bobwhite. We considered it a lost day when there was neither francolin nor guinea for lunch, and often happily ate it twice a day.

These lads are really such foolish fellows that it is almost a shame to shoot them, but like all African game, they can carry a lot of shot and still depart. The method of shooting was very simple. You drove down a road until you saw a flock scratching in the ruts or in the matted center grass, and then you stopped the car. You either ran like blazes and flushed them that way, or you waited until they ducked into the high grass and then beat them as grouse are beaten in Scotland. Or if, perchance, they congregated in a small clump of bush, you stood to one side and the boys chucked stones until they came boiling out, headed for Uganda. The only trouble with the boys as bird dogs was that they usually rushed after the birds and you were sore constrained to keep from blowing off the back of their necks. We finally trained a couple of them to hold to shot, and they were even excellent retrievers.

The spur fowl made excellent practice for a beginner, flying about as fast as our pheasant and presenting plenty of target. There was no given day when it would not have been possible to kill fifty or sixty in an hour's time, because I have seen as many as thirty roar out from the same scrubby bush. We never shot more than ten, since there was no refrigeration. And Ali the cook's cold, boiled spur fowl, with mustard-mayonnaise, was too much of a gastronomic delight to be squandered on the boys, who much preferred a fat haunch of eland or a rib section of topi to a silly little bird.

The francolin, about a zillion varieties of him, exists in such lavish quantities that Africa seems to be a farm devoted to his raising, but I often wonder how he exists at all. He is easy prey for all the smaller carnivores and the predatory birds, and he will sit stupidly on an anthill and look you in the eye while uttering a dismal *quarank, quarank* that sounds like a raven with laryngitis. And he tastes so good that he is a target for everybody – man, beast and bird. He nests on the ground, and he won't fly as long as he can run. But I love him, and wish we had him here. There are times when sport runs secondary to stomach, and I am hungry right now.

Unless you are the kind who crouches on a footpath and shoots off heads as they run, the guinea is fully as fine a sporting fowl as our wild turkey, and not a whole lot smaller. A big African guinea will run four or five pounds, with the vulturine of Kenya's Northern Frontier averaging larger, if more streamlined. He will tote lead like a turkey, too, and his big body makes his speed deceptively slow. I finally doubled my leads on passing shots, and guinea began to fall, whereas before they had looked back and sneered as they shoved off. If you are shooting guinea informally, the bet is with the bird, because you have to run at him at full speed to make him fly, and often as not he is nearly out of range when he takes the air. But the big speckled bum can climb like a pheasant, and at a startling and very deluding speed, so that you find yourself shooting under him.

He exists in tremendous quantities in Kenya and Tanganyika. On one morning Selby and I estimated we saw 3,000 of the speckled yelpers, and the day never passed when we didn't bump into a few hundred. We never made a point of concentrated guinea driving, but merely popped the odd one for Ali the cook to make immortal. Six, I think, was the biggest single total I compiled, but six was all we could use.

By waiting under their roosting trees, á la wild turkey, it is possible to bag scores as they fly in to roost, and the shooting is quite like bopping decoying ducks. Ours we invariably shot going away or, rarely, in passing shots overhead as the boys rushed around a point of bush and flushed them back at us. For my money the guinea fowl is a vastly underrated game bird. He is much more difficult than the average duck, for instance, and his vitality is enormous.

You could spend a very happy day on guinea fowl alone if your selfish employees would quit worrying about buffalo and leave you alone. In a spirit of bitterness, however, I recall that my asperity-ridden chum Selby never kicked or screamed when Juma, the headboy, fetched in a couple of breasts of the bird Harry scorned as game. It was touch and go as to who would seize the last chunk of white meat.

We never banged at the greater bustard, that largest of local game birds, but we saw the odd thousand. They are king's game in Tanganyika, and even if they weren't they comprise thirty pounds of shoe-leather that would need a rifle to bring them down. You can shoot them in Kenya, but you can't eat them, and that is very much for sure.

But the lesser bustard and his cousin, the black-bellied florican, is an ungainly, speckled, flat-crested fellow who flaps off at a creaky rate, but faster than he looks, and you have to stalk him to get within decent range. Him, too, we acquired as the opportunity presented; and while he's black meat, he is very tender, and nobody tossed him to the hyenas when Ali plumped him into the pot. Not much sport to shooting him, though, because his elongated superstructure makes him susceptible to shot.

If you are a waterfowl man, Tanganyika is your spiritual home. At some seasons the Ruaha River is congested with thousands of spurwinged geese, which are fat as butter and will weigh up to twenty pounds. There is a miscalled goose named knob-bill which runs five or six pounds and is delicious, and the black-and-white Egyptian goose is all you can ask of a goose except that not even the jackals would fancy him as an adjunct to their diet of carrion.

I blush to confess it, but our single specimen of spurwing was procured at a great distance, sitting, and with a scoped .30-06. We didn't have time that day for the shotty-gun.

Africa is duck-loaded with a dozen varieties of common migratory ducks, such as mallard, pintail, teal and widgeon, and fourscore varieties of its own, such as the yellowbill, or African mallard, and a dozen varieties of teal. Shooting is real simple. You can sneak 'em, or blind 'em, or drive 'em, and every marshy flat, lake, canal or waterhole will yield a *whoosh* of wings. We saw them by the thousands at Lake Manyara, where unfortunately we were after rhino, (*"And we'd best not spook the country with the shotty-gun, Bob"*) and in a marshy sector hard by Kiteti Swamp, where we were after oryx (*"Best not bother with the birds, Bob. We really want a good oryx"*).

The only bird I shot with the full approval of Master Selby, except for his greedy stomach, was a particularly brilliant brand of bluejay, which he desired as plumage for his girl friend's hat. As a collector on behalf of Cupid, I shot at it sitting on a branch to expedite matters. It flew off. It lit and I powdered it again. It flew off. I fired. Off it flew. At that moment there was a tap on my shoulder and the humorist behind me, Kidogo the gun-bearer, murmured quietly, "Bwana taka .470?" and handed me the elephant gun. Fortunately the jay decided to succumb, which prevented me from accepting the .470 and slaying one faithful gun-bearer.

In East Africa the much-sought quail is roughly as numerous as the weaver-bird, and the weaver flies in flights like swarming bees.

As you drive a car across fields of high grass, the little fellows literally get up in coveys of hundreds. We were continually killing quail with the radiator grill, and frequently had to stop to pluck them out of the grilling. My heart hurt when I thought how much emphasis I had placed on the little demons back home, whereas a twenty-minute stroll in Africa would flush the odd thousand or two. Too much of anything cheapens the product, and a poor native of Tanganyika sees more quail in a day then Bernard M. Baruch has been able to cultivate in fifty years. I shot exactly one, and that only for the record.

One of these days I am making another safari to Africa, and am taking with me only the shotty-guns, both *mkubwa* and *kidogo*. I aim to shoot nothing but birds, and with me will be a trained staff of non-sneerers who do not think Bwana Ndege is out of his mind because he wants to shoot birds. I am going to shoot birds in the morning, and birds in the afternoon, and I am going to thumb my nose at the kudus and the bongos and all the other rare beasts that command so much abstention from fun. I am going to make so much noise that all the rhinos in Tanganyika will commute to Rhodesia.

And in the meantime our friend Mr. Selby comes here to visit. As a neat bit of revenge I am going to sit him in a duck blind and freeze his East African fanny. Bwana Ndege's memory is long, and revenge will be sweet.

As I mentioned earlier, "The First Time I Saw God" and "The Truth About Safari" share the distinction of being the first of Ruark's Africa stories. They are tightly connected thematically, for "The First Time I Saw God" picks up and develops the idea Ruark touches upon in the conclusion of "Truth." Not until *Horn of the Hunter* would he again write so beautifully or so compellingly about the implications of a man discovering himself.

"The First Time I Saw God" appeared in the March 1952 issue of *Esquire* and was condensed in *Coronet* the following January as "The First Time I Met God." This is the original, full-length text.

Michael McIntosh

CHAPTER SIX

THE FIRST TIME I SAW GOD

I t was about 5:15 P.M., 108 miles northeast of Oran, I remember, when the starboard gunners shouted, "Torpedo off the bow!" The helmsman tried to swing her so the thing would run parallel to us, but the old bucket was bottom-heavy with about 9000 tons of high explosive and she was sluggish as a sleepy sloth. Whatever it was took a long time coming, but not long enough to dodge it. As I recall, I didn't pray, even though I had seen that afternoon, and on other days, what happens to a ship that gets smacked with a crawful of high ex. I felt a vague regret over the fact that getting blown up at the age of twenty-seven left a lot of pleasant things undone, and that was about all. Whatever it was hit us with a dreadful crash. The deck plates popped and spouted flame. The ship took a list, and was knocked heavily off her course. The feeling then was impatience that she didn't blow and get it over with. But no last-minute consignments of soul, no death-brink stammers of apology for what had been a short but gaudy life amongst the shattered Commandments. She didn't blow. And I uttered no prayer of thankfulness. I just figured that if there wasn't enough sincerity in me to pray ahead of it, there wasn't much point in praying behind it. The Lord and I did little business together in those days. It was more or less as if we had been introduced by the wrong folks.

If we can flash forward about nine years, now, I will tell you about a wordless prayer I said. I said it through my pores, sitting in a grove of trees in Tanganyika, East Africa, hard by a crocodile-infested river called the Little Ruaha. There wasn't anybody around at the time but the Lord and me and some wild animals. I didn't make any sort of formal speech out of it. Just told Him thank-you very kindly for not blowing up the ship that day in the Mediterranean, and for letting me live till this day. It was a little late coming, this thank-you note, but I never meant anything more vehemently. And so far as formal religion goes I am a very irreligious fellow, who smokes, swears, drinks whiskey, ogles girls and at that very moment was paradoxically interested in killing things.

I was very grateful to be alive, at that moment, for I was alone in the nearest thing to the Garden of Eden I ever expect to see. We had stumbled, while on safari, onto a piece of land which had largely been untrammeled by human feet, and uncontaminated by human presence. The exact location remains a secret. The place was too good for man to louse up. Its keynote was perfect peace.

We were out after kudu – greater kudu – one of the more elusive and possibly the most beautiful of all African game. He is as big as a horse, and as dainty as his tiny cousin, the dik-dik. He has enormous backswept upcurling horns that completely spiral twice, ending four or five feet from his skull in shining ivory tips. His coat is delicate grey, barred in white, and there is a chevron on his nose, and his heavy neck wears a long dark mane. Also he is ordinarily twice as wild as any animal, save possibly the bongo. A man is lucky to see one kudu in many months of hunting.

Here the kudu were comparatively as tame as the little Thomson's gazelle. I suppose we saw sixty or more in two weeks, and might have shot twenty if we counted the immature bulls. The cows were as tame as domestic cattle, nearly. I shot one kudu bull, because I wanted the trophy badly. The rest of the time we just looked around.

We marveled. Here was country as the first man saw it. We were camped on the river's edge, beneath a vast grove of acacias. It was like living in a natural cathedral, to look upward in the cool, created by the flat tops of the giant trees, with the sun dappling here and there to remove the dank darkness of moist forests. It reminded you of sunrays streaming in through the stained glass of a church window. The straw beneath the trees had been trampled flat by all the generations of elephants since the first elephant. The silence was unshattered by traffic sounds, by the squawk of radios, by the presence of people. All the noises were animal noises: The elephants bugled and crashed in the bush across the little river. The hippos grunted and the lions roared. The ordinarily elusive leopards came to within fifty yards of the camp, and coughed from curiosity. The hyenas came to call and lounged around the tents like dogs. Even the baboons, usually shy, trotted through the camp as if they'd paid taxes on it.

The eland is a timid antelope, a giant creature who'll weigh up to 2000 pounds, and who almost never stops moving. He is as spooky as a banshee, and unless you chase him on the plains in a car, a couple thousand yards away is as close as you're apt to get. Here the eland came in herds, walking inquiringly toward you. The same applied to the big Cape buffalo, who ordinarily snatch one whiff of man-scent and shove off. The buffalo walked up to us here, their noses stretched and their eyes placid and unafraid. We watched one herd of a hundred or so for half an hour, and finally shooed them into the bush.

The impala, lovely, golden antelope with delicate, lyrelike horns, are usually pretty cheeky little cusses, but here they were downright presumptuous. As we drove along the trails in the jeep, we would have to stop the car and drive them off the path. They leaped high above the earth for sheer fun, not from fear, and one little joker actually jumped completely over the car – just to see if he could, I suppose.

Even the crocodiles seemed unafraid. They slept quietly on the banks, and didn't bother to slide into the water at our approach. The guinea fowl, usually scary birds, were as tame as domesticated chicken. We must have seen at least 3000 one morning, and they neither flew nor ran to the nearest exit. They walked with dignity.

This place had been seen only by one other safari, and was not despoiled by natives. The locals lived eighteen hard miles away, and they were not a tribe of hunters. They grew crops and grazed cattle, and robbed wild beehives for honey, and generally did not even tote the customary spear, which is as much a part of native equipment as the umbrella is to the Londoner. One grizzled grandsire, eighteen miles away on The Big Ruaha, told us solemnly that he had lived there all his life and had never seen a kudu. We saw fourteen that day.

You felt that here was a capsuling of Creation, unsoiled, unspoiled, untouched by greed or selfishness or cruelty or suspicion. The white hunter, Harry Selby, whose life has been spent among animals, out of doors, gasped continually at the confidence and trust displayed by the profusions of game. We didn't want to shoot; we didn't even want to talk loud. Here you could see tangible peace, here you could see the hand of God as He possibly intended things to be. We left the place largely as we found it. We felt unworthy of the clean, soft blue sky, of the animals and birds and trees.

It was not until we found this camp that I became aware of what had happened to me in Africa. It had been happening daily, but my perceptions had been so blunted by civilized living that I had somewhere lost an appreciation of simplicity, had dulled my sensitivity by a glut of sensation and the rush of modern existence. All of a sudden I was seeing skies and noticing mountains and appreciating animals and cataloguing the flowers that dot the yellowed, grassy plains of Africa. I was tabulating birdcalls and marveling over the sheer drop of the Rift and feeling *good*. I was conscious of the taste of food and the sharp impact of whiskey on a tired man, and the warmth of water in the canvas bathtub, and the wonder of dreamless sleep. I was getting up before dawn and loving it. I was desperately anxious to win the approval of the blacks who made up my safari – me who never gave much of a damn about Presidents and kings. I was feeling *kind*, and acutely alive, and very conscious of sun and moon, sky and breeze, and hot and cold.

This has to be a paradox, because my primary business in Africa was killing. I was there to shoot. And I shot. I shot lions and a leopard and buffalo and all the edible antelopes and all the good trophies I could rustle up. But I never shot needlessly and I never killed anything for the sake of seeing it die. We killed for good trophies, and we killed to feed sixteen hungry people. Killing does not seem wrong in Africa, because the entire scheme of living is based on death. The death of one thing complements the life of another thing. The African economy is erected on violence, and so there is no guilt to shooting a zebra that the lions will have tomorrow, or a lion that will be a hyena's breakfast when he is too old to defend himself against an ignoble enemy.

This is a hell of a way to write for a professional cynic, but you see I'm not really cynical any more. What has wrapped us all in a protective armor, and insulation against honest stimulation, has been an artificiality of living that contrived civilization has thrust upon us to the detriment of decency.

Things are very simple in the African veld. You is or you ain't.

You are a courageous man or you are a coward, and it takes a very short time to decide, and for everyone you know to detect it. You can learn more about people in three days on safari than you might run down in a lifetime of polite association under "civilized" circumstances. That is why very few foreign visitors are speaking to each other when they finish a long trip into the bush.

There is no room for selfishness. A safari is as intricate as a watch. It is pared down to the essentials of good living – which is to say food, transport, cleanliness, self-protection and relaxation, or fun. It has a heavy quotient of hard work, in which everyone has a share. It is like a ship on a long cruise in that respect. There is a thing for every man to do, and if he fouls off his duty the failure affects everybody, to everybody's hurt. A sloppy gunbearer who lags behind can get you killed. Indecision on your part or the part of any vital member of your party can get you killed. Cowardice can get you killed. Lack of caution can get you killed. You shake your shoes each morning on the off chance a scorpion has nested in your boot ....

When you live among phonies long enough, when your life is a vast and complicated cocktail party of communication, pose, frustration, confusion, pressure, refinement, and threat of indistinct doom, you can forget that the human body is a very simple organism with very simple demands. It does not take much to amuse a monkey, but we have seemingly overendowed ourselves with playthings, with extraneous fripperies we call necessities, with gimmicks, gadgets, gizmos, and distractions that completely obscure the basic truth that a night's sleep, a day's work, a full belly, and a healthy elimination is about all a human organism needs for satisfactory existence. The refinements come later, of themselves.

I find today, to my dismay, that while I live in New York in an approximate palace – freshly decorated, at God knows what cost in blood, sweat, and money – I was happier in a tent. It kept the rain off me, needed no lease, was easily movable and did not require air-conditioning. The bed was a cot, and tired as I was nightly it could have been upholstered in spikes without disturbing my rest.

Now I'm back on my old routine of toying with a chop, and spending eight thousand dollars for a dinner I don't want, but I don't like it. I recall a fellow by the same name who used to pick up a whole guinea fowl and devour it with great enthusiasm, and who never cared too much whether the Tommy chops had been cooked sufficiently or not. Cold spaghetti tastes great out of a can. Beer is never better than when warmed by the sun, due to no refrigeration. I read a lot of mishmash about diet – in the words of my friend Selby, the hunter: *Gimme meat, and skip the extras.* In Tanganyika I ate like a starved cannibal and lost weight. There I was eating to live – not to sell books, not to be entrancing, not to be stylish. I was eating because I was hungry, and was burning up enough of what I ate to keep me thin enough to climb a mountain or crawl through a swamp.

You realize that a man who earns a living with two fingers on a typewriter has always accepted the A & P, the local supermarket, the utilities company, the waterworks, the central heating, and the highway department as part of his life. All of a sudden, save for a few conveniences, I was right back with the early man.

If we wanted light we either built a fire or turned on a very primitive lamp. Fire we always needed, if only to fend the hyenas off tomorrow's dinner, and always in the starkly chill nights to keep from freezing. So we had to pitch camp where dry wood was. And close to where water was. And where dry wood was, and water was, and food was, you had to travel. In the absence of a highway department you have to take a *panga* and cut your own roads through dense growth, or build your own bridge, or pave the bottom of a stream with rocks you have painstakingly gathered.

I had accepted light, heat, water, roads, and food. Especially food. You flicked a switch, screamed at a janitor, started the car and let her ramble, or picked up the phone and called the grocer. The most intimate contact with food I ever had was when I ate it and when I paid the bill. Now I was for the first time in the bacon-bringing business, which is to say that sixteen people eat or don't eat according to what I could do with the business aperture of a rifle. Not that my wife, the hunter, or I would starve, of course. But there were thirteen hungry black mouths, used to consuming ten to twelve pounds of meat a day – *each* – wondering what goodies *Bwana* was going to fetch home that day to plug the aching void. By goodies they meant *nyama* – meat. Zebra meat, eland meat, buffalo meat, any kind of meat. I was the Chicago stockyards, the slaughter pens, the corner delicatessen, in their simple and direct minds. This was a new thing. I hunted for it, and I found it, and I shot it, and we butchered it, and

Greater Kudu

then we ate it. What we didn't eat was made into *biltong*, dried meat or jerky. The hyenas, the jackals, the vultures and the marabou storks cleaned up the odds and ends.

There is a neatness in Africa that needs no sanitation corps, no street-cleaning department, no wash-down truck. What the hyenas and jackals don't get the buzzards get. What they don't get the marabou storks get. What else is left around the ants get. There is no garbage – no waste.

Maybe that's one of the things that hit me hard. No waste. Back home I seemed surrounded by waste – waste of money, waste of time, waste of life, waste of leisure, mostly waste of effort. Away out yonder, under the cleanly laundered skies, there seems to be a scheme that works better than what we have devised here. There is a dignity we have not achieved by acquiring vice-presidencies and a $50,000 bonus and planned economies and the purposeful directorship of the world.

The happiest man I ever knew is named Katunga. He is an old Wa-Kamba, whose filed front teeth have dropped out. His possessions are four wives, a passel of old children, young children, and grandchildren. And *pride*. Katunga is known as *Bwana* Katunga to white and black alike, because Katunga is the best skinner of animals in the whole world. He achieved his title because he once approached Philip Percival, the now-retired dean of all white hunters, and spake thusly:

"*Bwana*, I see that all white men are called *Bwana*. *Bwana* means Lord, or Master. Now I, Katunga, am an atheist, because my father was good enough for me. But to be called *Bwana* means that a man is master of something, and I am master of my knife. I am the best skinner in the world. Why cannot I too be called *Bwana* Katunga?"

"*Jambo, Bwana* Katunga," Mr. Percival said, and *Bwana* Katunga he has remained. He sings as he skins. He is a happy man, with a sense of humor, and he has never seen Dagmar or Milton Berle, and he disdains a gun as an unworthy weapon compared to a knife. Nor does he pay a tax or fret his soul about extinction. Death holds no horror for him.

One day just before I left East Africa I heard Katunga speaking more or less to himself, as he flensed a Grant's gazelle I had shot. He was surrounded by his usual clique of admirers, for Africans are great listeners.

"I am an old man," Katunga said. "I am not so very long for safaris. Someday soon I will die. But when I die – when I, who am now called *Bwana* Katunga, die – I will have left my mark. The safaris will pass my *boma*. They will see my houses, and my maize fields. They will see my wives and my children and my grandchildren. They will see what Katunga has left behind him, and they will say: "'*King-i* Katunga lived there!'"

And true enough, *Bwana* Katunga will have become King, since he realizes his worth and anticipates it before time awards it to him. Not many captains of our industry can say as much.

The best man I ever met, white, black, or varicolored, is named Kidogo. Kidogo is a Nandi boy, about twenty-eight years old, who was my gunbearer. He is rich according to his standards. He has wives and children and herds of cattle and grainfields. He has been to English-talking school and it has neither made him a scornful African nor a wishful Englishman. He will work harder, give more of himself to the problem at hand, sleep less, complain less, be more humble, more tolerant, and more efficient than any "civilized" person I know. With it he retains a sense of humor, too, and a vast pride in himself as a man. He hunts as a gunbearer for the best hunter in the business only because he loves the hunt and he loves the hunter and he loves the business of being with *Mungu*, which is God, no matter how you spell it or conceive of it. I feared the scorn of Kidogo more than ever I feared the wrath of God or man, and it pleased me that finally he approved sufficiently to make jokes with me. A joke from Kidogo was accolade enough to make my year. It told me I was a fairly decent fellow, worthy of association with a superlatively brave man, a tolerant man, a *good* man. Apart from the joking compliment, he showed no surprise when his bossman casually assumed that I would join them in a happy little adventure called "pulling the wounded buffalo out of the bush." Kidogo tracked the blood spoor for me, with his life on the line ahead of me. He seemed confident that his life was in good hands, since he had no gun. Adam, the other tracker, showed the same sort of confidence in Selby, and to be accorded a similar consideration as Selby was the deepest bow to my ego I ever experienced. Because Selby is the all-time pro at standing off charging buffalo at four feet.

I still thrill from time to time about the dedication to danger that was given me by three relative strangers. "Clients" are generally told to wait in the jeep until the dirty business of finishing off a wounded, dangerous animal is complete. If they are "good," or nonabrasive clients, they might be asked if they care to join in the dubious fun of extracting a sick, sore, and angry animal from his bastion in the thorn. We hit a buffalo hard. Twice he went to his knees, but nevertheless recovered and took off with the herd.

"Let's smoke a cigarette and give him time to stiffen," Selby said. We smoked the cigarette, Selby, Adam, and I. Kidogo doesn't smoke.

"Well," Selby said, directly to me, crushing out his smoke, "Let's go and collect the old boy." No ultimatum to wait in safety. No request as to whether I wished to play. It was assumed by Harry Selby, who is half buffalo and half elephant, and two lean blacks who live by danger, that I was naturally going to tag along. No Pulitzer Prize, no Congressional Medal of Honor, would ever give me the thrill I got that day out of casual acceptance as an equal.

You see there is a thing about the buffalo. He is a very naughty creature, as Selby might understate it. He is so bloody awful, horridly, vindictively naughty, after he has been hurt that he is almost impossible to kill. He will soak up bullets that would stop elephants cold, and still keep coming. He can run faster than you can. He can turn faster than you can. He will hide if possible and take you from the rear, and he can hide in bush that wouldn't cover a cat. He weighs in the neighborhood of 2,500 pounds. He will hook you with his razor horns – he charges with his head straight out and his eyes open – and then he will go and pick you up from where he has thrown you and he will throw you again. When you cannot move he will jump up and down on you with feet as big as flatirons and as sharp as axes. He will butt you and kneel on you and if you climb a tree he will stretch that big snout up and lick the flesh off your feet with a tongue like a rasp. When he is wounded and you are up against him there is only one logical development. You die, or he dies, because he will not run away. He just comes, and comes, and the brain shot sometimes won't stop him. Most wounded buffalo are killed within a hand's reach. The starkest fear I have ever known was given me by buffalo, until the fear became a fascination, and the fascination an addiction, until I was almost able to observe myself as another creature, and became bemused by my own reactions. I finally courted buffalo as a hair shirt to my own conscience, and almost would have been interested objectively to see how many possible ways there are to be killed by one.

In this trip to Africa, and in my association with Selby, Kidogo, Adam, and a few lions, leopards, buffalo and other vindictive insects, I had the opportunity to find out about courage, which is something I never acquired from the late war. I know now that I am a complete coward, which is something I never would admit before. I am the kid with the dry mouth and the revolving stomach, the sweaty palms and the brilliant visions of disaster.

But cowardice has its points, too. There are all gradations of fear, and the greatest gradation is the fear of being known to be afraid. I felt it one day after a lengthy stalk through awful grass after a wounded buffalo. When I finally looked at him, and he looked at me, and there wasn't any tree to climb and no place to hide, I was the local expert on fear. At less than fifty yards a buffalo looks into your soul.

I unlimbered my Westley Richards double-barreled .470, and let him have it where it hurt. Then I went off and was sick. And then for the next several weeks, I had to force myself to inspect his relatives at close quarters. I was frightened of embarrassing Harry and Kidogo and Adam by my own cowardice, so my cowardice conquered the minor cowardice, which only involved dying, and so we went and sought the buffalo. Ditto lion, leopard, rhino. Likewise snakes. A small cobra is very large to a man who fears caterpillars.

I learned, on this expedition, about such things as grass, and its relation to rain, and its relation to game, and game's relation to people, and people's relation to staying alive. There is a simple ABC here: When it rains too much, the grass grows too high. Also trucks get stuck, but the main point is that when the grass grows too high you can't get there from here. You stay where you are, and all the frantic cables from home can't reach you.

Also when the grass is too high the game is in the hills, and you can't get to the hills, and furthermore the carnivore which live off the game are out of sight, too, because there ain't no carnivore where there ain't no game. The lions and leopards and cheetah can't operate in the high grass because the Tommies and Grant and zebra and wildebeest know that the carnivore can't operate in the high grass. And it is an amazing thing that all the hoofed animals drop their young when it is raining so hard that nothing predatory can move much, which gives the young a short chance to stay alive. Me, I always thought pregnant animals went to hospitals when their time came on.

I learned something of females on this trip, too. Such as how the male lion seldom kills. What he does is stand upwind and let his scent drift down. Once in a while he roars. While he is creating a commotion the old lady sneaks along against the wind and grabs what she is sneaking after and then she breaks its neck. And brings home to father the spoils of her effort. We have reversed this technique in this country.

The emphasis on sex is very simple in Africa, having little to do with the citified voodoo with which we have endowed it. Sex is not really a symbol, nor is it hidden, psychiatry-ridden or obscure. There are two sexes –*doumi*, the bulls, and *manamouki*, the cows. They work and they breed and they die. There is no such thing as a sterile man, because the woman shops around amongst the village until she breeds. Breeding is thought to be highly important, since it begets *mtotos*, and children of both sexes are highly regarded as both nice to have around the hut and valuable in an economic sense. Neither sex of animal nor human group seems overworried about morality as we know it, or the implications of sexual jealousy as we know it. They got sex, and are content, and do not need a Kinsey lecture to impress its importance on each other. They also have sun and rain and seasons, and if they take the sheep and goats into the hut at night it is to keep the sheep and goats from harm while simultaneously keeping warm. It makes as much sense as tethering a poodle to a restaurant radiator.

What I have been driving at all along is an explanation of why I want to go back to Africa, again and again and again, and why I think Kidogo the gunbearer is more important to life than Einstein or Dean Acheson. It is because I discovered in Africa my own true importance, which is largely nothing. Except as a very tiny wedge in the never-ending cycle that God or *Mungu* or somebody has figured out. The Swahili say: *"Shauri Mungu"* meaning "God's business," when they can't figure out an explanation for why it rains or they lost the way to camp or there aren't any lions where there should be lions.

In Africa you learn finally that death is as necessary to life as the other way around. You learn from watching the ants rebuild a shattered hill that nothing is so terribly important as to make any single aspect of it important beyond the concept of your participation in it. You are impressed with the tininess of your own role in a grand scheme that has been going on since before anybody wrote books about it, and from that starting point you know true humility for the first time.

I believe today I am a humble man, because I have seen a hyena eat a lion carcass, and I have seen the buzzards eat the hyena that ate the lion, and I saw the ants eat one buzzard that ate the hyena that ate the lion. It appeared to me that *Mungu* had this one figured out, because if kings fall before knaves, and they both contribute to the richness of tomorrow's fertile soil, then who am I to make a big thing out of me?

It was not so much that I was a stranger to the vastnesses of Tanganyika, which are not dark but joyous. It was not that I was lost in a jungle so much as if I had finally come home, home to a place of serenity, with a million pets to play with, without complication with full appreciation of the momentary luxury of being alive, without pettiness, and finally, with a full knowledge of what a small ant I was in the hill of life.

I belonged there all the time, I figured, and that's why I say I had to go to Africa to meet God.

PART II

Mau Mau Years

In the spring of 1953, while Ruark's magazine stories and excerpts from *Horn of the Hunter* were appearing in print, extolling the joys and adventure of African hunting, the first shocks of the Mau Mau terror sent British East Africa reeling. For a few months, the matter of lead-time, or advance production, which is an inescapable part of magazine publishing, created a remarkable contrast between editorial content and daily news reports coming out of Nairobi.

For the most part, not even the weekly magazines in those days were geared to report hard news in a timely way, but *Life* somehow contrived to fit "Your Guns Go With You" into its issue of February 16, 1953. Ruark had been in Africa for about two months by then, and the upheaval he found when he arrived for his second safari clearly stirred his old instincts as a reporter.

Later, Ruark the novelist would take over, and most of the content of this article eventually appeared in *Something of Value* – either straightforwardly, as does the Mau Mau oath and the Christmas letter from the "Africans Communist Unit," or thinly fictionalized, as Andrew Holmberg and his gunbearer Njuguna became Joseph Watson and Waithaka, or as Kitty Hesselberger, Dorothy Reynes-Simson, and their boxers became Sally Henderson, Marian Sorrell, and a pair of Doberman pinschers.

Michael McIntosh

CHAPTER SEVEN

YOUR GUNS GO WITH YOU

It is very quiet and peaceful here in Kenya's Northern Frontier, where we have set up our hunting camp. This is a vast, sun-scorched desertland inhabited mostly by elephant, rhino and a few nomadic herdsmen whose first concern is water. It is angry-looking land, its bright red earth crisscrossed by dry, sand river beds and shockingly accented by carelessly strewn casual hills, buttes, mountains and peaks.

A group of Samburu herdsmen are camped half a mile or so up the road from our camp. They are an offshoot of the Masai tribe, corrupted possibly by interbreeding with the Somali, the Rendille or a touch of the Turkana. They are fierce-looking, tall men who go naked under a toga, who smear their faces and bodies with red ocher, who never move without the long spear of the *moran* (warrior) and who wear the *simi*, or short sword, stuck into their girdles. There are perhaps twenty of these *moran* watching me write. Some are standing on one leg, stork fashion, and leaning on their spears. Others are squatting on their hunkers, with the spears stuck butt-end first into the ground.

My pistol is in the sleeping tent – I suppose. I haven't thought about it for a week. There are about a dozen rifles, two shotguns and two more pistols, as well as a thousand rounds of assorted ammunition, somewhere about the camp. I imagine that Chalo and Metheke, the gunbearers, know where the stuff is. Up here on the Northern Frontier one can be casual about firearms and natives. Up here the natives still think it is the noise that kills. Nobody is apt to pinch a gun off you for the purpose of shooting you with it. This is the Kenya of the Masai and the Wakamba and the Nandi and the Rendille and the

Kavirondo and the Samburu and the Turkana and Boran.

In other words, this is not Kikuyu country, Mau Mau country. Here there is no fear and murder and brutality, no locked doors and barred windows, no vigilantes and counterviolence, no suspicion and hate and tension. This is not Nairobi or Nyeri or Nakuru or Thomson's Falls or Kinangop. They are in the country of the Kikuyu tribe – Mau Mau country. There a housewife goes to market with a pistol strapped around her waist. There you put the pistol in the soap tray when you take a bath, because you remember that Eric Bowyer of Kinangop was chopped up while bathing.

In the Kikuyu country your guns go with you wherever you go. In the daytime your pistol is around your waist or in your hand or by your plate. At night it is under your pillow. You know where your rifles are too. They attend the cocktail party with you, or rest against the hearth at dinnertime, or go with you to church, or are stoutly locked away. That is because you cannot afford to lose a pistol or a rifle. If you lose one or have one stolen, you are heavily fined or go to jail.

Mau Mau land today is a strip of high Kenya farmland, where one shoots intruders without question after dark, and any native (police excepted) possessing a gun, at any time, or a *simi* or a *panga* – a two-foot bush-knife – after dark is a candidate for immediate death. In Mau Mau land reserve police patrols cover the countryside and check nightly on the safety of the farmhouses. In Mau Mau land no Kikuyu tribesman is above suspicion, even if he has been your "head boy" for twenty years.

There often is no way to be sure that a servant is *not* a member of the secret terrorist society. The news may come some dark night when he opens the door to his fellow Mau Mau, who will chop you into small bits with *simis* and *pangas*. Many people are unwilling to serve as guinea pigs in this sort of experiment in loyalty. If you keep Kikuyu on your premises you are inviting murder. As a result, thousands of non-Mau Mau Kikuyu are beginning to suffer for the bloody sins of their brethren. They are being dismissed from jobs or packed off to the reservations, a process that creates resentment which leads easily to membership in Mau Mau.

The Kenya white man – the red-necked, horny-handed pioneer who has wrestled with the land for his rolling green acres, who has fought drought and locusts and lions and rhino and elephant and banks to make his property serene – will slap his pistol and laugh wryly about Mau Mau. He calls them "Mickey Mice" or hums a ditty which goes in part, "Mummy wouldn't buy me a Mau Mau. I have a strangled cat, and I'm very fond of that, but Mummy wouldn't buy me a Mau Mau...." The Kenya farmer, when he turns on his battery-driven radio for the news, will applaud and shout "bloody good show" when the announcer says that six more Mau Mau were shot near Nakuru or Nyeri yesterday by members of the organized native resistance.

A year ago Kenya real estate was at a peak of value. Today there is no reliable assessment on the worth of property in Kikuyu areas. According to the mood of the individual, you can buy a fine farm for nearly nothing, or find it impossible to buy one at all if its owner turns out to be a stubborn man who refuses to "get the wind up because of a bunch of bloody murderous Wogs." Yet this same man hides despair behind his arrogance and bravado. He does not want to leave the land he has painfully cleared and fenced and watered and planted. But the European is a tiny minority, some 30,000 in a sea of five million blacks, among whom a million are Kikuyu, each potentially a member of an organization so secret that the British do not even know what the name "Mau Mau" means. He knows that what is going on in Indochina, in Morocco and in South Africa is a trend. He has felt the first bite of the trend in his own backyard. Mau Mau has not spread to the other four million blacks of Kenya – yet. Nor has it infected Uganda or Tanganyika or Rhodesia or Somaliland – yet. He tells himself that Mau Mau will be stamped out as soon as the government and the people hit on the most practical method.

But he looks toward the morrow as embraced by a wave of dark nationalism everywhere, and he feels that the white man's day of minority rule over many is doomed. He tells himself he will fight, and maybe win, but he already has lost the security for which he shortened his life in the battle with the land. In less than a year, chaos has been created in Kenya by the secret society, Mau Mau, which has sowed a bumper crop of fear on Kenya's green slopes.

To me the scene in Kenya today seems remarkably similar to what we experienced in the U.S. during our colonization processes, when the sidearm was part of dress, and women took rifles to the fields with them. But we killed off most of our Sioux and Apache, our

Cherokees and Creeks and penned the rest in small reserves, and said, briefly, "Lo, the poor Indian – what there is left of him." In our days the only good Injun was a dead Injun, and the red man was listed as a varmint. The difference today in Kenya is that it would be rather difficult, not to say unjust, to kill off a million Kikuyu on suspicion alone. It certainly would cause some unrest among the other four million natives, some displeasure in the U.N. Assembly and high glee in Russia. The Kenyan cannot deal so summarily with the mass as we dealt bluntly and brutally with our aboriginals.

The native in British East Africa has been a special ward of the Crown. His lands are protected by the Crown, his rights at law are protected by the Crown. There is therefore a cleavage in opinion as to how to solve the Mau Mau question. The more ebullient farmers are for declaring a state of rebellion and hanging the lot – apart, of course, from those who are shot fleeing arrest. But a million Kikuyu would be fairly hard to hang. Government quite frankly doesn't know what it wants. It has sent the fuzzy-cheeked youths of the Lancashire Fusiliers out from the Suez Canal Zone to protect the settlers. It has allowed the organization of several preventive measures, such as the Kenya Police Reserves, the organized native resistance, an intelligence force and occasional special task groups for the hunting down of Mau Mau in particularly virulent areas like the Aberdare Mountains around Thomson's Falls, Nanyuki and Nyeri.

At the moment Jomo Kenyatta, the front man and accused head oathgiver of the Mau Mau, is in the midst of a long and windy trial, together with five associates, which has already been interrupted once by a separate contempt of court action. Kenyatta and cohorts are being charged literally with operating and managing an illegal society. Conviction on these charges would be a wrist slap. At the same time Michael Blundell, leader of the European Elected Members of the Kenya Legislative Council, has successfully wrought a bill to make the act of administering the Mau Mau oath subject to the death penalty.

The Kenya government is taking a long chance in another resistance effort. The good Injuns have been called in to fight the bad Injuns. I went to Nyeri the other day to pay a call on Muhoyo, the Kikuyu chieftain who is one of the leaders of the resistance. The Provincial Commissioner, Edward Windley, told me that Muhoyo was up in the mountains leading a sweep against an entrenched force of

Kikuyu who were hiding out in the Aberdares. The Athigani under Muhoyo are armed with spears, bows and arrows and an occasional single-barreled shotgun. They were effecting a pincer movement, backed on the other side by 100 Masai *moran* armed with the spears which they use so beautifully. The crusher was supposed to drive the fugitive Mau Mau into the waiting arms of the Lancashire Fusiliers and the organized police and police reserve.

At this time the native resistance force numbers 2,300 men at Nyeri, 1,600 at Kiambu, 1,080 at Meru and 1,380 at Fort Hall. The *moran*, the proud warriors of the Masai who once dominated Kenya with their spears, have offered some 3,000 spears if the government needs a blood-letting. Nothing would please the Masai more than to go out in a group and skewer a few "Kukes." It would be just like the good old days, when the *moran* raided and dipped their spears into all but the young girls and babies. Unofficially the government is quite worried as to the possibilities of creating a new and different blaze if it fights fire too successfully with fire. If the other tribes and the loyal Kikuyu get into the act with heavy success, there are some who wonder if this sort of achievement might not go to the heads of the resistance fighters, possibly encouraging them to start a holy war of their own which would make the isolated terrorism of Mau Mau look puny. Right now some Kenya officials figure it's a chance they've got to take, betting against the permanence of blood lust roused amongst the resisters.

It is the tacit opinion of many leading Europeans in Kenya that mass warfare is not the answer to stamping out the Mau Mau. They have lately launched an intelligence operation designed to correlate information with an eye to hunting down ringleaders – oath administrators in particular. Something of this sort was effected in the late fall after a series of horribly bloody murders had roused the countryside. Special small task forces composed of police, police reserve, intelligence personnel and professional white hunters went up into the hills to track down known Mau Mau, with considerable success. They snared quite a decent bag. Some were unfortunately shot resisting arrest. Friends of mine, on special duty, managed to find eight fairly high Mau Mau straw bosses in solemn conference, which was abruptly terminated by Sten guns. Others, hunted down and captured, were induced to unburden their souls of considerable information, leading to the capture of still others.

Sometimes the discovery of a Mau Mau in your midst turns out rather sardonically. For instance, Andrew Holmberg, one of the hunters on my safari, is short his best gunbearer, a man he'd known for eighteen years. Njuguna was a fine shot and a magnificent tracker, a superb hunter and companion in the field. But when Njuguna was found to be a leading practitioner of the Mau Mau specialty, and an oath administrator to boot, they had to clap him into jail pending trial. He was put in jail for the simple reason that, apart from him eminence in Mau Mau, all of the attributes which made the man a fine gunbearer also qualified him for the taking of Andy's head and weapons – heads and weapons ranking in that order as the most valuable things a Mau Mau can contribute to his cause.

Another hunter, Miles Turner, was something more than shocked to find that his lorry driver was No. 27 on the Mau Mau leader list, and was the chief recruiter for the Nanyuki district. Metro-Goldwyn-Mayer was also surprised to discover that a number of their lorry drivers, engaged in logistics for the film *Mogambo*, were Mau Mau members. A surprise raid on the M-G-M convoy left several of the heavy trucks sitting helplessly, driverless, by the side of the road.

We have had to fire all the Kikuyu but one from our safari gang of boys for a charmingly simple reason. My hunters are Harry Selby of Nanyuki and Andrew Holmberg of Thomson's Falls. Since both have been very active in counter-Mau Mau operations, both rank rather high on the Mau Mau list for extinction. In Nairobi, tremendous interest was evoked in the destination and time of departure of our safari. All the Kikuyu cabbies seemed vitally concerned with our welfare, as did waiters, room boys and others. (One of my boys at the hotel got his head chopped the night after we left, possibly for being uncooperative.)

No greater prize could be set before the Mau Mau council than the heads of Messrs. Selby, Holmberg, Ruark and Kronfeld, plus their equipment of guns, ammunition and vehicles. Ruark and Chester Kronfeld have no special significance except that we are classified as Europeans, which categorizes us as varmints who can be slain without license. Part of the Mau Mau oath deals with the separation of European heads from European shoulders as the classic example of exemplary conduct in the field. We do not fret about Chege, our

Waiting

Kikuyu lorry driver, because Chege is a very decent type. Decent types in recent murders have generally opened the back doors for their not-so-decent friends, but Chege is surrounded by a bristling array of filed-toothed Wakambas, plus some Masai and Swahili boys, and we are well out of Mau Mau territory. Even if my friend Chege were the No. 2 Mau Mau – and he might be, because it is impossible to tell by appearance or personality – he would not get very far with our heads while still keeping his own. The Wakamba would heartily disapprove. I keep hoping Chege *isn't* a Mau Mau, because he is my wife's birdshooting companion of old and they will spend an awful lot of time out in the bush when Mrs. R. arrives shortly.

One is apt to joke a little about Mickey Mice, but it is a fact that in most of the murders of whites the job has been arranged inside, generally by a trusted servant of vintage employment. Oddly, too, the murders have been senseless, since those chosen for mutilation have been gentle people with long records of kind administration of their own and other blacks. The classic case was the murder of Jock Mieklejohn and the horrid mutilation of his wife, a doctor who was known for her selfless devotion to the natives around the Thomson's Falls area. They slashed Mieklejohn to death with *pangas* and left Mrs. Mieklejohn, bleeding and unconscious, for dead. The house resembled an abattoir. The job was fingered by servants, who are on trial for murder.

Similarly Richard Bingley and C. H. Ferguson, two kindly farmers who were hacked in their home New Year's night a few miles from where our camp was then situated, were put to the *panga* for no real reason except that they were more or less available men who couldn't see harm in *their* Kikuyus. In the holiday week, when the Mau Mau promised twelve heads (native or white) to celebrate the Yule, and were pettish at having only produced eleven before New Year's, another gentleman around Thomson's Falls played into luck. He got drunk a couple of nights running, was forced to stay at a hotel, and thereby saved his skull. The Mau Mau came to call and found him absent. Local wags said a *panga* might have rendered him a less hurtful head.

But there is often a kickback, even to Mau Mau plans. Two lady friends of mine named Kitty Hesselberger and Dorothy Raynes-Simson, who live at a lovely farm high atop a lush green hill outside of Naro-Moru, rather conclusively dampened the festive feeling among the Mau Mau of the Nyeri area. Dot and Kitty – Dot tall and slim, Kitty a short, blond, determined lady – were sitting in their big living room among the homely treasures of many years in Africa. There is a big lion that Kitty Hesselberger's husband shot forty years ago in Abyssinia. The lion covers one end of the comfortable, easy living room. A huge leopard sprawls along the back of the divan. There are fine game heads everywhere, and two very good *sjambok* (metal-handled whips) hang by the fireplace. Dot has her favorite easy chair, close to the wireless, and Kitty has hers. Outside in the bright, flower-decked lawn a lantern burns bravely. The light can be seen for miles from the hilltop, and so long as it burns the patrols know that Dot and Kitty are all right.

It was 9 o'clock when Kitty got up from her chair to walk five feet to the table to crack a nut. They had just turned on the wireless. Two big boxer bitches, Damsel and Penny, sprawled on the floor. The cocker spaniel was asleep in a corner. They would have another cigarette and go to bed. Just then one of the houseboys came in with hot water, walking, Dot says, rather furtively and suspiciously. Dot was wearing her gun, a snubby .38. Kitty had taken her gun off. The automatic was in the chair. Kitty looked up from her nut-cracking chore, and stared into the face of a gigantic black man with a razor-sharp *simi* in his hand and a knobkerrie hanging from his belt. There was another man behind him. One of the men grappled with Kitty, forcing her backward over a chair. He raised his arm with the two-edged *simi* sharp enough to shave with, when Damsel, the boxer, came up from the floor with one long, smooth bound and sank her fangs in the Mau Mau's knife arm.

The confusion of snarls and gasps and screams, the room full of dogs, women, black men and strife, gave Dot a chance to unlimber her gun. Dot shot and dropped the giant dead on the threshold. She snapped one at the man wrestling with Kitty and the dog, and the gun misfired.

This turned out to be lucky, because she was aiming broad on the man's back, and the bullet conceivable would have pierced him and killed Kitty. She got in another shot, wounding the man, and another which accidentally killed the dog. The wounded man took off, and she sped him along with another round. Kitty recovered her automatic and the two valiant women went out into the dark, where they stumbled over the *simi* flourisher, dead among the flowers on the rolling green lawn. They reloaded, went back into the house, and seemed to hear the sound of war cries in an areaway. A body loomed in the dark hall and kitty cut down on it. This was the cook, one of the villains of the piece. Kitty killed him with one shot. One houseboy fled into the night, and has not yet been found. The other, he who led the men from outside, ran to the bathroom and locked the door. Kitty and Dot started blasting through the door. They wounded him, and he went out the window. They caught him later.

The two gals reloaded again, and remembered their distress signal – to put out the lamp. These are no ordinary ladies. Kitty raised her weapon, and sort of casually shot the lamp out over her shoulder. The next hour they spent in contemplation of the dead giant in the living room and the dead cook in the hall. They didn't worry about the defunct terrorist on the lawn. They worried more about poor Damsel, dead in her duty. Aid came within an hour. By that time the girls were cooled off again. But I noticed, some weeks later, that when Kitty gets up to crack a nut, the gun is on her hip.

The job here was completely inside. The cook and the two houseboys had neatly lined their shoes outside the door, ready for the rush exit. Ordinarily, a Kikuyu just steps out of his shoes and leaves them anywhere. One of the boys, outside to lock up, had spent about forty minutes on a task that demands five minutes. The houseboy let in the Mau Mau, who were carefully dressed, their pants bottoms tied with string to prevent catching in the bush when they ran, and their coats tightly buttoned for the same reason. The cook was hurrying off when Kitty nailed him. Kitty regrets the cook. "He was the best damn cook we ever had," she said.

This would be, I think, a first-rate example of the character of Kenya at the moment. I was mightily impressed with the ladies when I drove up the winding road to their aerie on the hill. The house is neat and well kept, a long-loved, long-lived-in frontier house whose gardens bespeak the character of the women. Two kinds of gracious ladies, having chopped a piece of pride and loveliness out of a hillside on the slopes of Mt. Kenya, will practice pistol shooting on the manicured lawn and offer tea, beer, cigarettes, candy or bullets according to the demand of the moment. Ladies do not shoot four nocturnal terrorists as a general thing, but the girls are still living alone on their high hill. The chances are they will not be bothered again, but if they are they will not run. They will not leave their land.

It is necessary to get the feel of the end product of Mau Mau before one attempts to assay it or explain it. You can get it in a city like Nanyuki when you see a lady shopping in an Indian market. She has three little blond girls with her, each in upturned, round schoolchild hats. The lady, buying cabbage and tinned goods, wears knife-creased slacks. Her pistol holster matches her general costume. You can feel it in the countryside where you see simple farmhouses guarded day and night by armed men. It can be had by attending a cocktail party or stopping for the first sundowner in a pub. The ladies have matching accessories – shoes, handbags and pistol holsters. The gentlemen rest their guns within reach before they order gin and French, or hitch their pistol holsters more comfortably to fit the bar stool. When we are in Nyeri or Thomson's Falls, I put on a gun before I tie a necktie.

It is possible to get the feel of Mau Mau even at our northern camp. You have only to switch on the wireless every night to hear a new tale of shooting, pillaging, cruelty and brutality — brutality of black to black, of black to white, of white to black and of black to animals. The Mau Mau make great use of highly contrived sadism. Their favorite symbol is a dead animal, hacked horribly, disembowled and stuck upside down on sticks, or crippled and left to suffer.

Sleeping at Andy Holmberg's farm at Thomson's Falls, or in a tent in the bush outside Nyeri, the .38 Colt seemed comfortable under the pillow. Nobody feels like a cowboy. There are too many bandaged arms and scarred faces about. There are too many pianos hacked to matchwood, too many fired drapes, too much smashed crockery, and too many violent reports on the local news program in the evening radio schedule. Too many neighbors are dead, their heads chopped to bleeding shreds. You must have tea with Kitty and Dot, or see people you know doing things they wish they did not have to do to get the feel of Mau Mau.

What is it? It is ostensibly a reign of terror inspired to drive the white man out of Kenya. That is its declared aim. It is implemented by many innocents at the direction of an evil few.

I am convinced that its prime exponent, Jomo Kenyatta, is by no means his own man. He was educated abroad, boasts of spending several years in Moscow, is married to a white woman, and is a highly intelligent fellow. Mau Mau's top leaders are unknown, but they have cunningly exploited the grievances of many simple, misguided people. It is quintessentially the old secret society that appeals to all men, everywhere. It combines the most evil aspects of religion, politics and savagery. It is implemented through fear, and its symbol is the ancient voodoo sacrifice of animal and man.

I have a copy of the letter, in which the Christmas killings were promised, that describes the Mau Mau as "The Africans Communist Unit." The letter, translated into halting English by an Indian clerk, bears reading. It says:

"Christmas Greetings from Kenya, to: The Africans Communist United. The Africans Government the truth.

"We are now reaching the place of having our self-government because when the Europeans was not present in this country, were keeped goats, cows and gardening but in the time we are very angry for Europeans to give the Africans much disturbing and to aim us with guns as a target mind you we are the human beings. Europeans are stagers [strangers] in this country no doubt we say in south this is the Africans Country. The Kenya Europeans government has no United Nations Charter. We leaved Athalita Hill and other crowds are leaving Mega Abyssinian boundry we are ready to reach in every direction in Africa. We wait to by visited by everyone who wanted us, who goes after a person does not miss him.

"We are wanting a dozen of heads for the Christmas of this Month. We are the Africans Communist Unit."

A childish letter, to be sure. But on New Year's Day they had eleven heads. Twenty-four hours later, with Ferguson and Bingley (the fourth and fifth white victims), they were over the quota. Since then there is no way of telling how many natives have been slain. Decomposed bodies are dug up nearly every day. Usually the bodies lack heads.

The Mau Mau initiation is pure voodoo. Two bent branches form the basis for a rude arch. It is covered with banana leaves and two sheep's eyes are stuck to the structure by thorns. The oath administrator is at one end of the structure and the neophyte crawls in the other side. The big oath is sworn to, and then the administrator breaks out the beer and they have a party. The oath runs roughly as follows: "If I am told to bring in the head of a European, I will do so, or this oath will kill me.

"If I see anyone stealing anything from a European, I will say nothing, or this oath will kill me.

"If I am called on by the Mau Mau in the middle of the night and am naked, I will go naked, or this oath will kill me.

"At all times, I will say that all land belongs to the Kikuyu, or this oath will kill me.

"I will not send my children to government schools, or this oath will kill me.

"I will not send my children to mission schools, or this oath will kill me.

"If I am called on to rescue Jomo Kenyatta, I will do so, or this oath will kill me."

The power of this oath on the superstitious individual is almost incomprehensible. Once sworn, the man is so bound that his bravery under duress is immeasurable. Pressures, some of which I am told are quite unpleasant, have been exerted on members in an effort to get at key men in the Mau Mau organization. Some will die rather than talk. The remainder largely tell lies.

"But they are plenty brave," one East African told me. "You have to give 'em that. Once they've sworn, all the old mumbo-jumbo takes over and they will put up with anything rather than talk."

The reign of horror has not, however, gone according to plan. Originally, I have heard, there was to have been a "Night of the Long Knives," heralded by "the sounding of the reed-buck's horn," at which time chosen Europeans were to be killed all over Kikuyu territory. Some of the bloodier-minded bucks got out of hand, and jumped the gun on the Big Plot. There were cattle slashings, and then murders, and by now there have been about 180 murders (eight whites) but no big "Night of the Long Knives." The Mau Mau organization apparently cannot control individual enterprise.

Most of the murders have been Kikuyu against Kikuyu, as a recruiting device. Several suicides have resulted among the natives, where individuals have hanged themselves rather than submit to torture. Three chiefs have been slain.

Chief Hinga, a resistance leader, was shot at Limuru, being wounded in the hand and mouth, in early January. He was taken to a hospital, and was followed by an assassin in a common taxicab. The killer told the cab to wait, entered the hospital, shot and killed Hinga and buzzed off in the cab. He has not been caught yet.

Chief Waruhio, senior chief in Kiambu, was coldly shot in his ear by a hired gunman. Chief Nderi, senior chief at Nyeri, was hacked to bits by *pangas*. Accompanied by three aides, Nderi refused to wait for further reinforcements before he tackled a Mau Mau meeting. They chopped up Nderi and cut two of his aides into small pieces.

In the Nyeri-Thomson's Falls area the Mau Mau have recently taken to potting at people as they pass in autos, without much success, and the cattle-sheep-dog-cat butchery continues. When sabotage is substituted for murder, it is quite appalling to assess the vandal wrath of the wreckers. When they take on a house, they crush, rip, burn, break and defile every single item that is ruinable.

Despite this savagery, it is safe to say that the Mau Mau will not chase the white man out of Africa, unless the movement spreads to the other tribes, joining up with racial strife to the south and all the way north. In Kenya the settlers will continue to fight, either as individuals or in groups, until they are killed. They feel the land is theirs, and that they bought it by painful effort. Whether Mau Mau spreads, whether it will be stamped out, how it all will end, nobody can say. The natives have an expression for it: *shauri a Mungu* – it's "God's business" from now on.

T he Mau Mau uprising served to heighten an already-growing interest in Africa, and that in turn offered Ruark the opportunity to broaden his scope. Like most of the stories in this section, "A Curious Community" has little to do with hunting but much to do with what Ruark had come to love about East Africa. It appeared in *Collier's,* August 21, 1953.

Michael McIntosh

CHAPTER EIGHT

A CURIOUS COMMUNITY

T he Northern Frontier of Kenya is a fierce, frightening, awesome land, bone-dry and sparse for most of the year – and impassable and forbidden when the twice-yearly freshets come roaring down the dry riverbeds like the Mississippi in flood, carrying huge trees and dead animals before their force and sometimes rising thirty and forty feet above their natural level. Then there is too much water, useless water.

In passing, the floods cut new riverways, twisting, turning, broad avenues of rock-strewn sand and tangled driftwood. Huge boulders stud the avenues. Along the banks the foliage is thick and green – thorn and myrrh and dwarf bamboo. Beyond, there are sparse dry hills of sand and rock, angry red mountains, angrier flats of ocher clay. And gray, twisted, stunted bush.

Isiolo is a tiny, shambling little town, with a few Indian and Goanese shops of tin and warped plank. Isiolo is on the main road north from Nairobi, only a couple hours' drive beyond Nanyuki, the heart of Kenya's Mau-Mau belt of murder and strife. It is the seat of the British District. Here the District Officer and the District Commissioner, the Game Department, the telegraph, the telephone and the jail: The tiny nucleus of the British raj, or what's left of it.

Here in the streets of Isiolo are slender, often beautiful Somali women in huge turbans and iridescent robes. Here are slim, handsome, hawkfaced Somali men, also brightly and hugely turbaned, each carrying his stave and somewhere a knife he is never timid to use. These Somalis are not Negroes, but an Abyssinian-Arab-Aryan tribe of nomads, cattle grazers, donkey raisers, sheepherders, goatherds, traders.

Here, too, are the Turkana, coal-black, fierce men, who are simply honest and magnificently ugly. The Turk wears a circular knife for a wristlet, and he can cut your head off with a swipe. He goes as nearly naked as possible, and even in the towns his women seldom wear more than a strip of cloth about the waist. He is a grand hunter, the Turkana, and a fine tracker, and his tribe is one of the two in Kenya that will eat elephant as a delicacy.

Here, too, in Isiolo are elephant. Wild elephant. In and out of the streets of the town, and stamping through the gardens. And here one night I ran smack into the middle of a herd of zebra, feeding in the middle of the main drag. When a speeding jeep hits a zebra, it makes quite an impact.

Isiolo is where you bid the civilized world goodbye. You cross a little palm-lined river, where the crocodiles snort and the monkeys play and the big blue pigeons swoop up and down the banks. You see a variety of direction signs: Archer's Post, Garba-Tulla, Shaffa Dikka, and a crossroads which says simply enough: Somaliland – Abyssinia, depending on which way you're heading.

But once you pass the majestic, beetling brow of huge old Ololokwe, the massive mountain, you begin to live on, and off, the luggers.

A lugger, or *luga,* or *raga,* is a sand riverbed carved out of the landscape by twice-yearly freshets. Around the luggers all life flourishes in the dry season, which is a good eight months a year. The main attraction is a chance for survival, for under the sand of the dry luggers is water. Awful, filthy, muddy, contaminated water. But water.

To me, this land of the dry oases is the most fascinating sector of the world – a place where man, beast, bird and reptile compete with one another constantly for water.

The luggers have lovely names. There is Kinya, and Sererua, Merille, Seralippe, Lasames and Koya. There is Kauro and UasoNyiro. Each is a community center. The peoples who live in and around and off the luggers – the Borran, expert cattlemen, the Samburu and Rendille, nomads today as they were nomads 5,000 years ago, the Turkana and the Somalis – take their camels and cattle and goats and sheep and donkeys from one dry oasis to another. The least anchored of the lot, the Masai offshoots called Samburu and Rendille, carry their entire wealth with them: their cattle and the few possessions they load

At the Luga

in sort of wicker hampers fastened to the backs of camels and tiny donkeys.

These nomads of the Northern Frontier do not camp for long. They throw up temporary huts of skins stretched over slender flexible branches. When the time comes to leave, the Samburu and Rendille tribes just touch a torch to what's left of their village and move on, pitiful little clans, struggling over the vastnesses of desert in search of another dry river with water under its sand.

In time I have grown fond of the Rendille-Samburu, who have managed to retain much of the quality of their cousins to the south, the Masai, and have lost some arrogance in the process. They are Masai in appearance. Their language is Masai. Their customs are Masai.

The men paint themselves in ocher mud, as the Masai do, and the young *moran*, the warriors, are just as lazy, spending most of their time making up their faces and tossing spears or running foot races and pursuing the opposite sex.

They circumcise their maidens as well as their young men. They smile a lot, and resist education entirely. They wear their tangible wealth on their backs, and live off blood, milk and an occasional goat. They also attract flies – billions of flies.

The ladies, when young, have fine torsos and good figures. If they forbore shaving their heads and washed oftener, you could call them pretty, because their grin is big, the teeth white, the skin light and features good.

The men have really beautiful features and wear their hair long in styles ranging from poodle-cut to page-boy bob. But there is no recorded case of homosexuality among the Rendille-Samburu. Their apparent femininity comes from centuries of loafing, of letting the women do the chores and of devoting their chief attention to their own adornment.

It takes an adult Samburu *moran* three hours of hard work, on the part of his wives, to make his face presentable for a day of chatting in the shade with his contemporaries. One top warrior, whom we called Gertrude, was as pretty a piece of flesh as ever you saw, male or female, and knew it full well. A tough boy, but a lazy cuss and very vain.

Let me try to describe life as we live it at Seralippe lugger. There was a big Samburu *manyatta* (village) a mile out of our camp, and square miles around the lugger were black with the cattle, the goats, the woolless sheep, the donkeys and dogs of the tribesmen. Each day the people marched the herds down to drink. It took half a day.

The cattle drank from hollowed logs alongside wells painfully dug into the soggy sands. The water was handed up by naked men or women from seepage in the bottom. In a dry year it is not unusual to have six men or women in a hole, each standing on a niche carved in the side, passing the water up to the cattle that the owners will not sell, but only hope to increase. (In the Northern Frontier a man's wealth is measured by the size of his herd.)

The competition with nature is most severe. Man must literally fight his way through beasts in order to drink and allow his domestic animals to drink. It is dangerous work. The luggers are boiling with thousands of elephant and rhino. Hundreds of leopard and cheetah haunt the edges of the luggers, looking for a cheap and easy meal.

The tower of Babel never heard more assorted shouts, screams, grunts, squeals and moans than a lugger in the dry season. There are hornbills that squawk raucously. There are greater and lesser bustards, millions of noisy guinea fowl, and untold grousy-sort of birds called francolin. There are gray, blue and green lories, and there are moaning doves and weeping unidentifiables. There are insects with trumpets and cellos and bass drums, and a maddening little fly which crawls into your eyes, ears, nose and mouth, and will not move even when you swat him.

The baboons and the hyenas growl, roar, scream and complain. So do the leopards. The elephants trumpet, and the rhinos grunt, and the cattle low, and the donkeys (worst of all the noisemakers) utter the sounds that have earned them the name of "Somali canaries." The sheep and goats bleat piteously, and the natives sing. It sounds rather like an interesting preview of the sounds in hell.

Hop into the jeep with Harry Selby, a professional hunter, and me, and we'll take a spin along the dubious road to Merille lugger to shoot some sand grouse, which for some reason drink there every day at exactly 8:12 A.M. The morning is still cool and fresh, but by noon the sun will be pounding with an unbelievable vindictiveness and your mouth will be blistered from thirst.

We bump along in the jeep over a road that is no road, pausing occasionally to let some elephant cross, or to shoo some giraffes or an ostrich off the road. We see herds of Grant's gazelle and a strange animal called a gerenuk, which is actually an antelope but has a neck like a giraffe and stands erect to eat dried leaves from the myrrh tree.

Once we get to Merille, we have to scare three or four rhino out of the track on the blinding white sand, rock-studded and treacherous, before we can pass. It's breeding time at the moment, and the cows are testy, the bulls formidable and stupid.

Grouse are beginning to fly in as we park the jeep and stand with shotguns behind a rock near the waterhole. Harry and I each have a gunbearer to collect the dead birds and a minimum of seventy-five rounds of shotgun shells. We shoot the sand grouse to feed the camp, not for sport. We shoot guinea and francolin as well, because meat won't keep in this heat and you must feed twenty people on a day-to-day basis.

The birds come in by the massed thousands now, pintails and some few speckles and an imperial or so. As desert birds, they drink only once a day and you cannot frighten them off the water until they've had their sup. They are not large – a pound apiece, perhaps – and they fly as swiftly as teal in a hurry. As the birds dip and bunch over the pool, Harry and I loose off both barrels. I imagine twelve fell to my gun, the same, or more, to Harry's. They come again, balled into a mass, and again we loose off the shotguns. Another double dozen.

The camp is fed, now, when you remember the guinea fowl that our other professional hunter, Andy Holmberg, and Chester (Blackie) Kronfeld, our photographer, will undoubtedly collect on their morning safari. We take a few more shots for the sport of it, then have a drink out of the canvas water bag that hangs from the front of Jessica III, the patient jeep.

This day we must have seen a dozen elephant, half a dozen rhino, a gross of lesser kudu and a couple of hundred other animals on the Merille lugger alone. On the plains, of course, a thousand or more zebras and gerunuks, and several herds of oryxes, a donkeylike creature with long, straight horns on his head and a foolish black-and-white face.

We reach Seralippe again about 4:00 P.M., and the place is full of Samburu braves, throwing spears and running foot races and attracting flies. A herd of sheep, goats and cattle is being driven through the camp. It's a typical afternoon on the lugger.

Eventually the constant activity of the dry oases spurred somebody in our camp to wonder how Hollywood had missed it. We were not wondering idly. Very shortly thereafter a messenger came with word that M-G-M had decided to shoot the big battle sequence of the Clark Gable – Ava Gardner picture, *Mogambo*, in that area.

Trucks creaked and groaned down the roads. Airplanes flew in from Nairobi every morning. A huge camp was set up at Archer's Post, and another – a false Samburu village and District Commissioner's house – was built under the sheltering arms of my fine old mountain, Ololokwe.

The only swimming pool in the vast burning expanse of the Northern Frontier, in which we used to lose fatigue after a hard day of chasing rhino, was suddenly full of starlets, ham actors and assistant directors. Scared the devil out of the animals, but entranced the natives, who performed as the wicked Injuns in the picture.

That was when we decided to leave, just before Clark and Ava and Grace Kelly came along to compete with the elephants. We felt that for once, the dry oases, the luggers, had overmatched themselves in the attraction of wildlife.

"He Fights Lions Barehanded" again shows Ruark the reporter, here exercising his instinct for a saleable, if essentially fluffy, story published in *The Saturday Evening Post*, December 26, 1953.

Although Carr-Hartley and his wild-animal business actually are little more memorable than a Sunday-supplement piece on teenage baton-twirlers, Ruark had a larger, far more serious project in mind. The incidents of Carr-Hartley becoming bewitched during an elephant hunt and subsequently practicing witchcraft himself reappear in *Something of Value*, performed by the character Henry McKenzie – right down to the detail of reviving the unconscious thief with a pan of dishwater.

Michael McIntosh

CHAPTER NINE

HE FIGHTS LIONS BAREHANDED

T he lion charged the man. The man had no gun, since his gunbearer had dropped it. So the man charged the lion. And swung a punch at her – she was a full-grown lioness – and knocked her flat. He is an impatient man.

He used the same tactics last year when the Mau Mau terrorist uprising erupted in full violence in Kenya, which is where the man lives. Returning briefly from a motion-picture safari, on which he was the paid chaperon of a flock of wild animals, the man went to check on the welfare of his farm, which is in a place called Rumuruti. His family was fine, but he was told by his panicked native employees that a message had come from the Mau Mau, mentioning pointedly that his head had an A-1 priority on the Christmas list that later was to collect thirteen heads through the holiday season.

The man speaks fluent Kikuyu, as well as Meru, Swahili, Nandi and half a dozen other dialects common to East Africa. He has a booming voice, which can be heard from Mt. Kenya to Kilimanjaro in Tanganyika on a quiet day. He used it now, in profane Kikuyu, the dialect of the Mau Mau sect.

"Tell them," he said, "that I regret I will not be available for their pleasure in the holiday season, because I must go to Uganda with the *Bwana Picha 'Mkubwa* (Metro-Goldwyn-Mayer). But tell them I will be back at the farm after the first week of January, and they are free to come and collect my head then – if they can."

This would be a typical retort from a black-mustached man named Carr-Hartley, who weighs some 240 pounds and has a barrel of a body; who refuses to tell his first name; who is a witch doctor of sorts; who lassos adult rhinos for fun; who has a tame wild leopard that regularly rips the shirt off his back; who supplies most of the major zoos of the world with animals he catches himself; who furnishes nearly all of the wild animals featured today in African movies; who has fought off bull elephants with an empty gun, and who is afraid of no thing, living or supernatural, from Mau Mau to lady lions with an evil disposition. It is unnecessary to add that he returned on schedule to his farm and still has his head.

Carr hasn't come through his thirty-odd years of African experiences without a few claw marks on both his hide and his psyche. He bears assorted scars from one rhino, two lions, one cheetah, one hippo, three elephants and a mongoose, which bit him severely. On one occasion – which will be described later – he was thoroughly bewitched by a Wakamba witch doctor, and it cost him considerable money and more face to buy himself loose from the hex. This resulted in his becoming quite a voodoo hand himself.

Yet he has maintained as steady a love for both animal and native as any man in that part of Africa, where love for animal and native is a rule among the white settlers. He still addresses a lioness that snapped off his finger as "my darling," and, as a matter of fact, calls most of his creatures, from Willie, the hyena, to the ugliest rhinos in the world, "my darling" and "my pretty pet." He is a trainer without cruelty, and to see the love affair between Hartley and Chui, the full-grown leopard, is an amazing thing, as, in the wild state, Carr "loathes and detests leopards above all other beasts."

Hartley cuts his life into about four sections. He is primarily a rancher. His biggest income derives from the sale of wild animals to zoos. He is a consultant to major movie companies that need animal sequences, usually providing the animals on location and putting them through their paces. Lastly, like every other able-bodied male in Kenya today, he is a Mau Mau hunter.

A trip to Hartley's ranch on the Laikipia plains is no journey for a fainthearted person. There are too many large things with horns, hoofs and fangs wandering around loose. The ladies of our party last spring went to the retiring room to repair their beauty before lunch and were rather rudely invaded by Tommy, a full-grown chimp that adores girls. The pilot of our plane, a brave man, was sitting on the hood of a truck when Chui, the mammoth leopard, flashed up and licked all the back hair off the pilot's neck. The pilot turned green and froze, which was just as well, because Chui is apt to be a little nervous around strangers. You might say that it takes a little daring to accept Hartley's invitation to ride one of his mature white rhinos, especially when the other rhino is heavy with calf and feeling testy as a result.

It's a beautiful farm, the buildings of native make, with high-peaked, thatched roofs, clustered under yellow thorn trees with the animal pens well away. But on moonlit nights it sounds like an animal hell. A dozen or more lions roar. The leopard coughs and grunts. The baboons and chimpanzees squeak. The elephants trumpet, the rhinos do whatever it is rhinos do, and Willie the hyena (he starred in *Snows of Kilimanjaro*) adds his own peculiar calliope chest tones.

Like so many other Africans, Hartley is a professional killer turned tender. He used to hunt for the game department. In four years he exterminated 1,387 Cape buffalo, and on elephant control he holds the record for one gun. He clobbered 518 elephant all by his lonesome, none of the shooting being done by game scouts or assistants. But the killing sickened him, and he turned in the gun for a lasso and a power wagon, and became a snarer of dangerous game for large-scale zoo supply and a director of fauna for the movies. The animal business is highly profitable today. Hartley's gross business to zoos in 1952 hit £15,000. Some forty percent is profit. He commands fancy consultant fees from the movies, and with meat at its current prices, he shows no loss on his cattle operation. The only thing that does not reimburse him is Mau Mau hunting, a painful but necessary occupation today.

Hartley's early professional hunting experiences are slightly fantastic. That episode of knocking out the lion – at least momentarily – saved his life.

"It was a lioness as big as Monty," Hartley says. Monty is his darling of darlings, his No. 1 film star. "She was wounded, and she jumped me and my gunbearer, knocking him down and knocking my rifle, that he was carrying, into the bush. She laid back her ears and came at me, and she looked a little scared. I said, 'You're windy, sister; come on.' I swung at her as she jumped, catching her on the head and knocking her flat, and then she walloped me right out from under my hat. We were both knocked out for a minute. Then she got on top of me and swiped me across the tummy with one paw, and I had horrid visions of my tripes tumbling out. I was trying to stick my arm in her mouth to keep her from biting my head off when the boy came up with the rifle and shot her.

"I was afraid to look at my belly. I hurt like dammit and I knew I was laid wide open. I told the boy to take the shirt off and tell me the worst. He was a Laikipia lad with a sense of humor.

"'*Nini?*' I said. 'What about my stomach?'

"'*Mafuta tu, bwana,*' he said. 'Only fat.' I was mightily relieved, I can tell you."

Hartley, sitting now at the bar of Nairobi's Hotel Norfolk, rubbed a livid welt on his head with a hand from which the tip of a finger was missing, because a tame cheetah had bit it off.

"What's the matter with your head?" somebody at the bar asked him.

"Tommy," Hartley said, speaking to me. "Since you were up at my place yesterday, I caught Tommy – the big chimp – sitting at my desk throwing papers up in the air and raising hell in general. When I shooed him away and sat down, he turned and belted me clean out of the chair. Quite a slugger, that chimp."

While Hartley was on elephant control, before the war, shooting rogues and depopulating farm areas of the huge beasts that trampled down native shambas, he had the usual narrow squeaks that are any elephant hunter's daily due. He does not, however, profess any great admiration for elephants' ferocity, although most professional hunters rank Jumbo at the top for unpredictable orneriness. Hartley claims to have turned several charges by ramming his empty gun in the face of the animal and scuttling away as it flinched and turned aside. This is not generally considered sound procedure – which may be why Hartley has been beaten up by elephants on three occasions.

What he remembers most clearly of his early elephant-shooting days is the time he became bewitched. He was shooting on control in the Wakamba country, and he had arranged a division of the carcasses between two separate tribal groups. (The Wakamba are one of the few East African tribes who fancy elephant meat.) He found a group of natives poaching on another clan's carcass one day, and cursed them roundly. When it happened again, he laid his stick to the backs of several. Next day, his headman came to him with a worried expression. "You shouldn't have beaten those people, *bwana*," he said. "They've put a curse on you, and you'll shoot no more elephants

After the Hunt - Cheetahs

here until the curse is lifted."

Hartley laughed in that tremendous voice. "I've been shooting half a dozen elephants a day," he said. "I'll keep on shooting elephants. There's nothing to this magic business. Tell those people if they poach those carcasses again, I'll beat them again."

At the hotel bar Hartley bit an inch out of his rum drink and went on with the narrative:

"You know, from that day on, for six weeks, I never fired a gun. I trailed elephants. I saw elephants. I started to shoot elephants. But every time I got close enough to shoot, something happened. Elephants meant money to me in those days. At the end of six weeks I was desperate. Times were hard and I might have lost my farm. I went to see an old Wakamba witch doctor I knew and told him the story. He said he'd cure me; lift the curse. For fifty shillings, one half in advance. I finally decided to pay him.

"He came up with a calabash full of cowrie shells and reedbuck horns and some bones and told me that I'd have to move the camp about a thousand yards away. He waved a stick at me – a stick with seven tails on it and seven knots tied in the tails. Then he built a brush fire at the end of the old campsite, cut both our fingers, mingled blood, poured some powder in the fire and spat in my face seven times. Then he told me to drive the vehicles through the fire and make a new camp. I felt a fool, but I did it. We squatted down before the fire at the new camp, and he began to talk.

"Don't get up early in the morning, *bwana*,' he said. 'Sleep late. Take your tea in a leisurely fashion. Shave. Have your breakfast served in your tent. On no account must you look for elephants. Elephants will look for you. The boy who brings your breakfast will show you three elephants, all big bulls. Don't hurry. Have your food. The elephants won't go away. Don't leave your tent. Then, after breakfast, after you've shaved, whenever you're ready, go and shoot them. You will shoot three bull elephants no more than a thousand yards from your tent.'"

Hartley investigated his drink again and looked seriously at me.

"I thought this was a lot of nonsense, of course," he said. "But next morning when the boy came with the tea, he chattered, 'Oh, *bwana, bwana!* There are three big bull elephants right out in front of the tent!' I had a look. There they were, three big ones, waving their ears not five hundred yards away. I started to grab my gun when I remembered what the old witch-doctor type had said. I told the boy to bring my shaving water, and then to fetch my breakfast. I wasn't going to muck up the old codger's spell.

"I shaved and I et my breakfast. I dressed and I called a gunbearer and went out. The elephants were out in an open glade with a nice piece of bush behind it. I stalked up, and the wind was just right. I got one with the right and one with the left. Ordinarily you'd expect the other elephant to be in Tanganyika by the time I'd reloaded, but he just stood there and I walloped him. Fine bulls, all, with fine ivory. I paced the distance from camp – exactly twelve hundred yards. I went back to the camp and waited for the witch doctor, and he came about dusk.

"'Now you must leave here,' he told me. 'The spell is lifted. Break your camp and go to Mbeyu. There you'll shoot seven fine elephants in one day. Then you must quit. You will shoot no more elephants this year. You may try, but it will be no use. I will go with you to Mbeyu, and you will see that I speak the truth.'

"We went to Mbeyu," Hartley continued. "It was just like the old boy said. I shot seven elephants the first day. I hunted for another three weeks to prove him wrong, and never loosed off the weapon. I was back again the next year, and the curse was on in full force. It was the same story all over again. It wanted the same remedy, and a slightly higher fee, to lift it. Back again the next year – hunted and hunted like a mad thing for weeks and never a shot. Bought the old boy off again, and he lifted the curse for the third time. I said to meself, finally, this has gone too far. I believe in it thoroughly, now, so I might as well join it. I paid the old man a whacking sum this time, and wound up with his paraphernalia – cowrie shells, calabash and the lot. The final cure was a horn I tied to my head. I've the horn still, and that's part of the sequel to the story."

The sequel, not related to me by Hartley, was simply that his skill as a caster of spells worked so potently that he is regarded as a tremendous *mundumugu* among the Kikuyu in his area and the slaughter of his cattle by the Mau Mau had ceased abruptly. Also, no further overtures had been made toward his head. What had happened was that Hartley had noticed much thievery among his native help, almost entirely Kikuyu, especially in such valued commodities as razor-sharp skinning knives.

There are several native tests to determine lying and thievery among the hypersuperstitious Kikuyu, one of which is passing a hot iron over the tongue. The theory is that the guilty party will be so nervous that his tongue will lose its protective moisture, so he who has the burnt tongue is adjudged the guilty party.

Hartley scorned such simple savergery. He dug up his sorcerer's kit, including the horn, and lined up his help. He announced that he was going to cast very possibly the biggest spell ever thrown by anybody, black or white.

"I tied on the horn," Carr says, "and got out the calabash and the cowries and some powder, and I made a few passes and spat in a couple of eyes, and then all the boys took off. All but one. He fell flat in his tracks, his eyes rolled back, and foam came out of his mouth. I was scared stiff. I thought that I was going to have a dead Kuke on my hands, and hell's own amount of trouble explaining it to the D.C. So I ran to the cookhouse, got a gourd full of soapy dishwater, hurled it into his face, made some more passes, shook my horn at him and spat in his eye again, and he came to. Went and got my knives, too, the blighter did. But I've been sort of chary of magic since then. These people take it too seriously."

Where Hartley wields his real magic is with animals. This has nothing to do with mumbo-jumbo, but consists of infinite patience and a vast amount of love. He can take anything, even a hyena, and usually bring out a softer quality in it - and when he fails, there are always Mrs. Hartley and the kids.

"Daphne's the genius," Hartley says. "She weighs ninety-two pounds when she's husky – right now she's less than that, due to the strain of this Mau Mau business, and I've packed her and the kids off to South Africa for a bit – but she can take anything that utterly defeats me, and love it into submission."

The rhino is generally known as the surliest, shortest-tempered, stupidest of all the African animals, but Gus and Mitzi, the two adult white rhinos that he raised after snatching them from their mother's side, have done steady palfrey duty for all the Hartley kids and the visitors who come to see his farm. Hartley treats the rhinos like a couple of cows, except that, at the moment, Mitzi's incipient motherhood has made her a trifle nasty.

Carr tickles his lions on the ears, and will reach into a cage and take two cubs away from their mother. His newest baby rhino, Sheila, is as tame as a Shetland pony.

A marvel of training success is Chui, the big tom leopard. For treachery, cruelty, stealth, unpredictability and erratic orneriness, the leopard is the worst of all the dangerous game, bar elephants, which are mainly big, mean and honestly murderous. Chui rubs against the wire of his cage, purrs and allows any stranger to scratch his ears and caress his nose. When Carr turned him loose in a big outdoor arena he uses for wild-game sequences, Chui flashed out of his cage, leaped a dozen feet through the air, and wound up on Hartley's back, tearing his shirt off. Hartley stood perfectly still. Chui released him and bounded off with Hartley's hat in his mouth, like a big and playful pussy. When it was time to go, and Chui had wearied of frightening the guests – he dived between my legs and scared me into mild hysteria – Hartley clucked at him and he scurried back into his cage with a feline sigh of relief.

The other training success Willie – or is it Wilhelmina? – the hyena that stole the show from Gregory Peck in the African epic, *The Snows of Kilimanjaro*. Willie is not only intelligent, for a hyena, and a superb ham, but he is one of nature's marvels, a true hermaphrodite. Many hyenas have both male and female characteristics, one dominant, one recessive, but few can completely change sex, as Willie can. Hartley ran a controlled experiment with Willie. He penned him once with two young female hyenas, and they soon had pups.

Later, Willie was again penned with four ostensibly female hyenas, and to his considerable embarrassment, was himself delivered of a thriving litter. At the moment, Willie is in the masculine, or Non-Wilhelmina, stage of his career, but seems considerably puzzled and not a little sheepish about the whole thing.

Hartley's roster of movie stars at the moment is quite large. In addition to Willie, and to Chui, which you might remember as the large beast that attempted to claw his way into Deborah Kerr's tent in *King Solomon's Mines*, there are Monty, Fanny, Mary, Podgy, Regular, Caesar and Brutus, all adult lions; Coco, an extraordinarily hammy hamadryad baboon; Tommy, the amorous chimp, and Clark and Ava – after Gable and Gardner, in Carr's last film effort – two starlet lion cubs. His other Wampus Babies not yet ready for stardom are Grace Kelly, a giraffe, and Sheila, the juvenile rhino. There are some several hundred extras, ranging from monkeys to mongooses to the surliest cheetah I have met lately. Carr keeps him in the house, hoping to sweeten his temper.

Hartley has worked on nineteen films, but is about to swear off, since he completed some chores for *Mogambo*, the all-time epochal epic which M-G-M shot in East Africa, to the consternation of most wildlife and practically all the natives from the Northern Frontier to the southern Masai. One of Hartley's chores was supervising a moth-eaten old black leopard that M-G-M flew in from America.

"Why," Hartley says, "the good Lord only knows."

"The cat got sick," Carr says, "probably pneumonia, due to being flown in at twenty-two thousand feet. I pumped him full of penicillin, and after 'twas all over – the shooting, I mean – they wanted me to put the poor old pussy out of his misery. I said, 'I've cured him once; damme if I'll kill him after I've cured him.' What with one thing and another, I gave up. Odd people, film people."

Hartley has lived all his life on the slopes of Mt. Kenya, and has been shooting and trapping wild animals since he was seventeen. He learned the use of the lasso from a troupe of Texas cowboys who were touring Africa, endeavoring to use the lariat on dangerous game. He catches rhino easily, once lassoing four white rhino in as many days. He throws his noose from afoot, ahorse or from a car. A power wagon is his favorite vehicle for coursing the bigger stuff. He races along at axle-smashing speed over rocks, through dry dongas, over logs and through thick bush, and snares the animal either with a swung lasso or from a noose on the end of a stick, with a running loop that dislodges from the pole. After years of experimenting, he has finally perfected a method of capturing a young elephant without killing the mother first – a delicate process of separating them and whisking off with the child while mamma squeals with fury.

Chasing beasts with Hartley is an experience. His burly vehicle romps madly over the terrain, knocking down trees with the abandon of a bulldozer gone amok. The animal is eventually snared – this is the easy part – and then must be either loaded into the back of the truck or walked, fighting all the time, back to camp where it then must be encouraged to enter the compound. This is a matter of ropes and

116

men, and great patience. In the purloining of cubs of the cat family, there is always the mamma, which is something serious to consider. The writer once went against a lady lion that had cubs, and we did not shoot her because she stopped at about a dozen feet. We were not attempting to steal the cubs either.

But there is a tremendous exhilaration to coursing animals, since the terrain is more dangerous than the beast, and a temporary breakdown, such as a busted axle, can kill you very surely and competently. Hartley thrives on it, seems to delight in the idea of death, violently administered. He seems disappointed not to be dead. Bullfighters of the old school experienced the same brief bit of hard-way ecstasy, I'm told.

Hartley does not course his animals to exhaustion for a couple of reasons. One is that it is inhumane, since African animals do not possess a tremendous endurance, and are likely to die if overextended. The other is that the Kenya Game Department, an inflexible organization, keeps a stern eye on Mr. Hartley's operation. He must obtain a special license, in advance, for every animal he wishes to catch, and the game department can be arbitrarily capricious. If he violates a tiny letter of its laws, it can put him out of business entirely.

He was in hot water once, in the filming of *Savage Splendor*, when a female rhino charged his vehicle and died as a result. They had been using five different rhino to film the sequence, and when the old lady kicked off, Mr. Hartley found himself in such a boiling situation with the game boys that not even Wakamba witchcraft could restore him to favor for some time.

Hartley's No. 1 customer for zoo animals today, which may seem odd, is Japan, which takes seventy percent of his stuff. The Japanese are primarily interested in monkeys, giraffe, zebra, rhino, hippo, assorted bucks, and carnivora, in that order. The United States, Europe, Great Britain and South America follow in demand for his lively stock.

The price list is somewhat as follows: Elephant, from £700 to £900 apiece; rhino, £650 to £850; leopard, £50 to £70; lion, £80 to £250; hippo, £650 to £950; buck, £20 to £180 (the highest priced is the red, heavy-necked roan antelope); giraffe, £200; and zebra, £100. Hartley buys about fifteen percent of his stock from other trappers and catches the rest himself. The last time I saw Carr he was greatly perturbed over the mislaying of a shipment of sitatunga, a rather rare, swamp-dwelling antelope which has the equivalent of webbed hoofs.

One might say that Hartley is possibly the happiest and best-adjusted man to his job in the world, since he knows animals, loves animals, no longer kills animals, and is surrounded always by animals. And he is raising a brood of likely successors, all boys – Kenneth Patrick, sixteen; Brian George, fifteen; Ian Roy, thirteen; and Robert Michael, eleven. They ride ostriches instead of horses, rhinos instead of hotrods, and take lion cubs to bed with them. Chimpanzees join in their games, and leopards sleep across their feet. They have cheetahs to hunt with instead of dogs.

Harry Selby, of Nanyuki, a professional hunter and no amateur with wild animals himself, has a healthy respect for Cape buffalo. He tells the following story: "I was up to Carr's one day to see a bull buffalo he had wandering loose about the place. I asked one of the kids to fetch him, and we discovered him behind the house. The buff was feeling pretty lazy and balky, and wouldn't move. So the kid went up behind him and bit him on the tail!" Selby, who has run his jeep over a wild lion's tail to get him to move, seemed shocked at the memory.

The steady pursuit of Mau Mau, which has disarranged the lives of all Kenya settlers, is cutting heavily into Hartley's business this year, but Hartley takes an occasional week off from command patrol in the Aberdare mountains to catch up a fresh batch of game and to check on the welfare of his beasts. He has just about decided to give up his movie work, at least for a while, until things cool down. This is due perhaps as much to exasperation with the odd ways of film people, both American and British, as to the tremendous pressure of his other duties.

"I have done a lot of things for films," Hartley said, rather wistfully. "I have vaccinated sick leopards and provided acting hyenas and arranged rhino charges and figured out elephant stampedes and done odd things with lions. But not so long ago some assistant director told me he wanted me to arrange a shot of some snowy egrets picking meat out of the teeth of some crocodiles. I speak English and Swahili and Kikuyu and Meru, and some Wakamba and Nandi and Masai, but I'm damned if I speak crocodile or egret. And short of being able to tell the creatures to get busy on the dental sequence, I'm stopped."

Hartley was squatted on his knees in front of his pregnant rhino, Mitzi, as he spoke. "I can talk a little rhino, though," he said, crooning, and shoving his arm to the elbow into Mitzi's mouth, to scratch her inner jaws lovingly. "Ah, that's my baby, my beauty, my darling, my pet."

A side from his "The Old Man and the Boy" pieces, Ruark wrote few short stories during the most fruitful years of his career, and "The Nairobi Incident" is the only one with an African theme.

It was published in *Collier's*, July 22, 1955, just three months after *Something of Value* appeared in print. The timing no doubt was meant to influence book sales, and the story itself may have even been conceived and written for that purpose alone. In any case, it's not a particularly serious piece of work, although loosely based on a true incident and quite well-written.

Michael McIntosh

CHAPTER TEN

THE NAIROBI INCIDENT

The other day in Madrid, I ran into Mark Manson. It was a routine business trip, and I had some time to kill – I'm a traveling man, so I always have time to kill. I sell hotel fixtures, and I sell them wherever anybody wants to buy them, which gives me a pretty broad beat. After twenty years in this business there may be one hotel I haven't visited, but you would have to go to Tibet to find it.

Except this new deluxe job in Spain. The plaster was still wet on this one. The elevator boys were still trying to figure out how to close the doors on the lifts, and the first chef hadn't been introduced formally to the second cook. It looked fine from the outside, though – a great big slab of granite front with a rich overlay of some kind of quartz that looked like jade. This was the latest twinklestar in the crown of Mr. Henry Hopkinson Hathaway. Old Three-H had finally circled the globe with his big, expensive boardinghouses, and he called this one the Flamenco-Hathaway. He could just as easily have called it the Hathaway-Flamenco.

Maybe he stole a couple of pointers from the Castellana-Hilton and the Fenix and the Ritz and the Palace, but he had what looked to be a very decent pub. The carpets were deep enough to drown in, and the doormen actually opened the door for you. The desk help was Swiss, naturally, with a couple of Spaniards added to lend a little local flavor. They had been educated at Harrow before they took their honors at Magdalen, which is pronounced "maudlin" and is located in an English college town called Oxford. They wore the usual black-coat, striped-pants, hard-collar uniform, so as not to scare off the sedate set. But the rest of the help was got up like *feria* week in Seville, in flat-crowned hats, short bolero jackets, high-braced pants, and you felt as though all you needed was to see Manolete come alive again and stick a bull in the green marble lounge.

The business was terrific. All the tourists that ever bought cameras were charging up and down the lobby. Just for laughs I walked over to the reception desk (which announced itself in French, Spanish, English and German) and inquired mildly if I might have a room for the night. The clerk looked at me as if I'd asked him to cut off Salvador Dali's mustache.

"I'm dreadfully afraid, sir, that we are booked solid through the festival of San Ysidro," he said, patting his marcel.

"When's that?" I asked him.

"A year from today," he said. "This year's San Ysidro ended yesterday."

"That's nice," I said, "but I can't wait," and stalked off to the bar.

In the cocktail room Spaniards and tourists were packed solid, and they weren't drinking *manzanilla*. They were drinking bonded Scotch at Heaven knows how much the hooker, and the best English gin. There was nothing doing in the bar, if it was a drink you wanted. All the early drinkers had staked their claims on space.

I mushed through the deep broadloom as far as the dining room, figuring I would test the new cuisine. It was only two o'clock, and ordinarily a Madrileño doesn't even consider the possibility of food before four. But the dining room was loaded and waited for. So was the terrace outside. This was no hotel: This was Fort Knox, Henry Hopkinson Hathaway version. They needed no fixtures from me.

When I was halfway to the street a hand dropped on my shoulder, and a voice remembered from other places said quietly: *"Jambo, Bwana 'Mkubwa."* I won't say I was startled, but so few Spaniards know how to say: "Hello, Big Master," in Swahili, which is a sort of trade language they use around Central Africa. I looked and there was Mark Manson.

Some of him looked like the old Mark Manson, the Mark Manson I used to know. His long, melancholy nose was the same, and so were the mournful brown eyes. But the double chins were gone and the tailoring was exceptional. The suit was a simple blue double-breasted, but obviously Savile Row. The tie was Charvet and the shoes were Peal and the silk shirt was born quite close to the Corso Umberto in Rome.

I goggled.

"Shauri gani?" I said, for lack of something better. It only means "What's new?" or "How's it going?"

"Hi m'zuri, m'zuri sana kapisa," he said, a long way to say, "Okay." He seemed to be glad to speak the language again.

"What are you doing in this town, in this joint?" I asked him, in English.

"I work here," he said. "I run this joint, as you call it. I am the managing director."

"But – "

"Let's go up to my suite and have a drink," he said. "You can't wedge yourself into that wretched bar."

"I know," I said. "I tried. But oh, how the pesetas roll in."

"It's a living," he said. "I'm successful at it. Let's go and have that drink."

I followed Mark Manson around some mahogany desks and he bowed me into a private elevator. In a few seconds we stepped out onto the hotel roof. There were a few acres of trees and clipped green grass; a small swimming pool and what looked like a bridle path, but probably wasn't. The bar he led me into was slightly smaller than Ebbets Field, but with better fixtures. I know fixtures.

The female fixture who came in after Mark had yelled "Hoy!" was quite something to see. She had that black hair and great violet eyes. And the baby she was carrying was a tiny carbon of her.

"This is my wife," Mark said. "My old friend Joe Patrick. And this is the heiress. Say hello, sweetie, to Mr. Patrick."

"Glop," said the heiress. "So nice," said the wife. "What may I do for you, darling?" she asked Mark Manson.

"See if you can get the chef to send us up a Madrasi curry and some cold guinea fowl," Mark said. "Lunch in about an hour. Right now, darling, if you'd excuse us, we've a lot of old times to talk about. You won't mind, will you?"

"Of course not, dear," she said. "I'll be seeing you soon and often, I hope, Mr. Patrick." She walked away with the angel child cooing over her shoulder. She walked like ladies walk when they've been ladies a long time. About three hundred bucks' worth of Balenciaga suit didn't hurt the exit either.

"The same," Mark said. He didn't ask it. He said it.

"Sure," I said, "Martini *a maui*," and grinned. A martini *a maui* was my contribution to East African culture. I taught the barman at the Livingstone Arms in Nairobi to make it, and the evil spread. A martini *a maui* was a triple, very dry martini "on the mountain" – *maui* being as close to "rocks" as I could come in Swahili.

Mark mixed the brain-busters, and he mixed them as well as the barman ever did. We touched glasses. "Bonzo," said Mark Manson.

"Bonzo," I answered.

Two very slow, very fat tears trickled down Mark Manson's face.

The first time I was ever really conscious of Mark Manson was some years ago, in Nairobi. Mark was standing in the middle of the guests' lounge of a plush hotel called the Livingstone Arms, of which he was manager. He had just been hit in the face with a bundle of laundry, thrown by a rich American lady. She had a throwing arm like Willie Mays.

"…It's not enough," the rich American lady cried, in a voice that had been tempered to a cutting edge on people she regarded as inferior. "It's not enough that the food you serve here would gag a buzzard, and that these thieves you call servants are stealing me blind. But I've had the last hole burned in my clothes with that special acid your laundry uses. Here's my dirty laundry. Wash it yourself. Also, you're too fat to be only thirty years old!"

I forgot to say that this happened in the middle of a birthday party that a few employees had decided to give Mark Manson, possibly in the hope of buttering him up for a pay raise. You can imagine how this little scene reacted on the help.

Manson fought his way out of the laundry and bowed, his face as red as the clay outside. "Yes, me lady," he said. "Immediately, me lady. Thank you, me lady."

The party drifted away. It was several days before anybody, even DaSilva, the dining-room steward, could bear to look at Mark Manson. And DaSilva was the closest thing Mark had to a friend in the Livingstone Arms. But I glanced out into the court the day after the party, and Manson was walking slowly toward Cottage 19 with his arms full of what appeared to be freshly washed and ironed laundry.

Manson never found anybody who could hold still long enough to let him talk about himself, so nobody ever quite knew how he got hooked up in the hotel business. But he fitted the business about as

Native Tracker

well as his clothes fitted him. They were obviously bought off the nail, and they seemed to have been hurled at him. He had longish black hair, which he coated with grease. From his accent you would gather he came from somewhere in the north of England, and he must have started in the hotel business as a dishwasher.

Personally, I always liked Manson. Maybe pitied him would be a better word. His eyes looked like a dog's – a dog that had been abused so much that he always expected a kick as a salutation. But DaSilva, the steward, and I were about the only people who had any time for him.

At that time Manson was very fat – not jolly fat, but sloppy fat. He had a skinny frame and the fat was laid on him in lumps, as if a backward child had troweled it onto him. His belly bulged and his thin-boned face was hung with extra chins and pouches. He looked like a young, badly dressed, dissolute pasha.

And he was lonesome, terribly lonesome. I'm a night bird, myself, and sometimes when I would come back from the Traveller's Club after a session with the boys, I'd see Manson stalking around the courtyard in the waning moonlight, just hoping he'd see somebody to talk to – maybe a fairy princess, for all I know. When the airline pilots and the pretty hostesses would come in after an evening's dancing and go off to somebody's cottage for the last nightcap, poor Mark Manson would sort of surface from the lilacs and say a long-drawn good night, hoping they'd ask him in too. They never did.

There was a New Year's party at the Livingstone one year, and Manson got himself slightly high on champagne. He lurched over to Peggy Something-or-Other, a cute little blonde air hostess, and planted a kiss on her. Mistletoe or no mistletoe, she slapped his face. When he reeled back, her boyfriend, a navigator, gave him the other half, but the navigator had his hand clenched. They hauled the manager off to bed.

I could case-history you to death with Manson's troubles, but it would take a couple of years. He couldn't manage his help. The firm that owned the hotel wouldn't give him a raise in pay. The food got worse. The service was so bad that people quit trying to use the telephones even in case of fire. One day a little hellion named Robbie McDonough succeeded in teaching his pet parrot to scream: "Manson's a clod!" every time Mark passed the cage in the patio. That same day

Mark had an argument with one of his reception girls. She hit him on the head with an inkwell, just as the airport bus disgorged a crowd of passengers. It was a lovely scene. You didn't know whether to laugh or cry over him.

The day after the inkwell incident, Manson was sitting all alone on the veranda, just under the sign that said: *All Dogs Strictly Forbidden.* It was teatime, and he was brooding into his teacup, fingering the bandage on his ear. His face was the color of putty, and there were brownish bags under his eyes. He looked as if he'd been left out in the rain too long.

There was a howl from the patio and the thump of a kick and a yelp of pain. Manson looked up, prepared to disapprove of the disturbance. The ugliest dog ever created dragged up to the veranda and skulked under Manson's chair, where it crouched and whimpered. A big porter hauled the dog out from under the chair and aimed another kick at it.

Manson looked at the dog. The dog looked at Manson. It was the kind of look that might pass between two strangers who suddenly discovered they were blood brothers. The dog slithered over on its belly and tried to hide itself behind Manson's legs. Manson looked up at the no-dogs sign and then he looked back at the dog. He patted the dog on the head. Then he jerked a thumb at the porter. "Leave him alone," he said. "Get the hell off the porch and go back to work."

The dog still whimpered and shivered. Manson picked it up – it was a big dog, but starved thin – and carried it off to his cottage. For a week you could see room service carrying a great many things – minced tenderloin steak, quarts of milk, eggs, raw liver, burnt crankcase oil, sulphur and flea powder – into the cottage. We didn't see much of Manson around the hotel for a week. He was nursing the dog.

One day he came out of the cottage and he was followed by the dog. It was the damnedest-looking dog I ever saw. It was part white bull terrier, and part African ridgeback, and part wildebeest, for all anybody knew. It had a long straggly tail, and one eye was circled with black. It had scabby pink patches all over its scruffy white body, where the hair was just beginning to grow back from a serious siege of mange, and suddenly we knew what the crankcase oil and sulphur were for; there never was a better mange cure. In a peculiar way, the dog and Manson looked alike. They kind of shambled, and didn't fit their skin or their clothes. They looked as if they had no business being there on the porch of a first-class hotel.

I walked up to the pair and made a joke. "Just what *is* it?" I asked.

"Don't be a fool," Manson said sharply. "It's a dog. His name's Bonzo."

"Bonzo?" I said. "There hasn't been a dog named Bonzo since the last century got tired and quit."

"His name is Bonzo," Manson said. "He reminds me of that dog I used to read about as a kid – the one with the big black circle around his eye. Buster Brown or somebody had him. He likes his name, don't you, Bonzo?"

Bonzo leered, and sidled over to nip me tentatively on the leg. "Ouch!" I said. "Take this monster off me!"

Both Bonzo and his master beamed with pride. "You see," Manson said, "He's getting his confidence back."

I must say that Bonzo got his confidence back faster than any dog, or man, I ever saw. Maybe it was the steady feeding that did it. It wasn't long before Bonzo had the run of the dining room. He had a table and chair of his own. He also had a chair at Manson's table. He was attended personally at meals by DaSilva, the maître de, and he ate off a plate – after one of the waiters, having been summoned by a bark, cut his food for him. He sat in his chair while he ate.

Bonzo had barely ironed the wrinkles out of his belly when he began complaining about the food and service. If the chops or the steak were tough or stringy, Bonzo raised his voice and disrupted the dining room. If the service was slow, Bonzo bit the waiter. In almost no time at all the hotel's food and service improved. So, as a matter of fact, did the clientele.

This monstrous dog also had his own chair in the lobby of the Livingstone Arms, precisely under the large sign that said *All Dogs Strictly Forbidden*. Bonzo enforced the law to its tiniest letter. No straggling mongrel or pampered poodle ever approached the veranda steps without sudden and violent assault by Bonzo, who now believed himself to be the house dick in addition to his other duties.

The private-peeper business was particularly noticeable at night. Bonzo would leap up onto the reception desk and sit by the register. Quite often he would stand on the register, feet firmly planted, his black eye as coldly suspicious as that of any house man in detective fiction. If he approved of a late-registering guest, he would loll his pink tongue and smile a welcome. If he was undecided, he would stand firmly on the register until he made up his mind. If he didn't like the smell of the guest he would growl, and Mark would be summoned to remove him from the desk. Nobody else could touch Bonzo when he was angry – not without losing an arm.

The hotel guests laughed at Bonzo's suspicions until something happened to convince them that dogs can detect evil intent in human smell, that a man frightened or up to something illegal smells differently because of a chemical change in his body. Late one night a lean, pasty, furtive-eyed type came in to register, and Bonzo uttered a deep growl and went for the man's neck. The man retreated, with Mark Manson hanging onto Bonzo's tail.

Manson apologized to the man, and that night Bonzo got his first and only beating. But then, two days later, the police caught the lean, pasty, furtive gentleman at the airport, with his valise stuffed with all the jewelry and cash he'd been able to scoop up in the hotel. Bonzo ate a specially prepared *filet mignon* that night. And Mark Manson coddled him like a widow with an only child.

Bonzo had one shocking weakness: He loved girls. He loved girl dogs, and quite often absented himself for two or three days, to return in a deplorable state of dissipation – his black circle blacker and the scars of amatory adventure etched deeply on his hide. Manson, the unsuccessful ladies' man, took great pride in Bonzo's excursions.

Bonzo loved girl humans, too, especially the pretty ones. He had a way of walking straight up to a cute young one, taking a firm hold on her skirt, and tugging her gently toward his master. Mark Manson met a lot of nice girls that way, because Bonzo was a wonderful go-between. By the time Mark had finished disentangling the lady from Bonzo's fangs, a please-forgive-my-dog drink was indicated, with Bonzo clearing the path toward the cocktail lounge, his tail carried like a pennant.

It was funny to watch. I was in and out of Nairobi a lot, since I was covering everything in the hotel line from Mombasa to Cape Town. As Bonzo developed, so did Mark Manson. It was almost as if they'd been waiting all their lives for each other, these two strays that nobody ever loved. The naked adoration in the dog's eyes was embarrassing to see. And Manson rarely moved an inch without Bonzo as escort, except on the few days that Bonzo went roving. Bonzo was the number one guest in that hotel, and the other guests profited from his presence.

Manson seemed to grow taller. He took time off from his work to take Bonzo picnicking, and he lost his flabbiness and sunburned his sallow face. He was spending so much more social time with the guests, now that the service had improved and the food was really excellent and there wasn't much to complain about, that he went out and got himself dressed up by the best Indian tailor in town.

He organized pleasant little extras for the guests – movies in the lounge on rainy nights, informal dances, flowers in the ladies' rooms and a gift bottle of whisky for the steady male customers. He kept his staff as sharp as a wait-a-bit-thorn. Maybe they were frightened of Bonzo, at first, but after the set-to in the kitchen it was Mark Manson himself who had the help's respect.

The set-to in the kitchen was something that has happened in a lot of hotel kitchens at one time or another. The second cook got sore at the chef and fell to brooding. He soaked his hurt feeling in the poisonous native booze that's sold in the bazaars, and ultimately took out after the chef with a long, wicked meat knife.

It sounded like an old-fashioned Masai slave raid. You could hear the shrieks and screams and the crash of crockery all over the hotel. Mark Manson was on the veranda, sipping a lime squash with a couple of customers, when the commotion started. Bonzo wasn't with him. Bonz' was off on a romance.

Manson got up and dashed for the kitchen. He burst through the swinging doors and found the floor covered with broken dishes, blood and scrambling people. Several waiters had the berserk cook treed in the corner, but the cook had added a cleaver to his arsenal and was waving it in circles over his head.

Manson didn't hesitate a second. He strode to the stove and picked up a caldron of red-hot pepper-pot soup. He let the cook have the full gallon right in the face. The cook screamed and dropped his cleaver and his meat knife. Manson kicked them into a corner, walked over to the screaming cook and hit him a hard punch under the ear. The cook collapsed.

Manson surveyed the carnage. "Call the doctor," he said. "Call the police. And clean up this mess. The dining room opens in ten minutes." Then he went and had the doctor treat his hands, which had been solidly blistered from the steaming caldron.

It is impossible to dislike a man who is so loved by a dog, especially such a personable cur as Bonzo. It was not very long before Bonzo's wry charm had split the hotel people into two forces: those whom Bonzo liked and those whom Bonzo tolerated. To be merely tolerated by Bonzo was like unto social ostracism. In order to gain Bonzo's esteem, people went out of their way to be nice to Bonzo's master. Bonzo's master reciprocated, and gained thereby an ease of manner and a modest charm that must have been buried in his unhappy bosom for a long time.

At the little hotel parties, Mark found female members of his staff approaching him to say coyly: "But, Mr. Manson, you haven't asked *me* to dance yet." Guests who used to mutter: "Oh, Lordy," when Manson entered the room, all of a sudden were clapping him on the shoulder, calling him by his first name, and demanding that he state his preference in refreshment.

The change – in less than a year's time – was startling. I walked into the Equator Club one night and nearly fainted. Manson, dolled up like Fred Astaire, was doing a very creditable rumba with the same airline stewardess who had slapped him at the New Year's party. When they walked over to their table, Bonzo got up to let the lady sit down. I noticed there was a bottle of champagne on the table, and that the lady sat much closer to Manson than she needed to even with Bonzo sharing the love seat.

This amazing social progress continued, until you would have sworn that both Manson and Bonzo had grown handsomer. But one day an end to their idyl came in the person of old Henry Hopkinson Hathaway, who was making a world tour to look over his hotels.

You've seen pictures of the old gent. He is about six feet five, with a shiny, bald head, and he doesn't weigh more than a hundred and fifty pounds. He always wears rusty black, and he looks like a string bean that's been bit hard by frost. He affects a stand-up collar, such as Herbert Hoover used to wear, and elastic-sided shoes. It is not necessary to add that he is a vegetarian, a teetotaler and a dog hater.

131

But he was accompanied by his niece, and the niece was fancy enough almost to justify old Three-H's existence. I didn't see her, because I was off in Kampala at the time, but I got the story from DaSilva, the steward. He said she had curly hair, cut crisply short, and eyes about the size of damson plums. She had a big red mouth and a figure that put cricks in the necks of all the gentlemen on the porch and in the patio. More tea got spilled the morning she walked in with her Uncle Henry than had been wasted since Mark Manson reorganized the Livingstone Arms.

Bonzo thought she was just fine, DaSilva said. She hadn't been out of her cottage ten minutes, after tidying up from the plane ride, when Bonz' bore down on her and seized her by the skirt. He delivered her to his master in the lobby. Manson had explained Bonzo and was leading the girl off to tea when old Three-H hove over the horizon. He took one look at Bonzo, gestured at the no-dogs sign, and opened his mouth to register indignation.

Bonzo bit him sharply on the shin. Three-H screamed louder than the cook had that time Manson doused him with the scalding soup. "… Fired! Sacked! Blacklisted!" were the only intelligible words that seeped through the splutters.

It was a pity. Actually the old gentleman had dropped off to check on his new fireball, young Manson, because Three-H always kept a vulture's eye on the books. The Livingstone Arms had just about doubled its gross in the last year, despite the Mau Mau uprising that was raising Cain with the tourist trade and the safari business, not to mention the movie-makings. There were a couple of sick hotels in the old man's chain and he had Mark Manson down as top candidate for the trouble-shooting job.

After the Bonzo incident, Mark was immediately relieved as manager of the Livingstone Arms. The old man didn't even grant Mark an interview. He added a month's pay to Mark's current week's salary and instructed the assistant manager to tell Mark that he and that blasted wild animal had to be off the premises within a week. And under *no* circumstances was Bonzo to be allowed in the hotel itself.

Manson took it well. Everybody in the hotel, nearly, came down to his cottage to say they were sorry, and to ask if there were anything they could do. As Mark said, smiling, it was almost worth getting sacked to find out how many friends he had.

One friend he hadn't counted on was this scrumptious niece of old Hathaway's. She came down the next day and tapped on his door. Mark invited her in, and Bonzo came over to say hello. He reared up, after she'd sat down, and gave her a great wet kiss on the cheek. Then he put his head in her lap. She rubbed his ears, and Bonzo produced a sigh like a steam whistle.

"I just wanted to say that I'm dreadfully sorry about yesterday," she said. "Uncle Henry was horrid. I think Bonzo's sweet, and I've heard all about him *and* you. I tried to talk Uncle Henry into taking you back, but he won't hear of it. But if there's anything I can do, later on …."

Mark thanked her and they chatted a while before she left. Before long he was calling her Carol. She gave him her addresses in London and New York and told him to look her up; she said maybe she could have a word with Hilton or somebody outside her Uncle Henry's empire. Mark felt pretty good, especially when she kissed Bonzo good-bye ….

I suppose you'll remember a part of this story, now, because it made every paper in the world. Although Mark was fired, that last week he still kept to his habit of making the evening rounds of the premises, with Bonzo at his side and a pistol on his hip. Ever since the Mau Mau uprising, everybody in Nairobi goes rodded up like in the old wild West days. Mark was walking on the back patio, looking up at the moon, when he stumbled over something.

It was the night watchman, dead. The man's neck had been slashed with a *panga*, one of those big bush knives the Mau Mau use in their terror raids. Mark pulled his gun. Bonzo growled and dashed straight for Cottage 1, the big deluxe job that Henry Hopkinson Hathaway kept reserved for himself and his guests.

Just as Mark and Bonzo hit the steps, a series of screams tore the night apart. The scene was what people in East Africa have come to expect these days. A tea service was scattered all over the room. A huge African had Henry Hopkinson Hathaway by the throat, and had bent him backward over a chair. In the Mau Mau's right hand was a long *simi* – a two-edged stabbing sword – poised high in the air, starting on the down stroke. Old Mr. Hathaway was kicking and screaming and flailing his arms.

Over in one corner, Carol Hathaway was yelling her head off. A smaller Mau Mau had her by the wrist and was trying to pull her over the back of a sofa, behind which she'd barricaded herself. He had in his right hand the bloody red-edged *panga* that he'd used on the night watchman, and he was chopping at her as he pulled.

Bonzo and Mark went into action separately. Mark shot the smaller African twice through the chest, and he flopped, his *panga* clattering to the floor. Mark wheeled then in time to see the larger Mau Mau dipping his knife down toward Henry Hopkinson Hathaway's breast. And then Bonzo leaped for the man's knife hand. Manson heard the crunch as Bonzo's teeth closed on the murderer's wrist.

Bonzo was a big dog, heavy with fine feeding. His leap pulled the killer off balance and carried him halfway to the floor. Old Hathaway tumbled off the chair and crouched behind it. Carol Hathaway had fainted.

The Mau Mau and the dog were wrapped around each other, Bonzo still holding fast to the man's right wrist. The assassin dropped the big knife and fell to the floor, with Bonzo on top of him. The fall broke the dog's hold, and he shifted his attack to the man's throat. Just as Mark Manson fired his third and fourth shots, the killer grasped the *simi* again, and plunged it deep into Bonzo's side.

The Mau Mau died immediately. Bonzo died a little later. He died on Henry Hopkinson Hathaway's bed, with his head in Mark Manson's lap, while Henry Hopkinson Hathaway stroked his neck.

M ark Manson mixed us another martini *a maui*, and we clinked glasses again. "Bonzo," he said. "I guess I owe him a lot."

"Old Bonz'," I answered. "You certainly do."

Mark took a drink, and wiped his mouth with a square yard of Irish linen handkerchief. "Funny thing about that damned dog," he said. "Just before he died, he looked at old Three-H and then he looked at Carol and then he looked at me. I swear, when he looked at me he closed his black eye in an outrageous wink. Then he closed the other eye and died."

Mrs. Manson called through the doorway.

"Lunch is ready, darling," she said. "Bring your drinks."

"Coming, Sweetie," Mark Manson said.

We sat down, the three of us, to tackle the Madrasi curry, which was just as good as it used to be at the old Livingstone Arms.

"Then it all worked out like in the movies," I said. "Bonzo saves the boss's life, you come out of the doghouse and marry the boss's beautiful niece, and everybody lives happily ever after. It's a good script, even if it is a little corny."

Mark Manson and his gorgeous wife began to laugh. When they quit laughing Mark reached over and took his wife's hand. You could tell they were very much in love. "This isn't Carol Hathaway," he said. "This is Sally Manson, nee March. I met her on the plane when I was flying over from Africa to build this hotel. She was a stewardess, of course, and I seemed to have formed the habit."

"Very persuasive lad, this man Manson," Sally Manson said. "We had a four-day wait in London, and when it came time to fly we were engaged. And he did it without that dog as a go-between, too."

"You've wrecked the story," I said. "How come no wedding bells with the gorgeous Carol? There must have been some pressure there."

Manson had the decency to blush a little. "There was," he said. "But I couldn't see working for *two* Hathaways at once. I didn't have to *marry* a job. The old boy was a touch cheesed off at me when I sprung the bride on him, but the hotel's a hit and the baby fixed everything else up all right. Old Henry's godfather, you know, and so we let him choose the name."

"We call her Bonnie," Sally Manson said, looking at me with those big violet eyes. "After all, Bonzo's such a silly name for a little girl."

A lthough the Mau Mau crisis didn't officially end until 1960, British military efforts brought the worst of the terror to a close in 1955. From October 1952 through the end of 1955, the body count amounted to 10,173 Mau Mau killed by the British, several dozen Europeans and untold thousands of fellow Kikuyu slaughtered by the Mau Mau.

Ruark's fascination with *fisi* began during his first safari. There are few places on earth where the continuous cycle of life and death is more obvious than in Africa, and in the hyena Ruark recognized a symbol for the impersonal brutality of nature – which, he believed, in turn defied the nature of Africa itself. All of which makes *fisi* the perfect metaphor in attempting to assess the aftermath of the Mau Mau.

"Land Of Violence" appeared in *Look*, November 15, 1955. It certainly was not to be his last word on the subject, but it's as concise and powerful a summary as any he ever wrote.

Michael McIntosh

CHAPTER ELEVEN

LAND OF VIOLENCE

There are people who shudder when they hear the word "hyena," as other people recoil when they hear the word "snake." I happen to respect hyenas, because to me the hyena in many ways typifies the tragedy of Africa. Known to natives as a *fisi*, to most of the tribes of Central Africa he represents the angel of death, and Africa is a continent that was built on blood and that lives off death.

I love Fisi for his virtuoso's voice. He can sound like a lion or a madwoman or a calliope gone berserk. He can sound like the howler on a destroyer, or as giggly coy as a tickled maiden. He is a dreadful beast really – hermaphroditic, stinking, an eater of offal, a skulker, a coward and a thief. But he is part of the African scene, and is as vital as the vulture and the ant to Africa's cycle of life-on-death.

I heard my first hyena symphony in Addis Ababa, high in the Ethiopian mountains, on a clear, crisp night, snapping with frosty stars. He was away outside of town, but his magnificent range of noises traveled clearly in the stillness. It sent a delicious shiver up my spine – a shiver I later saw magnified among the natives in Kenya and Tanganyika.

Fisi is a joke. God played a joke on him, and in turn, Fisi gets the last laugh. God gave him a lion's jaws, a dog's face, a crippled spine and the burly body of a bear. But his shuffling lope does not allow him to kill his own meat, so he must ever follow in the wake of the predator, whether the predator be man or beast.

Fisi may dine off the lion's leavings, but in the end, Fisi also eats the lion. Fisi is feared by the natives, because each native knows that, when the end comes, Fisi will be his tomb. It is the custom of certain tribes – who fear the curse of death which necessitates tearing down the hut in which the victim died, and moving on to another *shamba* – to leave their aged and infirm in the fields for Fisi to find alive, as well as their dead. Hence the sardonic lilt in Fisi's laughter, and hence the crawl of fear up the native spine when Fisi snickers, sitting on his haunches like a big dog, just outside the fitful flicker of the campfire.

The Africa I know is not the jungly Africa of the Congo, but the Africa of the great Rift escarpment, that enormous volcanic scar which splits a continent. My Africa contains the soft green plains of the high Masai country, and the broad, sere wastes of the North, where the big elephant and the rhino live. That red-clay Northland is so dry in the dry seasons and so wet during the rains that it is practically unlivable unless you are a Turkana or Samburu or Somali, happy to rove a million square miles with your belongings on your wife's back and in the wicker hamper of a tiny donkey, with your herds of sheep and goat and high-humped cattle bleating and baaing and lowing ahead of you. But whether the land is sere or soaking, hot or cold, ugly or beautiful, Fisi is right there to remind you of your miserably tiny place in a violently recurring scheme.

The violence of the continent is reflected basically in its physical appearance. The mountains and volcanoes are angry chunks of stone, seemingly strewn aimlessly by an annoyed Creator. It is not unusual to see a respectable mountain, colored harshly purple, red, black and white, standing lonely in the middle of a grassy plain as flat as your hand. When the flash floods come in the North, enormous trees are hurled thirty and forty feet above the riverbed. When the hot weather fries the plains, you can see a dozen elephants in a day, digging with their tusks for water in the dry river beds, the *lugas*, under whose sandy surfaces is a seeping ooze. The fight for water is as desperate as the fight for food. A rhino will walk twenty miles a day to drink, and a small tribe of herdsmen will rove thousands of miles, sometimes digging wells as deep as forty feet, to water their cattle and camels.

The struggle is endless. The rains come, and when movement by man and carnivore alike is restricted, the hoofed animals drop their babies in the wet. The young eat the tender green shoots and by the time the grass is high, and the cats are aprowl, the kids can take care of themselves. But the cats must eat, and so every night, something dies. The vultures know, although no one knows how they know, and

The Chase - Hyenas

the kill may be spotted next day by the birds circling and slanting and finally landing with a bump. The hyena is there before the birds, and finally come the ants and termites to clean up the bits and scraps. Somehow the inevitability of it all produces a curious peace.

I have known more happiness, more peace and more fear in Africa than in any other place in the world, and at no time did I feel like a "civilized" man loose in a strange place. I was no more than two hours out of Nairobi, on my first safari, before I felt as if I knew where I was headed – as if I had been there before.

At the first encampment, the night sounds delighted me. Half a dozen hyenas were ringed round the camp, drawn close by the smell of cooking meat. Away back over there, in a *donga*, or dry water-course, an old lion coughed and muttered and finally expressed his displeasure of the night with a ricocheting roar.

A leopard, hunting along the river bank, was having a personal exchange of hatred with a treeful of baboons, and at first the growls of both sounded exactly alike. It was only much later that I could distinguish the sawing grunt of the leopard from the sharper swearwords of the baboon. Apart from the carnivores, there are enough unidentifiable hoots, howls, cracks, pops and whistles to scare the daylights out of the tenderfoot, but curiously, I was not afraid.

Most normal killing, in Africa, is done at night. By day, I have seen half a dozen lions drinking at the same waterhole with a dozen antelope, and once I saw a lion loping along easily beside a herd of zebra, with neither lion nor zebra showing any concern over the other's presence. But when the sun sinks, and the sky streaks with blood, you will always note that the hoofed animals move out from the bush into the center of the plain. It is then that you hear the dying screams, as one world feeds on another.

The Somali say that a man experiences supreme fear three times – once when he sees a lion's track, once when he hears the lion roar, and once when he comes face to face with the lion. I experienced that fear once – and I suspect it was more excitement than fear – when I shot my first lion, at a range of about thirty yards. After that, although I later got into a nasty mess with nine lions at once, I more or less came to regard them as big, lazy dogs who would slink away rather than cause a scene. In the Masai country, where the lions are semi-tame, though wild, I once ran over the tail of an old boy who wouldn't get out of the jeep's way, and the look he gave me was the most reproachful I have ever seen on any face, human or animal.

The biggest fears I have ever known, including the war, were given me three times by buffalo and once by elephant. The Cape buffalo, wounded, is possibly the craftiest, most vindictive ton of destruction in the world, and I once was two hours in the bush after a sick one. At no time, for a million-dollar prize, would I have been able to spit. There was another occasion when a man named Harry Selby and I got trapped in a stampede of some 200 buff. Since there was no place to go, and no tree to climb, we did the best we could. We charged the chargers, waving hats and screaming, and the buff stopped. We shot the lead bull and they turned. On one other occasion, we were forced to sit motionless in a little glade while a herd of buff fed so close that I distinctly remember seeing the whites of a tickbird's eyes as it pecked, upended, seeking vermin in the nostrils of an old cow. She was no more than five feet away from me, and seemed to have more curiosity than is comely in a lady.

I look at a couple of enormous tusks today, and shiver slightly. In their original state, they were worn by about seven tons of angry bull elephant who charged us in the rain, after the wind changed and he caught our scent. We were obliged to wait him out and hope he had a sore foot and would step on a sharp rock, thereby giving us a corner of his shoulder to shoot at, because there is really no place you can shoot a charging bull elephant coming straight at you, at close range. It turned out this elephant *did* have a sore foot, and *did* step on a sharp rock, and *did* swerve enough to give me some shoulder to snap two bullets at. The elephant died 100 yards away, and I went behind a bush and was sick.

It was the life and beauty of Africa that enslaved me from the start, and I never troubled my conscience with the aspects of necessary death, since death made life, and one was completely adjunct to the other.

The picture of Africa as I like best to remember it was written a long time ago, after my first safari, when, I thought, I finally was leaving. It went like this: "We rode over the hills, rode for the last time, looking for the last time at all the landmarks we knew so well now – the cobbled hills there, the green knobby hills there, the long blue slopes there, the *baobab* here where the road crooks just before you turn in toward Kiteti, the rhino hill yonder, the lonely village of musky anthills, the broad yellow plain, the swamp where the buffalo were, the high hill where the other buffalo were, the sheer drop of the escarpment, the green strip of lush grass with the giraffes always standing solemn and ludicrous nearby, the little scrubby orchards of thorn, the fleets of ostriches running and pacing like trotting horses at the Roosevelt Raceway, the buzzards wheeling, the dew fresh on the drying grass, the flowers beginning to wither, the sand grouse specks in the sky, the doves looping and moaning lugubriously, the brilliant flight of the jays, the guineas running, the francolin scratching like chicken in the low grass between the ruts the car made, the weaverbirds swarming like bees and dipping and rolling like a tornado. This was what I wanted to remember of it more than what I'd shot, but the shooting was important because the presence of the animals in my home would bring it back as fresh and sharp as the air of this last morning; this last, sad morning." That was as close as I could come to putting it into one package.

When the Mau Mau invaded the Africa I knew, I experienced an anger that, I suspect, was first based on selfishness, because my Paradise was spoiled. Now the killing was useless – on both sides – since it served no purpose.

Where there had been peace and beauty, there were fear and ugliness. The literally lovely relationship between some whites and some blacks had been replaced by mutual mistrust and hatred. At first, there were revulsion and heartbreak among the settlers at the dirty task that fate had forced upon them – the awful reprisals in similar coin. A year later, on my third trip to Kenya, this revulsion and heartsickness had again been replaced by callousness, and the innocent suffered with the guilty. On the black side, whatever Mau Mau had started out to be, it had degenerated into a loathsome, bestial and brutal perversion of all the old good things. Nobody won, and nobody is winning – with one exception.

You may have been curious as to why I started this piece with a short dissertation on the hyena. Fisi won the battle of the Mau Mau. Everybody else lost, everybody but Fisi and the vultures and the ants.

Fisi will always win, which is possibly why he laughs.

PART III

THE OLD MAN'S BOY GROWS UP

I n August 1956, *Field & Stream* published the first in a series of special sections titled " The Sportsman's New World Today." This world, which in future issues would include such places as British Columbia, Baja California, and the Caribbean, was new, the magazine said, "because the old barriers of time and distance are gone" – because the newly burgeoning airline industry had created a world of "magnificent places now open to the average sportsman for the first time."

Because the average American sportsman of the 1950s could scarcely imagine a place more exotic, Africa was the first place featured in the "New World" series, and no American writer was better equipped to discuss sport in East Africa than Robert Ruark.

Ruark naturally had no idea that he was writing history, but from thirty-five years' perspective, "The Sportsman's Africa" is exactly that – an excellent overview of what African hunting was like at the end of a golden age that had lasted more than three generations.

Those who know something of African hunting today will find the sidebars – here presented together following the main text – amusing and bemusing alike. A $3500 price-tag for a month-long safari, airfare included, certainly seems bizarre by present standards, although at the time $3500 amounted to about half the "average" sportsman's annual income. But even considering that average income is considerably higher nowadays, the price has gone up: $3500 will scarcely cover coach-class airfare from Chicago to Nairobi and back, and the safari itself is likely to cost better than $20,000 a *week*.

In an introductory paragraph to the "New World" series, the editors of *Field & Stream* observe that "only a few years ago, none but the wealthy could hope to hunt in Africa." Hope, of course, is available to anyone, but African hunting seems to have come full circle.

Michael McIntosh

CHAPTER TWELVE

THE SPORTSMAN'S AFRICA

Not so long ago a safari – "a walking forth" in Kiswahili, the trade language of East Africa that was developed by the Arab slavers – was a thing that only the Prince of Wales, or perhaps Teddy Roosevelt, could afford. Up to the war, it was still an expensive playtoy, for the simple reason that so much time was consumed in getting out of New York or Paris or London on a boat, and getting back again, and bashing about in Nairobi or Dar es Salaam looking for porters and headmen and collecting equipment and trudging painfully in the smiting sun to where the game might possibly be. You did not have to devote a year to a safari, but you could use up the best part of nine months.

The old foot-safari, according to oldtimers like Philip Percival, Pat Ayre and Syd Downey, the youngest of the older boys, was quite a thing. It took a hundred porters to carry less than you can stick into the back of a fairly small truck today. For a fifteen to twenty-mile day, about sixty pounds was the most you could lay onto the back of an African. This considerably reduced the modern delights of safari – lush tenting, canned foods, whisky, abundant ammunition, good beds and such comforts. You ate largely what you shot, plus a few pickles to offset the hair in the stew. You carried a double rifle for the big ugly stuff, a shotgun for the fowl and perhaps a 9mm something-or-other for the middle business. The richer people, like Theodore Roosevelt, might employ Somali canaries (jackasses) to lug the gear and might chase lions on horseback. But there were few Teddy Roosevelts or Princes of Wales about. Mostly it was sheer shanks' mare and beans for breakfast.

It is possible that the first white hunter – so called because of the differences between a European pro and a picked-up guide from the first village along the way – was a gentleman named Alan Black, who undertook to show Lord Delamere the countryside in 1890. The next two names to come along were Fritz Schindler, a dashing Austrian, and George Outram. Schindler, a fabulous shot, used to hunt lions on horseback, but he made a mistake one day and the lion collected his headskin. The same thing happened to Outram, which convinces me that lions can hurt you if they try.

Along came a Mr. R. J. Cunningham, in the early 1900s, to take Teddy Roosevelt out a-gunning, together with Billy Judd, Leslie Tarleton, Philip and Blayney Percival. They're all dead but old Phil, who has just retired after twenty-five years as president of the East Africa Professional Hunters Association. Phil, who has survived alcohol, kidneys, cancer, Ernest Hemingway and assorted wild animals, including Tommy Shevlin, is past seventy and can't hear so well any more because of that shocking great .505 Gibbs sounding off in his ear, but he still goes out and bags the odd elephant. His brother Blayney died a while ago at eighty-some.

Pat Ayre, lean and sun-browned in his floppy double terai, is still around and active, although when Philip stepped down as president the other day, Pat departed his ancient post as V.P. Percival and Ayre have left a monument to hunting. What they know of bush they have communicated to most of the better current crop, including the young dean of the moderns, Harry Selby. Selby was Percival's mechanic, then his second hunter, and what Philip didn't know to teach Harry, Harry got from Pat Ayre.

Pat was the one who took out the late George VI and his pretty wife when Bertie was Duke of York and the current Queen Mother was a plump Scots lass. Gordon Anderson and Denys Finch-Hatton took out the ex-king, David Windsor, now the Duke, when he was the Prince Charming Prince of Wales. Of the older guard, Tom Murray-Smith, Sydney Downey, Donald Ker and sometimes Pat Ayre are the only members hunting today – unless you count Phil Percival, when he goes out for that occasional elephant or to ride herd on his buddy Ernest Hemingway.

Professional hunters are not to be confused with Game Department types, individual ivory hunters or farmers with a twitching nose for gunpowder. Old ivory poachers, like Karamojo Bell, who shot his elephants with a woodchuck rifle, or the farmers who shot their licenses dry in order to supply biltong (jerky) for their native help, or professional exterminators for the Game Department come into a separate category. J. A. Hunter shot a thousand rhino when Makueni district was being cleaned of rhino so that the thornbush could be leveled in order to eliminate the cattle-killing tsetse fly, so that the Wakamba tribe could extend its agricultural and cattle-droving activity. No one knows how many elephant Carr-Hartley killed when he was shooting on control, but he held the record for one gun. Eric Rundgren, at this moment working for control, was recently handed the assignment of doing in 200 elephant, near abeam the island of Lamu, in order to make room for resettled Mau Mau. When his assignment's finished, Eric will probably have 800 or so elephant to the credit of his .416.

A mighty amount of shooting went on in Kenya in the old days, which were just yesterdays. A certain Boer influence moved in from the Transvaal – a chronic Boer trait to shoot anything that moves, even across an impassable river, just to see it drop. The Boer, a frugal type, used to arm the entire family with full licenses – including Grandma, aged ninety-two – and shoot out the licenses, together with as much else as he could get away with, to supply biltong for family and native employees.

Meat poaching, ivory poaching and indiscriminate slaughter of Africa's best natural resource – game – is probably worse today than in the old days. There is a scandal in the Serengeti Plains at the moment, as the natives conspire with the Indians and Arabs in an illegal game-trapping, jezail (ancient musket) shooting orgy of wasted dead and painfully living wounded, for meat and money and stolen ivory and lion fat to cure the aching joints that gonorrhea brings, plus poached rhino horn to repair the lack of virility suffered by ancient Asians. Powdered rhino horn – it isn't actually horn, but compressed hair – is widely used as an aphrodisiac in China, Japan and India.

But there is still more game in East Africa than any place else in the world, and the East African Professional Hunters Association is jealously determined to guard it, in partnership with the Game Department and the people who run the national parks.

One of the most mistaken ideas of African hunting is that a man may step outside Nairobi or Arusha and do in the entire collection of African fauna without walking more than a couple of hundred yards from his jeep. Africa is a land of specialized hunting – and the special places can be a thousand or more miles from each other. Game follows grass, and grass follows weather – rain. But some game lives in mountains, and some lives close by water, and some lives on deserts, and some lives in jungles. You have to go to where the game is. This is kidney-jarring, dusty, sun-broiling work. Or, if you're too close to the rains, you see a truck mired or with spine snapped in a sudden flood.

This year I will shoot a greater kudu, a sable and a roan antelope. I will go to Tabora in Tanganyika, and I will go around December 1. That is not a boastful statement. I will go to the Ugalla River and I will shoot all three animals, for the simple reason that southern Tanganyika will be bone-dry at that time of the year, and these most elusive animals will have come down from the hills to the flats. They will have come down because of one sort of bush they eat at that time, and because there is no water in the hills. A man wouldn't go there at another time, simply because for most of the year the flats are sodden and you can't get a vehicle into the country.

There are certain places where a man on short safari can shoot a comprehensive bag – let us say the southern Masai. That has been closed since the worst of the Mau Mau business, but it's supposed to open up again soon. The Masai is candy-box country. The tsetse-fly portion is closed to the shooting of carnivores, but there is enough overflow on the fringe areas to allow you your lion or leopard legally. For the rest, you can collect a wonderful buffalo, if you work at it, and most of the common game like Grant and Thomson's gazelle, waterbuck and impala. I know one place on the lower Mara River where you can shoot a klipspringer, although they aren't supposed to be there – just as I know a place near Kiteti in Tanganyika where you can find desert animals like oryx and gerenuk, though it is right near low, wet country that resembles jungle more than any other country I've seen in Africa.

If you want the big stuff, you go north to the hot country, where the big elephant lives, where the long-horned rhinos are, and where there is probably the best bird shooting in the world. If you are hunting elephant or rhino, you hunt around the *lugas*–dry riverbeds named Kinya, Seralippe, Merille, Serarua – picking up the elephant's spoor from where he has come to dig for water beneath the wet sands in the hot season when all life is near the *lugas*.

You will find elephant all over the north and all along the Tana River, which spills Africa's eroding red soil into the Indian Ocean. It is not easy hunting, because the big beasts do not inhabit plains as a rule. They use clenched-fist forests of wait-a-bit thorn, of myrrh and sansevieria. A man can walk ten feet and disappear. You can't see an elephant more than fifteen yards away, when you suddenly stumble onto him. This is dangerous, unpleasant, sweaty hunting, where a stroll of twenty miles is nothing unusual – and at the end of it you find the bull you are following is a good bull, all right, but the unspeakable monster has only one lousy tusk.

Speaking of elephant, we get right back to areas. There are elephant in the Masai, a murderous horde of them. But they are small in the tusk and evil in the disposition. Nobody has successfully explained why, in the lush Masai, the elephants should run small to the tusk when the buffalo run long in the horn. Or why the desert lion, up north, should be maneless, whereas the lion in the south is wonderfully coiffured. I know there are huge elephant around Iringa in Tanganyika, because you see the spoor and hear them screaming. There is supposed to be a monster bull of 200 pounds tusk weight, each side. But he would be living across the river, in a tangled thorn-scrub which makes tracking nearly impossible. He'll stay there, for all of me.

The rains in Africa move from south to north; so the rains begin to pour, the *lugas* sometimes rise thirty to forty feet and the whole area is barred to hunting. You cannot hunt during the rains, and not only because your transport bogs. The animals, with plenty of water in every pig-hole, disperse all over the place. You might find them anywhere; but in a place the size of East Africa, if you have nothing to depend on but dumb luck, the chances are you won't find them at all. The *mtotos* (the babies) are born just before the rains, and have time to grow swift and sturdy before the long grass makes a natural camouflage for the cats.

You cannot hunt well in high grass. First of all, the game isn't there. It's up in the hills, where the grass is shorter, the water still plentiful in pockets, and the cats easier to detect. But anyway, you can't hunt in high grass because even if game is there, you can't see it. Hunting dangerous animals in high grass is as good a way as I can think of to invite a trip to the Hereafter.

This situation – hunting game after rain, when the grass is towering – tests the knowledge of your hunter. Geography having the same peculiarities as people, an intelligent professional hunter will know a little strip of land where the grass is never high. In June, when most of the territory is a forest of lush grass, a man like Harry Selby will have a spot like Ikoma, on the lower Grummetti in Tanganyika, tucked into the back of his mind. The grass is never high around Ikoma and the animals pour into the pocket in hordes. June is the time of massive migration. Millions of zebra and wildebeest migrate across the Serengeti Plains – and whither goeth the plains animals, so follow the carnivores.

Every hunter wants his first lion, and possibly his second, because he is shooting a symbol. After that you couldn't bribe him to shoot another lion unless it was in his lap. But the lion is on the list, and you may as well shoot one and get it out of your system. Shooting a very good lion is difficult, because lions salvage only about one cub per four, and most of them, being intelligent, hang out in reserves and national parks.

The easiest way to shoot one is to see one, hop out of the car, crawl a few hundred yards, and then wallop him in the ear or on the point of the shoulder, depending on whether he is sleeping or standing. Cats are soft-skinned and tender-boned. On a bet I will shoot a lion with a .22 Long Rifle, but off betting I will use Winchester's .375 magnum, which will depress him considerably, even if I gut-shoot him.

The tougher way to shoot one is to lure him out of the bush with a kill – say, a kongoni or a wildebeest. Once he gets into the free meal, crawl up close and bang! *Kuisha simba.*

Some you'll have to build a blind for, and get there either very early in the morning or very late in the afternoon. These could be the sophisticated types that need tempting, careful stalking and absolute quiet to collect. Apart from luck, this is the way you get most of them today, what with restricted areas, less lions and a general wariness.

Sudden Charge - Elephant

The lion, for my money, is not much trophy. A fine kudu, I would reckon, is the best, and there again you have to qualify. The noblest and most difficult is the bongo, a massive member of the bushbuck tribe. He lives high in the rain forest, and you have no chance at him unless you bait a salt lick for a year – *illegal* – or course him with dogs – *illegal* – or wait for every seventh year when the wild grapes die, and then just get lucky. Mostly when you hunt bongo in the twisted grapevines, in the rain, or the high Aberdares, you will hear him but never see him, although he will weigh 1,200 to 1,500 pounds. You will hear him snort and go away when the non-wind-carried scent of you circles out twenty yards and spooks him.

Next to the kudu, the sable antelope, with his sabered back-swept horns, would be my nomination for nobility, strength and beauty. Some people are peculiar. I would rather walk twenty miles a day hunting an elephant I might never see, or spend a lot of time trying to outwit a leopard I might never see, than do any of the others. It took the best leopard man in the world – Harry Selby – around five years to get the "camp leopard" in Ikoma into a tree and ready for the gun. I know quite a lot about leopards, but if you asked me how to collect one, apart from luck, I'd just have to quote Selby: "Hell! You have to *be* a leopard to shoot one."

The easiest and, for my score, least dangerous thing to shoot is a rhino. He is dumber than your dumbest cousin, can't see, and has as much target area as a tank. You can tell that he is about to charge – although he doesn't even know it himself – when the free-loading tickbirds jump off his back. Unless you want to shoot him in the sore spot under his Adam's apple, or wallop him in the armpit, you can always wait and bust his back when he gets close enough to lower his head.

The toughest of them all to hunt, most pros will tell you, is the old *ndofu*, the old Tembo, the elephant. I doubt if he sees too well, but with his big ears and his snaky trunk he hears and smells better than any other living thing. He is not the placid beast of the circus, the Indian elephant, any more than a Spanish fighting bull is the ordinary moo-cow. He can run fastest going up a hill, because his knees are backjointed; going downhill, he sits on his behind and slides. His trunk is elastic, so you may as well not bother climbing a tree. If he swipes you with his trunk, picks you up and throws you, kneels on you, tusks you or just runs over you, six or seven tons of energy are in there working, and you're likely to be dead.

The elephant is the only animal I know that will charge without provocation. The cows are the worst, especially when they've got Junior around, but the bulls – the lone outcast bulls – have always got a decayed nerve in the tusk or a sore foot or ants up the trunk, and are consequently hostile to the world. When you hunt them in thick bush, where there may be thirty or forty gray giants rushing about, a man feels stark-naked, no matter how big his gun.

Jumbo is difficult. When he is feeding, you can come up with him in ten miles or so, maybe even less, if you run through the thorn bushes. If he is migrating – using one of his well-marked trails – you may as well not bother. He's heading for some place 200 miles away, and you couldn't catch up to his amazingly speedy amble if you had a clear highway and a motorcycle.

For such an enormous animal, who stands maybe fourteen feet high and weighs about seven tons if he is a bull, Jumbo presents a very small target. If you go for the frontal brain shot, an area of about nine by three inches, you have to figure out a way to bend the bullet if he's charging and close. The professional technique is to give him one anywhere in the face and turn him, then wallop him in the heart or straight up the backside as he swerves. The classic shot is to hit him in the ear-hole if he's standing, or directly on a line between ear-hole and eye. If he's quartering, going away, a brain-seeking shot behind the flap of the ears is murderous. And you can always shoot him in the knee to anchor him, because the big animals can't make it on three legs.

Apart from elephant, the greatest sport with the big stuff can be the Cape buffalo. Everybody has heard how fierce they are, which is true in one way. Wounded, they develop an adrenalin that allows them to soak up bullets as big as asparagus, and they come and come and come and come until you poke the gun in an eye, fire, fall back and hope the old *mbogo* doesn't fall on you. They cut your trail, double back and crouch in a piece of bush that wouldn't hide a hare. They lie in ambush for you and come head-up snorting at you from fifteen feet. That's when they're *wounded*.

Unwounded, they are cattle – slobs – and you can make them do nearly anything you want. I have charged a herd of 200 buff and turned them. I have forced them past me by sending a boy upwind to let his scent drift down, and sat in the middle of 500 of them while they ambled past. They have very slow reactions, and if you startle them in any way they gaze dumbly for about twenty seconds which gives you more than enough time to shape your course, such as shooting the lead bull and crouching behind him while the others stream past. When they are milling around you – not stampeding – all you have to do is freeze, and the nearest cow is apt to start grazing on your mustache. There's been a lot of nonsense written about buff. Wounded they are the worst. Unwounded, they're just beef. But there is sometimes an exception which can kill you.

The common stuff is easy to come by, easy to kill, and worth the effort. The waterbuck is the most curious-minded of the big buck – he's elky-looking, has wonderful horns and a fine tweed coat endowed with a stinking insect repellent, and is completely inedible because his fat congeals and becomes unswallowable. But there is nothing nobler than waterbuck, aside from sable, kudu, elephant and buffalo, by way of trophy.

I think the most beautiful of all the little common types is the impala, whose coat is like a bright new penny, and whose horns spread back in a brandy-snifter shape. He is a leaper, and will jump right over your jeep, because he feels so good that day. He walks on little sore feet, with his heavy-horned head low, and is beautiful to eat as well.

But he isn't as beautiful to eat as the Thomson's gazelle, which can be shot, cooked and consumed in an hour. None are so cute as Tommy, with his switching tail – which stops switching if he's mortally shot – and none make such chops. Maybe his long-necked cousin in the north, the gerenuk, can challenge him in the skillet, but he gets no competition out of the Grant's gazelle. The Grant has beautiful horns, and the leopards love him as bait, but in the south he has measles and will make you sick, and in the north I would rather just wallop a gerenuk or an oribi and live high.

Of the edible animals, topi and kongoni are big enough and tasty enough, and so stupid that all you have to do to collect a three-day feed for the camp is to get out of the car, walk – not stalk – over to the nearest anthill, raise the rifle, and call the cook. It is always good to have a Mohammedan along to *hallal* (kosherize) the carcass; otherwise the Moslems in your retinue may not eat it, for fear of Allah's wrath. The *hallal* is supposedly done while there is breath of life in the animal. My boys cheat a bit – so long as I don't approach the beast until the operation is finished. Metheke or Chalo would cut the throat of a long-dead hairy mammoth and declare it fit for Allah, Mohammed and the Aga Khan.

One does not shoot ostriches, giraffe, colobus monkeys, except on special license. One does not shoot cheetahs any more, since they have been declared Royal game. They are supremely fast but stupid, make a lousy trophy, and are becoming extinct.

When I first hunted in Tanganyika, the game allowances were a scandal. They've tightened up some there and in Kenya, but there's still plenty of shooting.

You can shoot in Kenya today:

On special license -

1st Elephant	£75	Leopard	£25
2nd Elephant	100	Masai lion	20
Rhino	15	Giraffe	10

On full license - £50

1 Lion, not in Masai	1 Greater kudu, male only
2 Buffalo	1 Lesser kudu, male only
1 Eland	4 Wildebeest
1 Bongo	4 Topi
1 Waterbuck, *defassa*	5 Thomson's gazelle
1 Waterbuck, common	3 Grant's gazelle
3 Gerenuk	2 Impala
3 Zebra	1 Oryx Beisa
	1 Oryx Callotis

You can shoot in Tanganyika today:

On special license -

Elephant	£30	Leopard	£25
Rhino	25	Greater kudu	10
Lion	20	Sable	10
		2nd Buffalo	5

On full license - £50

2 Buffalo	1 Roan
	3 Wildebeest

3 Zebra	2 Topi
1 Waterbuck	2 Grant's gazelle
1 Eland	2 Impala

Bird shooting is getting to be bigger and bigger as a sport. I believe Africa has the best bird shooting in the world. I can get real emotional about it, whether I'm shooting a three-ounce African quail with a .410 or using buckshot on a thirty-pound knob-billed goose.

I suppose southern Tanganyika has the best birds, but I'm not knocking the Northern Frontier of Kenya. In Tanganyika there are the knob-bill and the spur-winged goose – especially around Iringa, on the Great Ruaha River. There are teal, a species of wigeon and pintail, and black mallard, a white-faced tree duck. There is the Egyptian goose. There is also an Egyptian ibis you'd better not shoot, even by accident, unless you fancy jail. There is a browny sort of duck, but if you want to leave the ducks and go upland you are in business.

The dumbest bird in the world, and I don't even except the dodo, is a thing called a francolin. Whether he is red-necked or yellow-necked, lesser or larger, he still sits on an anthill and goes *"quarank-quarank"* at nightfall. What makes him spectacular is that he is all white meat, even down to the feet. He is as big as a hen pheasant that is slightly stunted, or a grouse gone glandular. Boiled, roasted, fried or smoked, he is the gustatory king of fowl. He collects so easy that it isn't true. I used to shoot him with a shotgun, but the sport wasn't there; so I took up the .22 and collected him sitting. One day I shot five in line before the survivors decided that the noise they heard was connected with Eternity.

Close aboard the francolin is the guinea. You'll find the guinea every place. I do not consider the guinea as sport, either – unless, like my friend Mr. Selby, you shoot them *flying* with a .22.

Me, I am a biltong hunter. I have a special technique with guinea fowl, which average out at about three pounds of white breast meat. I approach the steadily trotting flock of guineas, racing down the sand riverbed. I fling myself on the ground and aim the left-hand barrel at the long line of heads. About ten to fifteen guineas die. Then with the right-hand barrel I knock off a flying refugee, which constitutes sport. This feeds people and saves ammunition.

The ammunition I save on guinea fowl I expend recklessly on sand grouse and green and blue pigeons. The sand grouse is a black-speckled tawny desert bird that drinks only twice a day, always at the same times. There are an imperial and a pintail. Big or little, if you can find a waterhole and get there at about 7:45 A.M. in Ikoma, or 8:15 in the Seralippe *luga* in the north of Kenya, you will certainly miss more birds than you ever thought possible. They have back-raked wings and fly faster than teal in a hurry, and if you take the passing shots you shoot your shoulder blue.

What is not generally known about East Africa is that its coastal waters and mountain streams provide some of the finest fishing, big and little, in the world. This is especially true of spear-and-goggle stuff, in the coves along Malindi and Mombasa, and off the reef that makes a shark-proof bathing basin of the East African coast. Outside the reef, there are big sail, big marlin, amberjack, kingfish, mackerel, bonito and tremendous shark. Eric Rundgren, a professional hunter for Ker & Downey, landed a 900-pound shark just a few months ago.

There is fantastic trout fishing in the mountain streams and rivers – according to Negley Farson, a fanatic fisherman, some of the best available internationally. In the big lakes, such as Lake Rudolph, the huge Nile perch run to hundreds of pounds, and the tigerfish, possibly the most difficult of all fierce-fighting fish to beach, abound. If you're just hungry, the twenty-five pound African catfish is lovely eating, and in the dry season you don't even have to fish for him. You just pick him out of the moist mud, clean him and pop him into the skillet.

In recent years, much of African interest has shifted from killing to just sightseeing around the reserves and national parks, equipped with camera and often sound apparatus. A certain amount of shooting is still necessary on a lens expedition, because you cannot tell a rhino to "Cut!" if he's headed your way. Also, baits have to be shot to provide lion and leopard footage, and there is, of course, the necessity of feeding the entourage.

You are allowed to shoot natives with a camera. Despite some ingress to the towns by Kikuyu, Embu and Meru, who center around white habitation in the Highlands, the majority of the bigger tribes are still present and largely unspoiled. The proud Masai still have their big *ngomas* (dances) self-adorned with fanciful paint jobs, lion-mane headdresses, marabou-stork leggings, colobus monkey cloaks, and long spears and buffalo-hide shields painted armorially in red and black. So do their cousins, the Wa-Ikomas in Tanganyika, the Rendille-Samburu up north. In the bush, the native is still African.

In Nairobi, a thriving boom town now, a lion occasionally prowls the streets, or a leopard gets into the hencoop, or they have to shoot the wildebeest off the airstrip. The Mau Mau crisis is nearly settled. Thousands were killed, and 60,000 are behind barbed wire. You very seldom see a civilian wearing a pistol any more, whereas two years ago every man, woman and child went armed. Nairobi today is considerably safer than New York City. And once outside the towns, in the bush, heaven is hostile by comparison. There are no locks on tents because none are needed. In the old days of the Mau Mau, I had a regular habit. When I went to town, I put on a necktie and a pistol. When I left town for bush, I took off the necktie and the pistol and heaved them into the corner of my tent.

The African is basically kind and completely cruel. The sight of suffering arouses mirth sometimes, but compassion, never. The African expects the unexpected. The African has a capacity for waiting, doing nothing, living in complete suspension. He will wait six days by a road for a bus to come, sitting in the same place, scratching white marks on his dusty legs with a stick. He will stand on one leg, like a stork, for hours.

Africans are enormous drunkards. They make a sort of mead of honey, or they ferment mealie maize, and the fermentation continues in the stomach. Central Africans throw their dead out for the hyenas to eat, and if Granny looks like she's on her last legs they pop her into the fields, still alive. This avoids the necessity of burning down the house and moving the shamba, the penalty for a death in the house.

Getting to Africa these days is the simplest part of safari. Two days take you from New York to Nairobi, with stopovers in Rome, Paris, Cairo. Compared to the one month it takes by boat to Mombasa, it's hardly any time at all.

The first thing a gent should do, if he is safari-minded, is put himself in the hands of an established firm with a reputation to maintain. There are so many no-hopers, what we call *shenzi* or *burri* types calling themselves white hunters, that a blind gamble will waste your time, money, and earn you nothing worth keeping.

Ker & Downey Safaris Ltd. is the firm I always used. Most of the good hunters – men who won't allow you to shoot cheaply, and who will get you the best in trophies, in country which isn't overrun by tourists and meat hunters – either work for, or have served an apprenticeship with, Ker & Downey.

A new firm has just formed itself, and it should be equal to the best. A bunch of old K & D hands split off to form their own operation: Selby and Holmberg, White Hunters, Ltd. They constitute a good portion of the cream of the Ker & Downey group – Harry Selby, Andrew Holmberg, Mike Rowbotham, Reggie Destro, Frank Bowman.

Still another firm of repute is White Hunters, Ltd., recently formed by Tony Dyer, John Lawrence, David Lunan and Jeff Lawrence-Brown, under Col. Douglas Brett. Bunny Allen operates independently and does a vast amount of film work. He possibly makes the best and most luxurious camp of them all. There is an independent operation by Stan Lawrence-Brown. For guided tours and interesting peeps at game farms, Carr-Hartley is excellent. You can count on any of these for a proper safari.

A proper safari is this: the best in vehicles, a truck for transporting tentage and provisions, and a Land Rover for hunting. The entourage should not be less than fifteen boys for a one-gun operation. The cook should be superb, and the icebox should work. There should never be more than two shooters to one professional white hunter, and no more than four licenses out of one camp. That is law now, and has put an end to outrageous "package" safaris, where fifteen people fell all over each other, wounded animals, and made a mockery of hunting.

On a decent safari, such as Ker & Downey or Selby-Holmberg mount, there would be a fabulous headman, such as Harry Selby's Juma, who is straw boss of the camp. Under him come two personal boys, who serve at table, wash, iron and wait on you hand and foot. Under the personals, but slightly separate, is the cook. If he is Selby's wonderful old Swahili gentleman, he can take a piece of meat that's been dead twenty minutes and make it taste like a slab of aged blue-ribbon sirloin. The food on a good safari is sensational.

Completely apart are the gunbearers – always two, better three, and always one to a gun. These are serious hunters, trackers and brave men who are at your shoulder with a fresh fistful of bullets or a spare gun when it looks as if you'll need them. To help you hunt, you often pick up a local tracker or two.

There is the kitchen *mtoto*, the cook's assistant, who is low man on the pole. Next to him in lack of prominence is the car boy, whose basic duty is to sit in the hunting car when you've left it to hunt. Then you have two or four porters who do the heavy work in making and breaking camp, gathering firewood, and suchlike.

And finally you have the scientists, the skinners. There are two as a rule, because when you get to shooting well, the game piles up. Especially with cats, skinning is a tricky business, because the hair slips unless you get the animal undressed quickly. Skinning out nostrils and ears, and removing the drop of fat from behind each whisker so that whiskers won't fall out is skillful work. There may be better skinners than our Katunga, who is half mad and bays like a wolf when the moon's full, but I haven't met them yet.

If you are asking where the white hunter comes in, I will cite you the captain of a ship. He is social equal, coordinator, navigator, administrative chief, assessor of the worth of animals, expert on the country, guide, drinking companion, victualer, explainer, expediter, fall guy, and is also the man with the big gun who keeps the leopards out of your lap, when necessary, the buffalo out of your backside, or the elephant off your chest. He an honorary game warden, and his pride is in shooting as little as possible and having you bring in trophy heads that will make him proud of his profession.

I doubt if there is anything more comfortable than a well-run safari. You sleep under double-fly double tents, with a bath tent behind and a sanitary tent to one side. The clothes you drop on the floor are washed that day and beautifully ironed. Your mess tent is a big square pavilion, open to the breezes. The headman and the two personals serve you in clean white *kanzus* with red or green bolero jackets and generally red fezzes – at any hour of day or night. All you have to do is holler "Boy!" and what you want, they'll bring you.

The nights are cold in the Highlands, and the fire leaps high. The stars swing low in the cold night sky, and the moon is a silver slice against blue velvet. The hyenas conduct their symphony, the night birds call, a lion complains, a leopard curses at a baboon, who curses back. As a man of poor appetite, I was suddenly surprised to find that

I was consuming four or five pounds of meat each day, and a whole breast of guinea hen was little better than an aperitif.

The longest journey you will make is from the cessation of shooting light until you arrive in camp, where a hot bath, a hot fire, a cold martini, a hot dinner and a warm bed await you. Twenty miles takes two centuries. Apart from a beer at lunch, drinking on safaris is done strictly at night. Alcohol and rhinos and double rifles just don't mix.

Clothes are just as important as your hunter's mechanical skill in repairing a foundered truck or a crippled hunting car. Clothes have as much function as a gun. You need at least two safari suits of khaki or green drill, the bush jacket equipped with bullet loops, and no breast pocket on your shooting side. Guns have a way of getting hung in pocket flaps. The pants should be long, and so should the sleeves; you accumulate less onslaughts from tsetse flies and mosquitoes that way.

The most important article of apparel is the shoe. If your feet hurt, you don't have any fun, can't run away from something that's trying to eat you, and can't hold your gun steady. Birdshooters of about eight-inch ankle height I reckon to be perfect. However, any ankle boot with a crepe or plain rubber sole is excellent.

In the hotter places a broad-brimmed double-terai hat or a light Stetson is handy, if only to use as a pillow or to wash your face in. Do *not* arrive in a pith helmet unless you want to be laughed out of town.

And finally we come to guns and shooting. You might as well start off by realizing that for the first day or so you'll be likely to miss everything, because the light is so tricky that what seems to be 100 yards away is just as likely to be 300 yards, and some freaks of light and haze can make a hare-sized dik-dik look like a bull buffalo. Curse freely, and in a day or so you'll be hitting what you aim at.

I will not attempt to expert you on guns. I started off with every caliber, and wound up with four – a .22 Long Rifle, a Westley Richards .318 for the middle stuff, a double .470 heavy rifle for the thick-skinned tough stuff, and a 12-gauge shotgun for wounded leopards and birds. I use a scope as little as possible, but a good scope on the middle rifle is invaluable for long shots when you can't stalk any closer or for hunting long-distance mountain game when your only chance for a kudu is apt to be at 400 yards.

The biggest mistake the amateur makes is coming out laden with a dozen different calibers. The ammunition is always getting mixed up, the right gun gets left behind, the gunbearer makes a mistake, and even if he doesn't you are disarranged emotionally by changing weapons all the time.

On dangerous game there is one cardinal rule: Get as close as you can, and then get ten feet closer. When you've killed it, give it the other one in the back of the neck, because it's the dead ones that get up and tromp you. And finally, never approach any wounded animal, even antelope, from the front. I knew a professional hunter who once was charged by a wounded dik-dik. A wounded oryx or sable is just as dangerous with his horns as a lion with his claws and teeth.

There is one final thing to say: Go out there expecting to learn something, and to enjoy the heat with the cold, the bugs with the dust, the mud in the waterbag and the busted springs on the hunting car as part of the spectacle, and you will have a wonderful time. Go out as an innocent, and you will come back wealthy and wise. Go out as a wise guy, and you'll hate Africa. I never knew a nice guy who had a bad time on safari. I never knew a sour apple who had a good time. Safari, like the sea, brings things out of man that he can camouflage in the city.

A man always finds what he looks for in Africa, even if it's only himself.

How Much Does It Cost?

TIME. With luck, you might get trophies of the Big Four of African game, together with plenty of lesser game, in as little as two weeks' hunting. But if you're making a trip to Africa, you'd be foolish to depend on luck. The best outfitters recommend that you allow three weeks for the safari itself, from the time you leave Nairobi until you get back. If possible, of course, allow more – but if you allow three weeks, you'll be about as sure as anyone can be, hunting wild game, that you'll get the trophies you're after.

Three weeks, then, for one safari. Allow two days in Nairobi, for preparations beforehand, two days in Nairobi afterward for details before emplaning. Add travel time, one and a half to two days by air each way between Nairobi and New York. Total: four weeks home to home, plus a day or two. Figure on the two days and call it one month.

MONEY. For the safari itself, one white hunter for one client, about $2,000. Two clients and one white hunter, $1,200 per client. Four clients, two white hunters – no white hunter may handle more than two clients, and a safari may not include more than four shooters – $1,100 per client.

Say you go with one good hunting friend, your safari cost is $1,200. That covers everything on safari, including fourteen native helpers – everything except liquor and your ammunition. You'll bring your own ammunition. Add liquor. Add a few days' hotel expenses in Nairobi at about $6 a day, including meals. Add extras for tips and for clothes you'll buy in Nairobi. Call it $1,400. You do not tip your white hunter.

Add game licenses. These differ somewhat according to territory and game. Tanganyika is representative. General license, plus special licenses to include all the Big Four, $450. Much of that is elephant. Include buffalo, rhino, lion, but not elephant, and the cost is about $250. All right, you want elephant, $450.

Add cost of taxidermy afterward. This will depend, obviously, on how much of what you get you want to keep. At a fairly generous guess – elephant tusks, rhino horn, buffalo head, lionskin rug, some antelope – say $500.

Add plane fare. Round trip New York-Nairobi costs $1,593 first class, $1,106.70 tourist. There is no tax to be added. First-class and tourist use same type of planes. On tourist flights you don't get free drinks. Off-season fares apply November 1 to March 31 and are slightly lower.

Add it all, assuming you fly tourist, in season. In round figures, $3,450. You can fly now, pay plane fare later in installments. You can arrange to pay both plane fare and safari cost in installments if you want to – twenty-five percent down, twenty months to pay the rest. You can postpone the taxidermy, you can shoot your elephant with a camera instead of a gun – you need no license for that and no taxidermist either. But figure it without cutting any corners at all – for the hunt of a lifetime, it's a bargain.

When to Go

As far as the game laws in East Africa are concerned, there are no closed seasons except in a few minor instances. But as far as the weather is concerned, there certainly are. Good hunting in East Africa, more than in most places, depends on the weather, which determines not only how well you can move around, but where you will find the game you're looking for.

East Africa has no winter, no four seasons as we know them. In general, the warm days are likely to come around Christmas, and the coolest months are July and August. But these variations are small; the greater temperature differences come with altitude. You might divide the hunting country into four main sections:

THE COAST – a belt extending some fifty miles inland, temperatures averaging 75° to 95° Fahrenheit. Climate much like that of Florida.

THE INLAND PLATEAUS – 2,500 to 4,000 feet above sea level. A dry area and hot – temperatures sometimes hitting 104 degrees.

THE LAKE VICTORIA BASIN – above 4,000 feet altitude. Warm days – 80 to 85 degrees – cool nights. At 4,000 feet or more you sleep under blankets.

THE HIGHLANDS – Days not quite so warm – perhaps 80 degrees – nights cold, down to 45 degrees. Mount Kenya, though almost on the equator, has glaciers and perpetual snow.

The controlling element in African hunting is rain. Many people think of a rainy season as a time of continuous downpour. It isn't. Mostly the rain comes as sudden, heavy thunderstorms, with hours of sunshine between. Any day without some sunshine is exceptional, and even at the height of the rainy season, five hours of sunshine a day is not unusual.

But the rains ruin hunting. Travel becomes not merely difficult but dangerous and often impossible. With pools of water everywhere, the game scatters all over. And the grass grows tall, so that even if you could get to where some game is, you couldn't see it. The time of the rains, in East Africa, is the time when hunters stay home.

The best months for hunting are July to November; the worst, when the rains come, are March, April and May. June, December and January are variable, not so much from year to year as from place to place; a good white hunter can still find game for you in those months, but you probably have to travel farther and work harder to get it than you would have in the best season. If your time is limited, stick to July to November.

What to Take With You

GUNS. You will want three rifles on safari – a light but high-velocity one, caliber .22 to about .25; a medium, caliber .30 to .375; and, for elephant and rhino especially, a heavy, .450 to .475. You will want scope sights for the light and the medium rifles – 2.5X is about right – but not for the heavy rifle; the big animals are shot at short range. You will also want a shotgun for birds. You can, if you wish, rent rifles and guns in Nairobi, but you will obviously enjoy the shooting more if you bring your own. Do not bring handguns; you will have more trouble getting them through customs than they'll be worth. Do not bring more rifles than the three you'll need; you will be shooting with native gunbearers, and three sizes of rifle ammunition to keep separate and ready for you in the field are enough.

AMMUNITION. For a three-week safari you will want for the heavy rifle about fifty rounds of ammunition, thirty solid and twenty soft; for the medium, 120 rounds, thirty solid and ninety soft; for the light rifle, 150 rounds, soft. For the shotgun you'll want 300 rounds Nos. 4 and 6. If you can give your outfitter enough notice, he'll lay in your ammunition for you and save you the trouble of carrying it or shipping it ahead.

CLOTHES. Most of your hunting clothes you can buy in Nairobi. Get measured as soon as you arrive, and your clothes will be ready for you the next day. They are not expensive. You can get boots in Nairobi too, but you may prefer to bring your own. You'll be doing a lot of walking, and you want to be sure of having footwear you can depend on. Bring along a sweater or two. If you have woolen pajamas and a woolen bathrobe, bring them too; the hunting country is warm by day, but cool after sundown. Do not bring any large supply of underwear, handkerchiefs, socks and things like that; on safari, laundry is done every day. If you happen to have a sun helmet, leave it at home. In East Africa sun helmets are jokes. Plus bring binoculars, preferably 7 X 50 or 8 X 40, in a good case as near dustproof as you can get it.

Bring a camera. A 35 mm is probably easier to use and carry, but any good camera you're used to will do. Unless the camera you bring is 35 mm, you'd better bring your own film, as stocks of film of other sizes in Nairobi are undependable. Put your camera in a dustproof case and bring along equipment for cleaning it. Bring a light meter; the light in Africa is like no light you ever saw before, and without a meter you're sure to misjudge it.

You know the rest. If you wear eyeglasses, bring an extra pair. Bring sunglasses – two pairs. Just remember that although you live well on safari, you won't see any kind of store except a native fruit market for three weeks. Bring what you know you'll need for comfort and good hunting, and bring spares.

Get Ready, Get Set …

If you're going to Africa, you can't start this minute. There are certain necessary preliminaries. You will need a passport and visa. For the State Department to issue a passport takes three to four weeks. There is one visa that covers Kenya, Tanganyika, Uganda and Zanzibar; that's the one you want. To get out of East Africa, you must have a valid International Certificate of Inoculation against yellow fever and an International Certificate of Vaccination against smallpox. The sensible thing to do is get both before you leave home; they're good for several years. You will also probably want to get shots or boosters for typhoid-paratyphoid, cholera and tetanus. You must make a date with an outfitter in advance and get plane reservations to and from Nairobi.

OUTFITTERS FIRST. There are several good ones, among them Ker & Downey Safaris Ltd., Selby and Holmberg , White Hunters, Ltd. All can be addressed at Nairobi, Kenya, East Africa. Names of others can be obtained from Professional White Hunters Association,

Nairobi, or from East Africa Tourist Travel Association, Dept. A, 295 Madison Avenue, New York 17, N.Y. Ker & Downey are represented in the U.S. by John Hart, Reliance Travel Service, 143 West 49th Street, New York 19; and White Hunters by T. W. S. Pasley, Continental-American Travel, Inc., 465 Park Avenue, New York 22. Three-week safaris in Northern Rhodesia, run by the government there, are somewhat different from safaris in Kenya and Tanganyika but cost about the same. For information about these write Continental-American or Tourist Office, Northern Rhodesia Government, Livingstone.

TRAVEL. Airlines flying New York-Nairobi are British Overseas Airways Corporation (BOAC), Trans-World Airlines (via a link-up with Ethiopia Airways at Cairo), Scandinavian Airlines System (SAS), Air France, Sabena and El Al, the Israeli airline. All have offices in New York. BOAC runs thirteen flights a week each way; flights of all lines total about twenty a week. Fares on all lines are the same.

PACKING. Weight allowance tourist is forty-four pounds, first-class sixty-six pounds. If your outfitter can get your ammunition for you, fine. If not, sending it ahead by ship takes four months; sending it ahead as unaccompanied air baggage costs about the same and is much faster. Guns, ammunition and clothes *must* all be packed separately from one another. Ammunition sent by air *must* be packed in sealed metal containers enclosed in a wooden box.

Take extra time if you can. Wherever your airplane puts down – London, Paris, Rome, Cairo – you can stop over and see the town at no extra cost except, of course, your expenses while there. To go on safari, allow a month, home to home; if you can take a couple of weeks more, you can hit many of the high spots of Europe besides, all on the same ticket, providing you notify the airline in advance. To stop over, you will need appropriate visas. Get them before you leave. The main thing is to plan ahead.

On the first safari, Ruark learned that most professional hunters held a low opinion of photographers and motion-picture crews, and subsequent experience led him to adopt a similar view. In "Darkroom Africa," published in *Esquire*, September 1954, he argues the difference between hunting and the specious humaneness of big-and dangerous-game photography. Murder, he says is murder; hunting is something else entirely.

This theme, developed in beautifully lean, tight prose, is one of Ruark's most valuable legacies. The conflict it treats hasn't changed in the past thirty-five years – except, perhaps, to grow even more rancorous – and those of us who love and understand hunting can find in Ruark a powerful voice in support of good sense and a point of view seldom heard these days.

Michael McIntosh

CHAPTER THIRTEEN

DARKROOM AFRICA

The Masai warriors were pretty tired. Their lion-mane and ostrich-feather headdresses were rumpled and weary. They found their forbidden (by local law) buffalo-hide shields a little too heavy for comfort. They did not flaunt their spears. They leaned on them. A long line of these warriors, the most fierce, the least tamed of all of the African natives, stretched from Narok, the center of culture for the Masai nation in Kenya, to the straggling hills abutting the Loita plains. Their ocher-clay war paint was mussed and running, and about them was a general air of fatigue. They had *not* been in battle with their hated friends, the Kikuyu.

We drove the jeep alongside a couple of the more wilted gladiators.

"Shauri gani?" I said. "What gives?"

One of the braves twitched his goat-hide cloak a touch more demurely about his nakedness, stood on one foot, like a stork – a slightly overhung stork – and leaned on his third-degree *moran*, or professional warrior's spear.

"Bwana 'Mkubwa Queeny," he said. *"Ngini, Keshu, kuja M-G-M."* More or less translated, this meant that Mr. Edgar Queeny of the Monsanto Chemical Queenys was back to make still another African film on tribal life, and that tomorrow, or any day now, Metro-Goldwyn-Mayer would be along, full of high plans and baksheesh. The *moran* was right, too. Evidently the jungle drums had spoken, because the next bright day was darkened with scout planes searching out a location on the Mara River where Mr. Gable and Miss Gardner would fit nicely into the other wildlife.

If you stalk onto the veranda of the Norfolk Hotel, or into the drinking room of the New Stanley Grill, the chances are excellent that you will run into eager rich people in stiff new khaki bush jackets, with light meters slung around their necks and their heads full of *f*-stops. Or, if you pursue the bush from Egelok in the southern Masai to the road which says "Shaffa Dikka – Garba Tulla" in the Northern Frontier of Kenya, you will trip over multifarious moving-picture safaris, each equipped with a full complement of young women in pedal pushers and dark glasses, questing airplanes, grumbling trucks, and assistant directors made up to look like assistant directors on location. This is what is sometimes called "darkroom Africa," out of respect for the scourge of photography that has beset the land.

In the past few years, due to cheap labor, fairly constant blue sky, innumerable free extras in the form of wild animals, and nearly free extras in the person of the local natives, Africa has become a sort of extension Hollywood. And for the amateur photographer on vacation, it is almost El Dorado. The major safari companies such as Ker & Downey, Safarilands, or Lawrence-Brown and Lunan of Nairobi, will tell you that where once safari takers came primarily to shoot with guns, they now come to shoot with cameras. The combined process has succeeded in spoiling the natives as picture subjects, frightening fauna, and killing more animals than ever were killed when the initial aim of the African safari was to procure a few select trophy heads to hang on the wall.

The natives, whether they be Samburu or Borran or Somali to the north, Masai to the south, or Wa-Ikoma in Tanganyika, have resolved the ingress of bulb snappers and moving-picture safaris to their own satisfaction. Over the length and breadth of Central Africa, it is impossible to buy a snaggle-toothed beam from the mangiest nomad for less than two shillings. Flash a camera and the fly-hit aboriginal flatly refuses to pose unless you bless him with trade goods, namely shillings. He has never seen a movie, and perhaps he has never seen a still-picture print. But he knows all about that little box which whirs or says *click*. It means that the mad white man is doing something nefarious for his own gain, and there's *shillingi mingi* mixed up in the magic. I have recently encountered tribes whose primitive habits haven't changed since the beginning of time, with one exception. They don't understand penicillin, and they think that the noise from a gun is the killer, but they savvy the *picha* as fully as Josef von Sternberg ever did. They will dance, and flourish spears, and paint themselves up real fierce, and say "ugh-ugh" on demand – for a handful of silver and a billing in the screen credits.

There is a little village in Tanganyika, where the leopards scream and the lions abound, and in this village every buck has killed his own lion with a spear. This is *wild* country, three days' hard driving from Nairobi, mostly on no roads, over mountains, across deserts, over dry riverbeds, across treacherous cotton soil that would mire a thistle in the rainy season.

As far back as two years ago I went into the Ikoma village one day to talk to the chief, to arrange a very fierce, spectacular, Technicolor lion dance. The chief, after a respectable time, came out from his *boma*, followed at a decent distance by a gross of wives and tribal elders. The chief was blowing on his fingernails, which were bright pink. In one hand he held a bottle of Revlon nail polish.

We asked him what the going price for a big mad dance might be.

"Sixty bucks," he said, in the Swahili equivalent. My hunter, Harry Selby, screamed in anguish.

"It was only thirty bucks last year," Harry said. "Look, chum, I live here. You know me. Bwana Naraka, from Nanyuki. Let's have no hanky-panky on the prices."

"Sorry, old friend," the chief said. "But the price of war paint has jumped. It's hardly worthwhile for my men to go all the way into the Indian *ducca* to buy paint to dance at the old prices. There's not enough margin of profit to even buy beer. There was a war on, or something. Anyhow the price is sixty bucks for the *ngoma*, or we don't dance."

We paid the sixty bucks, and the local lads turned out in all their finery: lion manes, colobus monkey-fur cloaks, marabou-stork anklets, and similar trappings. They danced, and were drunk off the native beer for about six days. The chief bought more nail polish.

The animals have not solved the situation so glibly. They still do not understand that the sun must be *behind* the picture snapper, or at least in a cross light, and that certain twiddlings must be effected to change lenses, reload magazines, or adjust focus. Nor do the bigger, more dangerous brutes understand the word "cut!" A charging rhino is apt to keep on charging, even after his horn fills a one-inch lens, with more or less disastrous results either to the rhino, who must be shot, or to the valiant photographer. Nobody has yet succeeded in convincing an irascible cow elephant with a young calf that the man with the shiny box in his hand is really a friendly fellow, who only wants to capture her image on film. Even in the national parks, where shooting in self-defense is frowned on, the ruder creatures such as elephant and rhino haven't sorted out the difference between friend and foe. The elephants that died in *King Solomon's Mines* and *Ivory Hunter* were shot out of stark necessity. Just recently I've had to shoot an elephant *and* a rhino, on successive days, to keep them from mangling a photographer and me. This never happened when I was a shooting man instead of an unpaid flashbulb holder and photographer's general assistant.

The most puzzled of all of the beasts are the zebra, the wildebeest, the wart hogs, the topi, and the kongoni, all animals which are rather liberally located on a full license. These poor creatures cannot understand the difference between being shot for their hides, heads and tallows, or being shot to provide a dinner for a lion or leopard, so that the *Bwana Picha* may get a real dandy-peachy close-up of a lion for his photograph album or his home movies. The poor old zebra or wildebeest reckons that he is just about as dead in one condition as in the other.

Roughly speaking, the only animal who has really solved the photography business is the lion. In the tsetse-fly area of the Masai reserve, lions are not on license, while most of the common game is shootable. These Masai lions – who are named Hector, Tiberius, or Nero, and who are labeled according to their locality, such as the Egelok pride, or the Jagatiak pride – have entered fully into the spirit of photography. If you shoot off a gun on the upper plains of the Masai, you are apt to be engulfed by a pride of twenty lions, who have learned to identify gunshot with dinner. They come tearing out of the bush, panting for that juicy topi or zebra the nice man has just walloped, and are willing to pose at five feet in payment for their reward. The average lion, when he sees a hunting car passing, does not look at the car. He adjusts his gaze to about twenty feet behind the car, where a carcass of some antelope is sure to be dragging. One might say that this sort of deliberate enticement is frowned on today by Maj. Lynn Temple-Borum, the game warden of the southern Masai, and most reputable hunters such as Harry Selby won't do it. Tantalizing rhino and elephant from a speedy jeep or power wagon is also *verboten* for picture purposes, but it still gets done, and nearly every day. There is a fine line between "approaching" a wild animal with a camera, or deliberately inciting it to violent action, but the camera bug seldom sees the line. His eye is pinned to the viewer, which is generally bulging with beast.

The Masai lions have hit a stage of tameness that is almost unbelievable. Recently, one was enticed to jump into the back of a truck in which a carcass had been placed. Harry Selby, in an open-topped, doorless jeep, in my presence, has run over the tail of a lion who wouldn't get out of the way. Selby has also smacked a lioness in the face with his hat, to force her to desert a wildebeest carcass that we wanted to move for better lighting. One of my gunbearers has gone into the bush with a full-grown male lion in order to tie a rope to the leg of the zebra on which the lion was feeding. Selby has fixed an ailing gas pump in the middle of a pride of six full-grown lions, getting out of the jeep and going about his mechanical chores while whistling cheerfully. My wife, no heroine, has sat semi-happily at six feet from a dozen adult *simbas*, with no doors on the car, no top on the car, and no gun loaded. There is only a small chance you take – that there will be the one odd lion who doesn't like people, doesn't like cars and hates cameras. There's one like that in the Masai, which I hope Maj. Temple-Borum has shot by now. There's another in Tanganyika – a lioness who is going to chew the head off some happy photographer someday. She has charged, with no provocation, at least five open-faced cars, and if somebody doesn't shoot her soon she will give photography a bad name in greater downtown Ikoma.

B asically, big-game photography – dangerous game photography – is considerably more dangerous than gun-hunting, because even in national parks the animal is still wild. This is especially applicable to rhino and elephant. It is not especially dangerous to the camera-wielder because he will have had the forethought to have hired a competent professional hunter to back him up. But it's dangerous to the pro, and it's sort of fatal for the animal here and there.

What makes it dangerous is the basic difference between gun and camera, especially the moving-picture camera. When you are shooting trophy heads, your main idea is to pick out one especially choice item and shoot it as swiftly and competently as possible. You want to get as close as you can without disturbing the beast, and then to shoot it dead so you won't have to follow it into the bush and risk a charge from a sick, angry animal at close range. And generally speaking, the sportsman is shooting lone males – old boys who were past breeding, expelled from the herd, and wearing enough mane, horns, or ivory to make them a welcome addition to the wall. The trophy hunter shoots sparingly, because he only wants the best.

The photographer wants it dramatic, of course, and he wants as many animals as possible, at once, with the sun right, and close as he can get. This means that the animal must be agitated, must be disturbed, and must be rendered irritable and nervous. Eventually his patience dissipates, and he charges. Somebody has to stop him, or somebody gets gored or trampled.

Ordinarily I will run from any rhino, or backtrack softly and quietly if I stumble on some surly old gentleman who is snoozing beneath a thorn tree and who won't like it if you wake him. In a recent movie-making safari, I had to stand pat for five rhino charges to keep the cameraman happy. One of the poor old boys I had to shoot, and I had to break his neck at about fifteen feet to keep him out of my lap. The rest of the time I stood and quivered and sweated horribly from the brow and palms. The reason we had to shoot the one lad was that he was keeping company with a lady in the bush, and seemed to resent it when we chased the cow out of the bush. He foreswore romance and took up murder instead.

The rhino is the patsy in most of the big, super-epic movies you see, dating as far back as the supposedly humanitarian Martin Johnsons. The late Johnsons killed more animals than a plague of rinderpest, just to get pictures, as a perusal of Osa Johnson's old book will plainly show. In filming the ancient movie, *Simba*, they not only killed considerable lions callously, but they got several natives killed and clawed up in the process. Old Pat Ayre, a professional hunter, was piqued thirty years ago when Martin Johnson was dissatisfied with a close-up of a rhino being shot, and insisted that Ayre "drop the next one in his lap." Pat dropped him in the camera's lap, all right, but he didn't like it. They abused at least three rhinos – I recently viewed the old film – one of whom was a half-grown calf, and Osa took the credit for the kill in a clever cut-in shot. At no time was the rhino actually charging, but merely running up and turning away.

In a more recent effort, *Savage Splendor*, no less than *five* rhino were used in one sequence, and when one of them died as a result of being teased into butting a truck, the professional who arranged the sequence temporarily lost his license. The hunter, Carr-Hartley of Rumuruti, Kenya, freely admits the facts of this particular business. If it's a rhino charge you want, Hartley can arrange it for you, as can any other professional hunter with a badge to pin on his hat. But he'll have to kill the rhino if the close-up is a good one.

There is no danger to leopard photography, largely because there *is* no leopard photography except by rare accident. Most movie companies which need leopard footage rent Hartley's semitame leopard, Chui, who cavorts in a special arena Hartley has built to conform to the rugged standards of the wilds. A really wild leopard is largely a nocturnal animal who comes to a bait just at nightfall or after.

In the national parks, where you're not supposed to get out of your car, and where signs read "Elephants have right-of-way" and the general admonition is to please don't be beastly to the beasts, you can still get into an awful lot of trouble, which sometimes necessitates shooting. A good many elephants have been shot in African national parks in recent years in the process of picture taking. Tony Dyer had to wallop one at Ambozeli, in Kenya, during the making of a British film called *Ivory Hunter*. Tony was the professional hunter on the film safari and it was his job to agitate the elephants.

"After the fifth day," Dyer said, "I was so bloody nervous I was going out in the morning with my gun in one hand and a bottle of brandy in the other." Dyer is a man who doesn't drink much.

After some time of stirring up an average of 250 elephants daily, an old one-tusked bull broke off the herd and gave spirited chase to Mr. Dyer and the cameraman. Tony finally turned, fell on his back, shot the elephant in the face, and then walloped it through the heart as it swerved. They measured the imprint of Dyer's rear end from the last print of the elephant's forefeet. Distance: nine yards. Too close.

The dramatic scene in *King Solomon's Mines*, of a bull elephant breaking off from the herd, charging, and then being struck down in its tracks, with spurts of dust coming off its skull as the bullets hit, was also an actual hunk of necessity. Stan Lawrence-Brown was the hunter. The old bull got testy, charged, and the camera crew took off, leaving some electrically operated cameras whirring. Lawrence-Brown belted the bull in the skull and again in the shoulder, and down it went, and that is what you saw in the beginning of the film, before Hollywood started painting donkeys to resemble zebras and speeding up the film on giraffes. They *did* paint up the donkeys, and they *did* employ phony tarantulas and a tame leopard to claw at a tent. But the elephant operation was brutally real.

Sequel: In the confusion, the elephant, which had only been stunned, got up later and went away. The Game Department authorized the hiring of Frank Bowman, another professional, to take a small plane and go off in search of the wounded bull, who would be ripe and raring to trample a few luckless natives.

Elephants can be pure poison in the business of picture-taking.

In the national park around Lake Edward in Uganda, an old lady elephant with a calf chased Harry Selby and me in our truck a good thousand yards, screaming with rage, her trunk outstretched like a cannon's barrel, the hole in the end looking as big as a manhole cover. We were doing better than forty miles an hour before we commenced to gain on her.

The very next day we were taking pictures of a herd of some sixty elephant when the car suffered a grievous wound in its left hind foot and we had to change the tire in the middle of the mob. There was *no* place we could go. The same old lady was in the herd. There was a gun in the back seat of the Rover. National park or no national park, if the old gal had continued her yesterday's hostility, I would have shot her first and worried about the Rt. Hon. Kenneth Beaton, monocled warden of the area, a little later on. Seven tons of angry elephant is a fearsome thing indeed, and much faster afoot than you'd believe.

We mustn't sneer at the fortitude involved in this kind of photography, since the audacity involved is considerable. You are inviting trouble when you hunt with a camera, beckoning the trouble on, cocking a snoot at common sense. The gun's there, of course, but it is a last resort gun on the dangerous stuff, and you are fighting, as the bullfighters say, on the terrain of the bull. This is what kills matadors – and photographers' assistants.

I believe that all photographers and the people who assist them are just a mite goofy, because they seemingly are willing to die to get the best possible picture, be it moving or still. I found myself infected, finally, with an urge toward self-destruction, and certainly we did some things with animals I wouldn't ordinarily attempt, such as sending a gunbearer around to let his scent drift down the wind into a herd of buff so that the buff would charge *our* way. Charge is not precisely the word. Stampede is better. But when you are sitting unprotected on an open plain, being very still indeed, and 500 buff weighing a ton apiece come thundering down, and finally you must charge the buffalo, screaming in order to stop them and hoping to see a tree, then the imminence of the idiocy strikes you and a camera does not seem worth the trouble. It is so silly to die in order to qualify for Picture of the Week, or Year.

But you must never believe the photographer when he gives you that holy word about imprisoning the thing in print, and not killing it, but capturing its essence while letting it live. Of the two, the big-game hunter and the big-game photographer, the first is a humanitarian and the other a callous killer. The photographer couldn't care less about death, especially if somebody else does the dirty work of shooting it first, poking it in the eye to see if it's dead, and then hanging it in a tree, or dropping it on a plain, or shooting it in desperation – according to what exposure the humanitarian has just twiddled into his camera. Murder is murder, according to the victim's view, and it is difficult to find any nobility in the assassination of a zebra to make a lion look homelike, or the killing of a rhino who has overstayed his welcome in the lens.

R eporting the difference between fact and popular belief always was one of Ruark's favorite ways to build a story. He used the approach again and again, in sporting and nonsporting pieces alike, and his masterful skill at it had much to do with both the depth and breadth of his reputation as a writer.

"Lowdown On Leo" is an example of Ruark at his best. It appeared in *Esquire*, March 1955.

Michael McIntosh

CHAPTER FOURTEEN

LOWDOWN ON LEO

T he first wild lion I ever saw yawned at me. I did not yawn back. I was not bored. Then the lion got up, leisurely, and went away. I got up, non-leisurely, and went away. In the opposite direction.

The first lion I ever shot came awake in camp, after he was already dead. Somehow you do not notice the thorns on the thorn trees when you are climbing one. You only get stuck painfully on the way down.

The last lion I shall ever shoot was of no particular problem, but he had some ladies with him. Four badly disposed ladies, one of whom wound up in my lap. The next day, when I went back to pay a call on the harem, her disposition had not improved. She charged me and the jeep, which had no top and no doors on it, and her teeth clicked within a foot of my rather ample posterior.

With all these preliminaries finished and done, I then proceeded to learn a lot of things about a lot of lions. And the first thing I learned was that the lion is not the King of Beasts, and never was. He just looked like he ought to be the king, because of a certain stuffy nobility of countenance, plus the ability to kill anything he swipes at with a right or left hook. The elephant is the undisputed king; the lion is the old politician, and the leopard is the knave.

A lion is a lot of things he isn't supposed to be. He's a sneak. Unless you hurt him he's a trouble-dodger, and mostly he's a dope. He is so lazy you wouldn't believe it. He is greedy and he is selfish. He is killed by his own sons or dies of old age. He is a dirty feeder, will eat carrion. He is more dog than cat, is many ways, and he believes sincerely in allowing the women to do all the work. He smells bad, and is generally infested with flies. He slouches when he walks – but when he comes in a hurry he can do 100 yards in just over three seconds, in leaps of more than twenty feet each.

A lion can, and does, climb trees. There are lions in India, but no tigers live in Africa. Successful matings between both beasts have been arranged. The offspring of a male lion and a tigress is a *Liger*. The other way round it's a *Tiglon*. In both cases they look a little discouraged, as if they wished they'd had less adventurous parents. Lions, facially, differ as much as people. I have a blond lion friend in the southern Masai of Kenya who looks exactly like Bert Lahr. I have seen lionesses who could be described as very ugly, and others who would make Marilyn Monroe look seedy. There are more maneless lions than there are lions with manes, and a Leo of Metro-Goldwyn-Mayer is very seldom seen. Maned lions vary in coloration from cherry red to albino blond, and I have seen a couple who were solid black all over. They hate two other creatures badly – buzzards and hyenas. They are friendly with tiny bat-eared foxes and jackals, and with all hoofed animals – when the lions are not hungry.

Lions do not, actually, except under strange conditions, fear anything. They love people, if the people feed them, and they tolerate them under most circumstances. They leave the African elephant severely alone, and the big, old seven-tonner is happy to reciprocate. Donald Ker, a professional hunter, has seen a lioness dead under the body of a female giraffe, which had trampled the lioness to death with its hoofs. I have seen a leopard eating a dead lion, but a close inspection showed that the lion had been mortally wounded by a Masai spear. The leopard came along as an afterthought.

Unlike the leopard, the lion never kills for fun. She – and I use the female pronoun on purpose – kills only when she is hungry, or has been attacked and wounded and fights back as a reflex. The male lion often feels it beneath his dignity to slay his own supper. He is surrounded by a harem which usually has nothing to do but sleep in the sun, and the old boy sends the old girl to market. This is done very simply. Himself may go for a stroll around a herd of zebra or wildebeest, to let his scent drift downwind, and, if he's feeling liverish, he may roar a couple of times just to tell the simpletons that Simba is about. While he is providing the window decoration, the old lady flattens herself in the grass, with her ears just peeping above the eye level, and walks on her tippy-toes. She creeps as close as she can, and then she sticks her tail out as stiff as a broom handle and takes off. I know of nothing non-mechanical that can go as fast as a charging lion for a matter of yards.

The old lady lights on the back of her quarry. Usually she hooks her hind feet into its rump, and her teeth are sunk into its neck. If she doesn't kill with her teeth she puts one forepaw around the victim's neck, for purchase. The she reaches out with the other paw, seizes her dinner by the nose, and hauls the head around. *Crack!* Dinner is served.

The feeding operation is a matter of whim. Sometimes the old gentleman won't let his women and children eat until he has filled himself so paunch-heavy that his belly is dragging the ground. Other times he allows the ladies first-crack at the carcass. On occasion he will invite everybody in for their fill, and you will see a dozen or more lions all facially blood-red, tugging in opposite directions at their meal. For some reason, mostly known to themselves, they aim for the viscera first, and dive headfirst into the tummy of their kill. They eat until gorged, and then lie up until the digestive processes have leaned them down again, when a new kill is indicated.

The jealousy of lions for their kills is amazingly contradictory. I have moving pictures of a lion taking free-handed swipes at a vulture who had walked too close to Pa's repast. You can entice the most cowardly lion out of the safety of bush if you can induce one single vulture to volplane down out of the sky and look enviously at a carcass. One evilly grinning hyena, sidling out of the bush, will cause a mass exodus of all the lions inside the bush. Yet it isn't unusual to see a bat-eared fox or a tiny jackal feeding right alongside old Simba, and even jostling the so-called King of Beasts away from a choice morsel.

It is just as well to discuss man-eating here, in the feeding habits of lions. There never was a lion who would take on a man as a light lunch except for one or two exceptional reasons. You have to approach the reasons gradually.

One is this: The natives of East Africa have a dread superstition of death. A person who dies inside the lodge haunts the whole premises, necessitating a move. So, when Grandpa and Grandma get real sickly, their relatives really don't give the old folks a good chance to die in the house. They lug them outside and leave them in the bush.

They die all right, usually from fear as well as from degeneration of tissue.

Lions love carrion. Lions get old and slow afoot.

It is easy to understand, then, how an old lion, maimed in a battle with his sons, rheumatic or just plain sick and tired, or expelled from his pride or group, might start haunting native villages to clobber the odd bullock or sheep. In the course he comes upon the corpses, or the near-corpses, usually after having had a taste of man-meat when, from fear, he has accidentally been forced to kill a herdsman whose cattle he was attacking. Once the taste of man is firmly in a lion's mouth, he finds man an easy dish.

J. A. Hunter, in his book, tells how he was forced to exterminate a hundred lions in the Masai district because a variety of circumstances, including defense of cattle, killed enough natives to give the lions a zest for human food. The story of the man-eaters of Tsavo, when a very few lions ate up the road gangs who were building a railroad in Kenya, is classic. Once they even went into an office and removed the superintendent. Evidently there is something about human flesh which is habit-forming for big cats, since Jim Corbett recounts tales of single tigers in India who've eaten hundreds of natives as a matter of simple preference.

The compressed force in an adult lion is almost unbelievable. A mature lioness will weigh over 300 pounds, and at least one male I shot was estimated at over 600 pounds. When you consider that most of this is lean, coiled-spring muscle under a velvety hide, with no horns to weigh it down, and it has never been subjected to tobacco, nicotine or drug, and moreover has lived its entire life on a diet of pure protein, sunshine and slumber, the potential strength and agility is nearly impossible to contemplate.

I know of one occasion when a leopard, the cousin who is only a fifth as big as a lion, took a zebra foal weighing anywhere from 300 to 400 pounds all the way to the top of a tree. A lion can pick up a dead mature zebra in its jaws – and a dead mature zebra weighs about 700 pounds – and drag it off. A man in a lion's mouth is only a tidbit. The man-eaters of Tsavo used to leap into the railroad camp, choose a coolie, and bound over the *boma* with the man firmly clamped in their jaws, and the bound might be one of fifteen yards!

Skillful Hunter

The lion's killing apparatus is extensive. He has a set of teeth that shear past each other like chisels. His claws are curved scimitars. He has a dewclaw, well up his forepaws, that juts out horizontally when he attacks. It's a terrible sort of longshoreman's ripper hook, which would make him formidable if he had no other weapon on his person. Adding the massive muscle in his forearms, and the electric spring in his spine, plus the accumulated decayed flesh that make both his talons and his teeth deadly poisonous, and you have an animal that combines the best attributes for destruction of a tank, a serpent and a poisoned well.

Yet he is such a gregarious creature that on many occasions I have seen lions running as members of the herd with zebra and wildebeest. I've seen him drinking at waterholes with impala, Grant's gazelles and Tommies, and the antelopes paid him no mind. Even in the presence of man you seldom see him dash off in a panic. He looks at you, shrugs and ignores you – or just gets up and shambles off, high-humped and angular under his slow-slipping hide.

As for ferocity, there are certain bad-tempered ones. But I have seen a man hit a lion in the face with his hat and drive it off. I have seen a man in a jeep run over the tail of one. I have seen a man – in this case, me – take a haunch of zebra away from one in order to move him to a better piece of sunlight so that pictures could be made. You can get them to leap into the back of trucks, if you put a piece of meat there. A recent picture taken in a national park in Africa showed a lioness standing on the hood of a tourist's car.

I mark a lion by its expression, as you might judge a person. When I find a surly one, a nervous one, a just-generally-mean one, I do not deal at close range with that beast. An ordinary lion is as good-natured as old Uncle Josiah down in Paducah, a-settin' in the sun and contemplating the next sour-mash bourbon.

My wife, who is not the bravest woman I ever met, has become accustomed to sitting in a topless jeep, with its doors off, while we play with mature lions – including mothers with cubs – at a range of very often under six feet. My wife will not go buffalo hunting or elephant watching with me, which is the best justification of the pleasantness of wild lions that I can offer. You can do *anything* with a lion of even temperament. A buffalo, an elephant, a leopard, a rhino – they're all unpredictable.

Midday – Lions

We have had lions in our camps like dogs, on one occasion brazenly pinching three Grant's gazelles we had hanging for food. They roar at 100 yards' distance, and the noise is musical. Lions are nice people. They are, except when very, very hungry, the best example of *laissez faire* I ever saw.

Speaking of roaring, a lion does *not* roar when he's angry. He roars because it's a damp night and his rheumatism, to which he is susceptible, afflicts him. Or he roars because he is feeling pretty good and the moon's bright. Or he roars because he is in love, or hungry.

Like your bachelor Uncle Henry, he mostly mutters. It is a mutter with an asthmatic catch in the throat, and is repeated over and over again. He is a grumbler. If he's wounded, he growls; it is one of the more horrifying sounds of the world, a deep-chested, angry rumble. I think actually that he made his reputation on his roar, which is considerably more amiable and less infectious than either his bite or his snarl.

For hunting purposes, the lion is about the easiest quarry I know. You can drive him, you can lure him with a kill, and you can really walk up pretty close to him. There's a village I know in Tanganyika, and several in Kenya where the Masai live, where every young buck who has killed a lion has his own lion-mane headdress.

The accepted Masai method of killing lions is to drive them with the young *moran*, or warriors, into a cul-de-sac, from which the cornered lion is forced to charge. A young Masai warrior takes the charge on his shield and is very often killed in the process of acceptance. Whilst he falls to earth, and the lion is mauling at him, another brave type hauls at his tail, and the others fall upon him with *simis*, or two-bladed short swords. Generally speaking, a mature lion may cost you one dead warrior and several scratched up. But the man who wins his mane will not let a stranger touch it, nor will he let any other man wear it.

The Masai of East Africa, plus the safari hunters and the farmers, at one time reduced the lion population to such dismal numbers that there were only about four shootable lions left in the whole Masai area. This, in nearby Tanganyika, already had become apparent on the huge, sweeping Serengeti plains. The season was closed in Kenya and the Serengeti made into a preserve. Today it is very easy to see a couple of dozen lions in a day of casual driving, and they have no fear of man. This preservation has allowed sufficient lions to move out to the fringe areas to give the sportsman his trophy, if he wishes, without actually damaging the reservoir.

The largest pride of lions I ever saw numbered twenty-one. The family is administered by the old man, and his sons are allowed to hang around if they behave. The old gentleman services all the lionesses. There may come a day when the biggest, burliest Junior decides that Pop's had his way long enough, and a ding-dong battle is pitched. The average result would be that the youngster either kills or so severely cripples his father that the ex-head of the house moves out and becomes a maverick, and that's when he has his best chance of learning how easy it is to kill cattle first and man later. But I once shot a boss lion who had just killed his son. The boss lion bore the wounds to prove it, the mature son, who I'd seen that morning, was no longer with the pride, and the buzzards were gathering over a piece of impenetrable bush. Harry Selby once found and dispatched (with a pistol) a mature lion whose back had been broken by his son. The wounded lion was in the second week of starvation, was ringed round by hyenas, and the maggots were already at work on him.

Lions follow the huge game migrations, and you can always find lions by the state of the water and the grass. But once settled in an ample reserve, they are creatures of firmest habit, and just will not, like the Rock of Ages, be moved. There is an old black-maned dweller in Tanganyika whose mane comes down past his knees, like an apron, who has been haunting the same terrain and sneering at hunters for better than ten years. I know families in the Masai – such as the Jagatiak pride and the Egelok pride – that never move more than a few miles from base. I also remember Mama.

Mama was a nasty-tempered old girl in Tanganyika. She did not greatly admire me, because I walloped her old gentleman one day, and Mama decided that people who came in hunting cars were not nice people, and she charged me and permanently stunted my courage.

I went back to see her the next day, and she charged the car – which, being a doorless, no-topped jeep, had all the protection of a broomstick. Harry Selby went back to the area three months later and the old lady charged his hunting car. Andrew Holmberg or Tony Dyer,

I forget which, went back six months after that, and the old girl came at the car like a bullet. You can talk all you want of an elephant's memory and a lion's average stupidity. All we know is that this gal had a vengeful memory, and she knew very well a man was a man, in or out of a car.

The breeding habits of the lion are more or less irregular, as in humankind. Some lions are monogamous, cleaving strictly unto one wife. Others will serve a harem. I have seen prides with several lionesses and several sets of cubs, in different age groups – and the odd thing is that the non-mothers eagerly perform as babysitters and protectors of the other girls' children. The average litter of cubs is two, but quite often the mother will drop four. It takes a young lion about eighteen months before he is adjudged big enough to look after himself.

Lions are the only animals I know that take a definite honeymoon. The swain goes off with the lady and for a couple of weeks they make love, and rarely bother to eat. At such a time Pop's temper is absolutely foul. One of the most foolhardy acts ever committed in the bush was committed by Harry Selby, who crept up to a pair of courting lions and managed to take several snapshots of the propagation process without having to shoot either.

The period of gestation is roughly sixteen weeks. While the cubs are very small and nursing, other lionesses in the pride do the hunting for mama and children. A lion's life can be up to twenty years, but maturity is reckoned roughly at seven years. Unless shot, they can figure on a span of about twelve years. At that time disease or injury makes them easy meat for the hyenas.

It is hard to say what, exactly, determines the size of mane in lions. The lions of the Northern Frontier of Kenya are largely maneless, as are the lions in the high plateau of Tanganyika. The most luxuriantly maned fellows I know are those around the Serengeti area of Tanganyika, and its adjoining southern Masai of Kenya. In those areas, despite any talk of thornbush keeping the mane short, there are occasional magnificent old gentlemen with manes as lush as any zoo lions.

The lion got around the globe real good. He got as far as India from Africa by crossing through Arabia, and he got into England from Asia Minor to Western Europe. He was found in France and Germany and in Palestine. There are many references to lions in the Old Testament and their fossilized remains have been found in England. He was in Macedonia and Crete and Persia and Mesopotamia. His killing was always the sport of kings.

You do not find him in North Africa any more, and in the last hundred years he has nearly disappeared from India. The survivors, strictly protected, are mostly in the vicinity of Kathiawar. They are still found in Ethiopia, and possibly a very few can be found in Uganda and around the Congo. In Uganda they are classed as vermin.

The only animals I know that are capable of killing lions are elephants and, in rare instances, giraffes and crocodiles. The lion has no truck with the elephant. Crocs often have been known to seize and drown a drinking lion. Giraffes will fiercely defend their young if famine is such that the Simba decides to clobber a small giraffe for dinner. But mostly the lion dines off zebra and wildebeest. These creatures travel in vast herds and pose no problem whatsoever in the killing. Yet I have shot zebra with well-defined claw-marks on their withers and rumps, proving that even the enormous strength, speed and armament of a lion are not always infallible.

Probably the finest lions ever shot by visitors in East Africa were shot by Duncan McMartin, a Canadian sportsman, Ben Finney, an American, and the Duke of Gloucester. A true black-maned lion is a rare sight, and these were magnificent examples. The average lion, even if dark, is dark only on the tips or coarser hairs of his mane, and is light underneath. One of mine had a mane of bright cherry red and exceedingly green eyes.

According to personal quirks of character, lions are tamable, semi-tamable, and completely untamable. A lioness named Iola was, even when full-grown, as tractable as a Newfoundland puppy. A lion I know named Monty seems conditioned to his status as Carr-Hartley's best pet and movie property. But Hartley, a wild-animal collector in Kenya, is missing fingers from other pets.

I have mentioned that I will never shoot another lion, which is not quite true. If I am ever back around Ikoma, in Tanganyika, I am going to shoot that surly lioness, if only to keep some tourist from being gnawed loose from his camera. That dame is strictly no good, and as Mr. Selby once remarked, she has an awful ugly face for a lion.

I n the latter 1950s, a keen interest in leopard replaced Ruark's earlier fascination with Cape buffalo, as the preponderance of leopard stories written during these years suggests. In some ways, the leopard is the most demanding of African game, requiring finesse, providing tense drama and an underlying sense of danger that Ruark found strongly appealing, and he responded with some of the best narrative writing ever done on big game.

"Camp Leopard" was written after a safari Ruark made in December 1955 and was published in *Field & Stream* in July 1958. Its flaws, which mainly lie in Ruark's regrettable weakness for stiff, stilted, hyperbolic dialogue, are few, and in narrative structure, it's among his best magazine stories.

Michael McIntosh

CHAPTER FIFTEEN

CAMP LEOPARD

T his has all the advance indications of being an unusual story. It is solemnly promised that it will *not* hang together, because it is a story of purloined pigs, treason, friendship, leopards, aircraft, faith, money, rainbows and the mumps. With virtue – mine – eventually triumphant.

Let us begin with people and pigs. And treason. As some readers are likely to know, a professional hunter named Harry Selby is my best African friend, and his son Mark is also named Robert, being my godson. I am very fond of Mark, because he repaid his father's treachery in kind by giving Harry the mumps, but that comes later. One of my next-best friends is a hunter named John Sutton, who is also more or less in the family.

It was in the high Masai some years ago that John Sutton and I fell in love – with a pig. A warthog. This was the most beautiful warthog that ever lived. His warts were as big as Irish potatoes. His mane was a rich, ugly red. His tusks stuck out of his horribly beautiful face like evenly warped baseball bats. Elephants have been shot with smaller ivory, or so it seemed every time we saw this pig. The tusks were so heavy up front that the owner was barely able to keep his hind feet on the ground.

Selby was off coursing Mau Mau or getting engaged or something equally dangerous when Sutton and I spotted this pig. We hunted him day after day, almost getting him but not quite. We would take a long-range shot and miss, or he would fade into the gray bush. It was as close to Cap'n Ahab and Moby Dick as you'd be likely to come in modern times.

The safari wound up and it was time to head home. Being trusting souls, Mr. Sutton and I, over a sarsaparilla, confided our emotion about this pig to Mr. Selby, who, false friend that he is, seemed unduly sympathetic. Mr. Selby placed me on the aircraft for Entebbe with tender solicitude, even standing several rounds of near-beer before he waved me off into the wild blue.

And before we were clearly airborne, he whipped into his Land Rover, collected a gunbearer and a tin of corned beef, raced off to the Masai and shot *our* pig! Not just *any* pig. *The* pig of Bwana Sutton's and Bwana Ruark's.

That was several years ago. I went back to hunt again recently, and the talking drums spoke steadily. *Don't trust Selby*, the drums said. *Any man who will shoot another man's pig is no true friend—especially when the pig's tusks measure eighteen inches outside his face. A pig stealer,* the drums said, *will suck eggs as well, and probably beat his wife.*

Mr. Sutton and I confronted Mr. Selby with this information. "Did you shoot our pig?" we asked.

"Yes," said Mr. Selby.

"Where are the tusks?"

"I ain't saying," replied Mr. Selby.

"Do you beat your wife?" Mr. Sutton asked.

"Would you suck eggs?"

"Why not?" replied Mr. Selby. "I shoot other people's pigs, don't I?"

That ended the conference. It is difficult to confer with a man of no moral standards whatsoever.

Time cures most things, even base treachery, and it so happened that I forgave Mr. Selby to the point of shooting greater kudu and sable with him in December of 1955. Apart from the fact that warthogs never entered the *chakula* conversation, things were as before. We shot a pretty good sable in Tabora, Tanganyika, and were up at Singida looking for the kudu when Mr. Selby got carried away one night over an eggnog and confessed that he, too, was in love.

"There is this leopard," he said, "a *chui a campi*. A camp leopard who thinks he owns us. I have his picture in my notecase. Look."

Sorting through the several thousand pounds sterling he has made off me during the last few years, he produced a color photo of a leopard so fat from free feeding that he looked like a jaguar.

"I got this photo at night," Harry said. "I tied a trip string to the bait and hooked it up with a camera that had a flash apparatus. Beggar came as usual after dark and tied into the wart – no I believe it was a Grant's gazelle – and we got this glorious picture."

Harry's eyes misted. "Two years," he said. "Two whole blessed years I've tried for him a dozen times. So has Andy Holmberg, Frank Bowman, Eric Rundgren, Reggie Destro – everybody. The damn cat lives in the camp at Ikoma. He walks into the lavatory tent. He steals from the kitchen. He does everything but pinch the Land Rover for a joyride. But he will *not* feed in his pet tree until after black nightfall. I sometimes get the feeling that this is not a leopard at all, but something supernatural sent to haunt me for my sins."

"Are we going to Ikoma? After all, it's where we had the first safari years ago. I'd like to see it again."

Selby looked at me keenly. "No," he said. "I don't think so. Ikoma's for first-timers. You're a specialist now."

"Hmm," said I, and the conversation dropped.

The next day hunter Selby's appearance had unsubtly changed. His face was as big as a basketball. His eyes were slits. He had aches and pains and fever. Away back in the Tanganyika bush, John Henry Selby, the great white hunter of song and story, had the mumps.

The mumps had been bestowed on the great white hunter by Master Mark Robert Selby, aged then about three. The mumps had barely disarranged young Selby's constant habit of saying "No!" to everything or his dislike for going to bed before midnight. But son's mumps lit on the father like a vulture on a carcass. A slight reattack of malaria, hand in hand with pneumonia, came to infest the mumpy hunter, and I got scared stiff.

We telegraphed for a plane, in the best Hemingway tradition, and it arrived in Singida just before the hunter embraced the final process of dying. The plane bore a Mr. Frank Bowman to replace the mump-ridden Selby, who sped off to doctors and a hospital in Nairobi. Frank and I shot a pretty nice greater kudu, and he asked me what we were going to do next, and where we'd do it.

"Ikoma," I said. "I do believe there's a sort of special leopard there."

"Oho," said Mr. Bowman. "So you know about that pet of Harry's?"

"And yours. And Andy's. And Eric's. And Reggie's."

"Be very dicey trying to get to Ikoma now," said Bowman, hooding his eyes. "We get stuck in that Serengeti if the rains – I know where there's some awful fine guinea-fowl shooting. It's down – "

"I know too," I said. "And it's on the way to Ngorongoro, and Ngorongoro is over the top leading to the Serengeti, and at the other end of the Serengeti is Ikoma, and the camp is just under the old German fort, and don't give me no con, bud. I was hunting that area when you were back in Australia shooting crocodiles, and your pet gunbearer, Kidogo, was my special boy. Shall we proceed?"

It was a *shauri a Mungu* – God's will – that we got there in time to beat the bad unseasonable rains by a literal inch. They followed us in frightening big black clouds, and once they caught us, and then we lucked out and got ahead again, and finally managed to cross the Grummetti River just before the skies cried. It was close. I shot the only piece of meat we were to shoot for a week – a topi – through a downpour so heavy that I couldn't see more than a blur of the critter through the scope. You just bang and hope for the best, and this time I heard a *tunk* as the bullet hit, and at least we ate for the week we sat in a tent, considering whisky as an antidote to the torrents that coursed past in the hurriedly dug runnels that allowed the water to course to the river. There was no question of going anywhere, because we had forgotten to bring a steamship. Or even a canoe. That topi was awful high when we ate the last of him.

Brother Bowman had a wife and a new baby and Christmas was coming on, and the hunting was nothing; so the iron bird arrived again at our hand-hewn airstrip, with its toilet-paper markers and a windsock of smoking green wood. This time the plane disgorged Don Bousfield, a nice kid who had just left the game department to be a professional hunter. I had known Don briefly when I was up north eating *posho* porridge and stewed elephant heart with Eric Rundgren, who was shooting elephant on control to make room for the grateful ex-Mau Mau. Don had been the game ranger for the area around Lamu. I think I was his first client in the professional hunting business.

The rains had stopped. The news was that Selby had had a terrible recurrence of the mumps, but was going to live.

"What do we do here?" Bousfield asked, after the plane had disappeared.

"We shoot a leopard," I said. "A very special leopard. The *chui a campi.* The fattest leopard in show business, because you guys have been free-feeding him for years."

"I know about elephant control," Don said. "I don't know a hell of a lot about leopards."

"That makes us even," I said. "I've shot a couple, but Metheke here has been in on the death of about two hundred, one way or the other, between Philip Percival and Selby. He'll tell us when we're wrong."

Metheke, a Wakamba, grinned his cannibal's grin through the vacant space in his mouth where the teeth had been knocked out ceremonially a lot of years before. *"Hapana,"* said Metheke. *"Hapana, piga chui. Bwana Haraka."* He shrugged eloquently. He was saying that we were very unlikely to shoot this leopard if the Bwana Harry couldn't.

"The Bwana Haraka," I said to Bousfield, "is not invincible. He's got the mumps." I puffed out my cheeks for Metheke. *"Shauri a Mungu."* Metheke laughed. *"Mimi na piga chui,"* I said in my impeccable Swahili. *"Wapi* the bloody *miti?* Where's the tree?"

"Pandi hio," Metheke said. "The other side of the river."

In shooting leopards the tree is the all-important thing. I have never had much trouble with leopards, because Selby thinks like a leopard, and the correct tree is the tree where, if you were a leopard, you would like most to be for a free lunch which somebody – again, a *shauri a Mungu* – would be likely to hang you a free lunch.

This was a fine tree. It was just off the river. It had plenty of bush behind and around it, so that the leopard – which dislikes open spaces vehemently – could come to the tree without exposing his flanks. The first fork of this tree was just a comfortable leaping distance for a leopard, and the bole was angled nicely aslant. The feeding fork, where you would fix the pig or the Grant's as bait, was also on a nice slant, so that the cat could sit on his haunches and feed from the bottom to top of the maggoty, ripened bait.

Blinds are illegal in Tanganyika, but there was a piece of bush about fifty yards away that made an acceptable hideout if you swished a *panga* enough to clear away a little underbrush. More important, it had a natural approach for the *man* – which is to say that you could hide yourself in the bush without ever crossing open country, whether it was in black night to wait until morning, or early in the afternoon to wait until dusk. This damned leopard should have been dead years back, because when I left the area I had five big toms feeding in much less delectable trees. Far as I know, they're still feeding, but they had gotten so brash that they were roosting in the trees all day, save the noon hours, and were coming to feed again as early as 4 P.M.

This particular tree had a hollow at the bottom of the trunk. That hollow became important. The tree was creeper-twined and it had leopard claw-marks all over it. It also had a straight, slim sapling close aboard, where the Bwana Haraka had arranged his night-shooting camera. This tree even smelled of rank cat smell.

The leopard hadn't left. I was sitting in the latrine tent one day when he almost knocked on the door flap. Another time he looked in on Juma, the head boy, and scared Juma into a small conniption. "He's not a leopard," Juma said. "Bwana, this is *djinn*, an *afrit*, a devil."

Bousfield and I assassinated a pig and stuck him exactly, precisely, in the tree. We got up in the middle of night and walked precariously through the bush until we had to crawl to enter the narrow game trail that led to the impromptu shelter. The leopard was already in the tree, chomping away at the bait. We could hear him chew, but we couldn't see him. And we could hear the soft *skush-plump* when he leaped out of the tree as the moon waned and the sky pinkened with early morning light. *Hapana chui.*

We arrived then each day, walking carefully, quietly, at 3 P.M., remaining until well after dark again. The night would fall, and twenty minutes later you would hear the *scrutch* of his claws as he headed for the mizzen of this tree. Then you would hear the clash of fangs on bone and the contented grunts as he fed sumptuously off his maggoty big porker. I swear I heard him burp. But no shooting. *Hapana piga.* I saw him again as he skirted camp by daylight, and I promise you he looked as big as a tiger.

Don and I kept the faithful vigil. Five A.M. until early morn and then back again in the afternoon until well past dark. It appeared this boy had one magnificent appetite, because the pigs and Grants were dwindling down to a precious few. This leopard could eat enough for two leopards, and I wondered how the battler eagle that was his daytime vigilante was getting enough scraps to survive.

One morning, just as dawn came, there was a scrutching sound of claws on bark, and a dark shape, big, very big, blacked out the early light next to the half-eaten pig. The arriving shape and the pig merged, and Don touched me gently on the arm and pointed with his chin. Eating sounds occurred in the delicate morning air. It was still too dark to make out anything except two blending blurs, but there was a big cat in that tree, and from the eating noises it sounded like it was staying there.

The sun was rising, bright red, and the first faint pink light had widened into gold when I saw the cat. It was daytime, or at least early morning now, but the tree was so darkly held in the bosom of bush that the cat was just a shape, lying full length on a branch, digesting its meal. Four or five hundred years passed before I could make out which end was which, but finally we decided that the end that had a tail hanging from it was the end we weren't going to shoot at.

H ere we must do a little cliff-hanging. I own a scarred, battered, magnificent .30-06, Remington by brand, which has a special talent. It has never missed a leopard, whether I was shooting it or whether it was on loan to a friend or a client of Selby's. Its scope, a Lyman Alaskan, seems to see leopards better than other guns. I consulted silently with the gun, which said, "Shoot, little man." and I shot.

We were too close to hear the bullet hit, but the solid *blonk* that cat make when it struck the ground was *not* the sound of a missed leopard, or of a wounded leopard. It was the sound of a dead leopard, except that with a leopard you had better not wager that it's dead until you've skinned it out.

"That's a big cat," said Mr. Bousfield. "I think we collect the prize. Let's give it a little more sunshine before we embark on the horrible business of seeing whether it's dead or just slightly annoyed."

There is a thing about looking for leopards that may be dead or annoyed. You fan out. One man always has a shotgun loaded with buck, and the man with the rifle holds it in front of his neck for the leopard to bite on, as there is no possible purpose in trying to hit a charging, wounded leopard with a rifle bullet. I am the cautious type, and Selby had taught me a trick. I had a thick sweater and I tied it around my neck. In the time it takes a leopard to bite through a thick sweater and a rifle, somebody might just come up and shoot the creature off you.

We went into bush which was so tightly clenched that you had to part the thorns with your hands. Metheke and Chalo were spread out ahead, and Don had the shotgun off to the left. You could see from the freshly bruised limb of the tree where the cat had been hurled backward from the shot.

This is where I brag.

Metheke has eyes like a vulture, but I scooped him on the little patch of yellow, black-polka-dotted fur a good thirty yards from the tree. It was a leopard that was never going to be any deader.

This is where I do not brag.

It was one of the biggest female leopards I ever saw. The bossman was still at large.

Mama Chui explained a lot of things – such as why so much bait was eaten nightly; such as why we always heard the male cat come just after dark and leave before morning's brightness. *Two* leopards were feeding out of that tree, and Papa was doing his eating in the middle of the night. To all of us this was a new thing, because usually a leopard guards his personal kill-tree so jealously that he'd bite a chop off the wife of his bosom before he'd share the cache with her.

This was a lovely cat, a little light on the golden side but beautifully rosetted. I looked at Bousfield. Bousfield looked at me. We both shrugged. "There goes the license," he said. "And the Selby Memorial Leopard is still abroad in the land."

"Let's go shoot some sand grouse," I said. "Or something."

"As a matter of fact, let's go send a telegram," Don said. "I have to go to Musoma anyhow. It's only a hundred miles or so. My wife's pretty close to having a baby, and that *bilharzia* she caught swimming isn't helping her any."

So this is how the plane came again, to collect Mr. Bousfield and to unleash a Mr. John Sutton, accompanied by a Mrs. Virginia Ruark. Mrs. Ruark is used to this nonsense, including airfields striped by toilet paper.

"Howdy, Buster," she said. "What's new?" The last time I'd seen her was in Spain.

"We got some leopard problems," I said.

"Oh, God," she replied. "Couldn't it be elephants or buffalo?"

Prized Possession - Leopard & Gazelle

"Leopards," I said firmly.

"Well," said Mama brightly, "at least I brought some good books."

John Sutton is small, but only in proportion. He is built like a pocket Hercules. He plays a dashing polo, is a good boxer, and was once a very fine football wingback. He can drive 600 miles a day in a Land Rover and still survive, and for him a short stroll after elephant is twenty-five miles out and twenty-five miles back. This I can verify, because once I got carried back from a short stroll of twenty-five miles out.

"You shot a leopard?" asked Little John.

"Yes." I said. "The bitch. There were two of them. That's what had you people foxed."

"The male's still around?"

"Yep. At least I haven't shot him."

"Hmmm," said Little John. "I think maybe we change camps."

"I already switched," I said. "I got tired of the leopard organizing the household. It made a servant problem. We're on the other side of the river now."

"Let's go see it," John said. "And then we talk."

We settled into the new camp and then John said, "Let's go inspect the tree."

We went and saw the tree. "It is a very nice tree," John said. "What's this hole?"

"Bees," I said.

"Hmm," John said. "Bees, eh?"

We went back to camp and had some drinks and dinner. Over the coffee, as the fire blurted its lovely light high into the purple, star-dappled sky, John said, "Bees."

"Bees?" I asked politely.

"Un-huh. Bees"

"What's with bees?" Mama asked, looking as if she didn't care to hear the answer. She has been through what she calls "leoparditis" before. She knows that all leopard hunters, buffalo hunters, elephant hunters and duck hunters are nuts.

Little John was talking to himself. "A bee'll bite a dog," he murmured. "If it'll bite a dog, it'll bite a cat. A leopard's a cat." He looked around, challengingly, as if he expected a fist fight over whether a leopard is a cat.

"Maybe that's why he only comes after dark?" I was venturing, not stating. "After the cold has put the bees to bed?"

"That could be. I don't know." John was still talking to himself. "But here we have a thing. We didn't know he was married, and we shot his wife. Or you did, anyhow. That'll shake him a touch, break up the old routine. We changed the camp, huh? That'll change the routine. So suppose we switch his tree, too, and put him more securely in the bush than he's ever been. Maybe he's tired of bees. We'll disturb his security."

"I think you people are completely crazy," Mama said.

"It figures," I said. "I got a pig in the tree now, and it's not dark yet. Let's go take down the pig and drag it around a touch, and then plant it in another tree. Our pal can follow it from the bee tree. Maybe if he hasn't got bees but plenty of fresh security, he'll start to feed earlier. Now his wife's gone, I mean, if the approaching bush is safe enough. I mean for him to approach."

"It better be the thickest, and maybe only one branch to see him on," John said. "And to take the chance that somebody better kill him real dead if we get a shot."

"We can't take him from too far away," I said. "Not for damn sure in his pet tree. And there ain't but one other tree that a decent leopard would light in. And there's no hidey-hole for the hunters that isn't a hundred and fifty yards away."

"Can you crawl?" Sutton asked.

"Been known to," I said. "Don't like it, but I can."

"All right," John answered. "If necessary, we crawl."

"You forgot something, little friend," I said. "We ain't got no license to shoot a leopard, unless you've got one for Tanganyika. They only give you one to a customer now, you know."

"I guess that finishes the leopard," John said. "Quite apart from a special license, I haven't even bought my general license for Tanganyika yet. It costs seventy-five pounds, plus leopard and such, and I am kind of broke."

"So am I," said I, "but there must be a genial, foolish kind of banker in Musoma who will take a check. What is a lousy hundred pounds if our reputation is at stake? I mean to say, it's only a hundred miles each way, over a bad road, with very few detours from the bridges that've been washed out. We can easy make it back the same day if the nice man'll take a check...."

(This is known as a leopard you bet on beforehand. And you haven't seen that road during the rains. Nor have you seen Metheke's face swollen from bee stings when we changed the pig from one tree to the other.)

Leaving Mama alone to be devoured by the hyenas, we took the jeep and made the murderous drive to Musoma. And whether you believe it or not, we found a banker who had read a book of mine and was so beautifully silly as to cash a check.

"What do you need the money for out here?" he asked. "I mean, you usually can sign a chit for most things you get at the *duccas*."

"We are in love with a leopard," I said, "and being men of honor, we would not like to shoot this leopard off license."

The banker shook his head. "Did you ever shoot a leopard?"

"Three," I said. "One last week."

"What do you want with another one so dreadfully that you're willing to spend a month's salary – my salary, I mean?"

"Well, It has something to do with a pet pig –" I started to explain, and he waved his hand wearily. "Take the money and go," he said. "I'm *troppo* enough in this hole without any additional help."

As we drove back over the awful road Sutton looked at me with real admiration. "You'd make a wonderful confidence man," he said.

"How so?" – blushing a little at the praise.

"You sounded so stupid you just got to be honest," John said, and I unblushed.

"We got a new license to shoot a leopard," I said. "An unshot leopard that you people haven't been able to shoot. A hundred quid is $280, plus the mileage on the Rover, plus the petrol, plus wasted time, plus the average cost of a safari, plus the transport from Europe, plus your salary, plus the plane that flew Harry out, Bowman in, Bousfield in and out, and now you and Mama. Not to mention guns, whisky and other ammunition."

"I must say, old cock," John said, "one must admit you have faith."

On the way back there was a likely looking impala with ugly horns and a family problem involving mass infidelity with his male cousins; so I shot it. Anybody who talks about God's wonderful gentle creatures should have seen the way my impala's male cousins roared – literally – and gored their chum, savaging him over and over until we had to beat them off the body with a stick. This impala was only fit to be a bait by the time his chums finished with him.

We slung him in the new tree, next to the dilapidated pig. The widower might have been mourning his departed bride, but his appetite was holding up fine. Usually it takes a couple of days before a leopard starts to feed on a new bait in a strange tree. He was stuck into this impala six hours after we hung him up.

Day came and there was a rainbow, aimed directly at the new tree. "There's your pot of gold," Sutton said.

"Where?"

"Not in the bloody tree," Sutton said. "Off bashing around in the bush."

"He'll come," I said. "I got a feeling." So we walked back to camp, cursing as we stumbled.

Mama was waiting. "You see the rainbow?" she asked.

"Sure," I said. "Pointing right at the tree."

"*Bees,*" Sutton said. "It has to be the *bees.*"

Mama made a banker sound. "Oh, God," she said. "Leoparditis. I got some martinis mixed."

"Lemon squash for me," John said. "This needs sobriety."

Several days passed. Baits were digested, but we noticed that he was leaving later in the morning and coming back just a little bit earlier in the evening. He trusted that tree, because it was surrounded by the nastiest piece of bush I ever saw. Only one branch of the tree was clearly visible, and that was the feeding branch.

One night, just an hour before dusk arrived, we got fed up and started to leave.

"Wait a minute," John said. "I'll glass it one more time for luck."

He swung his binoculars. I could hear him suck in his breath. He handed me the glasses without a word. A long tail, spotted, with an insolent curve in the end, hung from the topmost rigging. All you could see was tail.

"We got to get closer," John whispered. "We'll never be able to see him enough to shoot from here."

"How?"

"Crawl. That fallen log. You can see him from there."

"It's a good hundred yards over clear ground. There's no cover."

"Clouds," Sutton said. "We'll use clouds."

And that is just what we did. The clouds were shifting, and it only took us an hour to move 100 yards, crawling and freezing until the shadows cast by the shifting clouds gave us cover. After what seemed a lifetime, we achieved a fallen log that had accumulated bush. It was good cover, and only thirty-five or forty yards from the tree. I collected my breath and very slowly raised my head. We had no way of knowing whether our boy was still there or not, but there he was. He had dropped down to the horizontal branch next the bait. He was sitting on his haunches like a big dog, and he was proceeding to eat as methodically as a house pet.

The only trick about shooting leopards is to get them in the tree. We had this kid in the tree. The gun aimed itself and went off. You could hear the crash as the cat flung himself through the branches and the *blonk!* as he hit the deck.

Kuisha chui. Finish.

We waited until Mama, who had heard the shot, came racing up from camp in the jeep. She came with Metheke, who had been off seeing to another leopard tree I was baiting for a friend. Much drama had occurred. Metheke, not the world's best driver, had played about a little too close with two male lions – this was mating time – and one of them had jumped *through* the back seat of the jeep, and had taken a chunk out of the ceiling. His teeth marks and some hair remained. But for the fact that the other gunbearer was in the front seat with Metheke, we would have lost us a man.

"Piga chui?" Metheke asked.

"Kufa," I said. "Dead."

"I don't believe it," Metheke said.

"Come on," I said. "Mama, you button yourself up in the jeep."

"No fear of me doing anything else," Mama said. "Try to come out of that bush alive."

"I'll do that," I said.

Here is where I brag some more.

I scooped Metheke again. I found the leopard first for the second time – heart-shot, shoulder-broken, neck-broken as the bullet angled upward. Poor old Metheke was so downcast when I hollered that the leopard was over there, *kufa*, that I eventually had to give him a very fine British waterproof coat to soothe his hurt feelings. This cat also cost me a set of gold teeth for the headman, Juma, who lost his religious reserve – he is a Moslem priest of sorts, and about half Arab – and reverted suddenly to savagery when he saw the cat.

It took four men to haul that leopard out of the bush. It was black night when we got back to camp, but I stood around the fire as the skinners undressed him. He was so fat from over-feeding that the boys scraped off, collected and sold more fat than you'd get off a prime lion, or nearly as much as from a fat zebra stallion! The gunbearers and skinners split a small fortune when they sold the fat to the nearest Indian *ducca* as a specific against gonorrheal rheumatism.

I have shot a 115-pound (each side) elephant, and I have shot some tigers and most of the big trophy stuff, lions, buff, kudu, sable, rhino – the lot. But never have I seen such a celebration in camp as when we dragged that leopard in. Every man knew him. Every man had seen him and heard him sawing insolently within a long block of the camp. The camp went mad.

Sutton and I discussed our heroism for several days, until Mama threatened to intern herself in the nearest Mau Mau camp. Mama reckoned that leoparditis was bad enough in advance, but retroactively, it was completely horrible.

Tracing our way back to Nairobi, we stopped off in Musoma and sent a cable to the convalescent Mr. Selby. The cable said: "Tanganyika now safe for photographers and bird watchers and this will teach you to keep your dirty hands off other people's pigs."

It is a matter of medical record that when Harry Selby received the cable he had another relapse.

R uark's interest in African wildlife naturally included some of the more exotic non-game animals as well as the traditional species. Because he was wont to rely upon his own experience and that of people who, in his opinion, "ought to know," his natural history isn't always wholly accurate; hyenas, for example, are not truly hermaphroditic, and female crocodiles do provide some care to their hatchlings.

Such minor failings aside, however, Ruark had a deft, imaginative touch with natural-history writing, and judging from the quality of "The Vulgar Assassin," published in *Field & Stream*, March 1961, it's a pity he didn't do more of it.

Michael McIntosh

CHAPTER SIXTEEN

THE VULGAR ASSASSIN

On the premise that even a wart hog thinks another wart hog is pretty, if the moon is right and the sex divergent, and that the hyena in full voice adds glamour to the night scene of Africa, even the most unattractive animal seems to have something to recommend it. And actually the wart hog is almost beautiful in its extreme ugliness, while the hyena excites a certain pity with his dog's head, bear's body, and crippled hind end.

But up to now I have failed to find anyone with a kind word for the crocodile, including the Romans who named him *Crocodilis vulgaris*. Even the people who kill him for his hide hate him and the work that translates him into a lady's handbag or a pair of sporty pumps. Certainly there is no imagination sufficiently elastic to conceive of the croc as worthy of sporting attention, unless one fishes for him in a manner I'll describe later. He is indeed so utterly awful as an adult that he has no close confidants, possibly because of a halitosis so overpowering that even his best enemy wouldn't come close enough to tell him. This halitosis I can vouch for, since I once propped a croc's mouth open for a picture and nearly fainted from the rush of stinking breath from his cargo of putrid meat.

A fact like that is obvious, but in reality nobody really knows the definitive truth about the crocodile. A lot of arrant nonsense has been written about him, a flock of exaggerations have been set down as gospel about his size and habits, gustatory and otherwise, and he has become legendary to most of the native tribes who live in constant fear of him.

You can call a croc stealthy, cruel, frightening, wicked, awful, powerful, canny, deceitful, omnivorous, intelligent, powerful, amphibious, slimy, determined, reasonable, unreasoning, menacing, hungry, cowardly, brave, cannibalistic, dentally miraculous (as soon as he loses one tooth another replaces it), quiet, noisy, and enigmatic. And you may always refer to "crocodile tears" when spurious sympathy is demonstrated by the banker just before he forecloses the mortgage.

Beyond this it is difficult to generalize, except that there is no such thing as a sympathetic croc, a charitable croc, a lovable croc, a pretty croc, a kind croc, or a cute croc. The crocodile is an individual, a callous criminal, and surprisingly little is accurately known about his breeding, length of life, and family habits. It is still not generally believed by scientists that he can, and does, hibernate underwater – in one instance may have lived in hibernation for as much as eighteen months.

I have heard story after story about crocodiles nipping off an arm or a leg, as a shark might shear off a member. This is not so. If a man lost an arm or a leg to a crocodile, it would be because he was tied or chained to a stone or a tree the croc couldn't haul into the water, together with the man; then the limb would be pulled out of the body. No man is powerful enough to cling to a tree or a rock and thereby lose a leg when the croc sets his teeth and yanks.

The truth is that old *mamba* can neither chew nor properly bite. He has a rudimentary tongue that is fastened securely to his lower jaw, so what he ingests must be swallowed whole. His lower jaw is immovable, and the upper lifts like a manhole cover with spikes in it. He can maul but he can't munch. This is why he stores his food in muddy underwater caverns until it is rotten enough to be torn into edible bits. And this is why the flesh he consumes is generally so foul (unless it's a small fish or animal or child) that his breath is worse than any hyena's.

The vast rows of teeth are awe-inspiring; if they worked together as cutting agents, a grown crocodile could snap a cow in two. But they perform only as the jaws of a steel trap, to clamp and hold. The teeth fasten onto the prey and lock; the croc has a lower fang that grows straight up at the end of his lower jaw and fits into a hole in his snout tip, effectively locking the jaws. (Note to Editor: I have hand-operated this business, using a just-shot croc, and if bonuses ever are given for research, I qualify.)

Potential Danger

The *mamba* kills by vising onto his prey and dragging it into the water where he sinks to the bottom and drowns his victim. The variety of victims is almost limitless. It certainly could include a young elephant – although I have no eyewitness accounts to offer – since the trunk of a drinking elephant would make a tempting target. But there are several documented cases of crocodiles drowning full-grown African buffalo, and on the Tana River, in Northern Kenya, a crocodile dragged a mature rhino into the drink. Certainly a fearful toll is exacted among young hippo, and any ordinary animal that comes to the water's edge is a fair prospect.

As an offensive weapon, the heavy, sharp-horned tail – as big at its base as the body – is a vicious flail, comparable in use to the elephant's thick trunk as a fighting tool. A flirt of this spined extension is enough to break the legs of any ordinary animal on land. Waterborne, the croc uses it with tremendous efficiency against native canoes. He will charge a dugout, swim by close alongside, swerve, and knock the boat galley-west with a swish of that tail, which approximates a limber, pointed, jagged, iron train rail used as a quirt.

I'm not acquainted with the mechanism that submerges the crocodile. This I know from firsthand: A croc shot dead in the water will sink and remain on the bottom for several days, rising finally to wash ashore. A mortally wounded croc will not choose to die in the water. After several hours he will swim in, haul himself ashore on the shingle, and expire there. Of the scores of crocs shot on Lake Rudolf in recent years, the mortally wounded have a way of turning up next morning to die on their favorite lee shore.

My friend Harry Selby, the professional hunter who runs a fishing camp at Rudolf, and I were croc shooting one day a year or so ago at a favorite sunning site of the saurians on Molo Island, down the beach a piece from a small fishing village of the decimated Molo tribe. A small mountain tops the beach, and we stalked over the lava cobbles to the summit. There was one big croc lying below on the shale in a line of his snoozing relatives, which looked like dirty driftwood. Selby made a long shot with a .243, a remarkably flat little rifle, and dotted the big chap beneath the eye bumps.

"I think that got him," Selby said, "but I'll give him the other half."

The croc moved just as Selby fired again, the distance being downhill and about 300 yards on the flat. The bullet struck too far aft, and the croc made the water and disappeared. Harry shrugged. "We'll find him on the beach tomorrow," he said. "That's a dying croc. Maybe he doesn't know it yet, but he'll come ashore to die."

We sat and smoked a cigarette, and away off in the distance a pair of knobs showed out of the water. It was a good 600 yards.

"Maybe that's our boy," Selby said. "I'll have another bash at him."

He took very careful aim, bracing the rifle with his elbows on his knees, aiming just under the knobs. I saw the bullet smack in the right place, making a little splash. The croc turned over, sun flashed on his belly as he thrashed, and then he quit flailing the water and slid into the deep.

"That is a stone-dead croc," Selby said. "He'll sink straight to the bottom and wash up in four or five days. But the other – if it was another. We'll just fish a while and watch. That other chap'll head for the beach."

We fished for a couple of hours, then ran the boat down to the end of the island. There was a big croc on the beach. Selby glassed him.

"That's our boy," he said. "The first one. You want to go ashore and finish him off?"

I said sure and jumped down into the dinghy with one of the native sailors. We rowed as close as we could get to shore, and I held the scope on the croc. Blood was trickling from a head wound, all right, and there was another hole a little behind the shoulder. Harry had told me to shoot him "behind the smile," the point where his mouth ends in a cynical grin, so as to nail him in the spine and anchor him. (The other shot is for the brain, about two inches below the eye knobs.)

The boat was bobbing up and down in the breeze, the boat boy trying to hold it steady with a paddle stuck into the mud. I waited for the down bob and squeezed as the crosshairs rode onto the top of the smile. The croc's legs shot out and I could see him quiver, exactly as a brain-shot elephant quivers.

"That did for him," Harry shouted. "Wade shore and finish him off, then come on back to *The Lady*. We'll bend a line on him and tow him home."

211

Largely by accident I had immobilized the critter with the spine shot, but he was still very much alive. They don't die easy, these chaps. He was already incipiently dead from Selby's first two shots, but the awful gray-yellow snake eyes were open and malevolent. He was breathing. I poked the rifle muzzle close to his head and blew the brain pan off. It took the best part of an hour to lay a line on him and to tow him home, but when we horsed him up onto the beach with the Land Rover his heart was still going. This wasn't surprising. Denis Lyell, who wrote a book called *The Hunting and Spoor of African Game*, once butchered the heart out of one, laid it on the hot metal deck of a launch, and held a watch on it. The severed heart was still palpitating at the end of three-quarters of an hour.

This fellow of mine was a big croc, about twelve feet long, and a male. There is no certain way to tell a big female crocodile from a male except at close hand, which means a dead crocodile. The male's sexual organs retract into his body and are covered by a flap over the vent, so that his underside is completely smooth.

The Molo fishermen cut this one up; they, like some tribes on the Zambezi, greatly esteem the croc as a delicacy. I fiddled with the idea of trying a piece of him fried, figuring he'd be fishy at worst, and not worrying too much about his carrion-eating habits. But a whiff of that fetid, reeking breath when we were taking the pictures put me off crocodile – or any other food – for quite some time.

So we had proved that a mortally wounded croc comes ashore to die. A few days later the Molo reported that the other croc (the second one) had washed in. He was torn up pretty badly, but the head was intact, and Harry's long-shot bullet had taken him just under the eyes and had blown his brains out. So we had also proved that a stone-dead croc will sink until such time as bloat-inflation makes him lighter than water and fetches him to the surface . But why does it take him so long to surface? The one I shot was easily waterborne behind the boat, and was tremendously bloated an hour or so after death.

The tenacity of life shared by most reptiles is of considerable importance in the procurement of crocodiles for the hide market. He must be killed and collected immediately unless he's harpooned.

We slit the belly of the first croc and found him full of fish, with a few stones for digestive aid. The fish diet was not unusual, because Rudolf is practically solid with the giant Nile perch and the tasty tilapia, and few animals inhabit its edges. Baby hippo and fish would seem to comprise the basis of the Rudolf croc's diet, as the fishing Molo never seem to be taken, although, wading naked in the water, they net tilapia in croc-filled shallows. The children are never taken either as they drink and play at the water's edge. And the solitary fishermen spear peach from a raft made of two logs lashed together that floats half submerged.

A crocodile will eat literally anything, and his digestive juices must have the consumptive force of corrosive acid. Certainly the bones and small horns of his prey are dissolved. He kills untold thousand of Africans annually, and since he cannot munch the bones, some special agent must dissolve them. You will find old bracelets and any number of stones in a croc's belly, but seldom bones unless the meal has been a recent one. Since he can't chew the bones into smaller bits, his digestive juices must resemble those of a boa constrictor or python, which also eats its dinner whole.

One thing, one other nail to add to the general loathsomeness of the beast. *He dotes on hyenas!* Jack Bousfield, a professional crocodile hunter from Lake Rukwa in Tanganyika, once took a hyena by accident in a crocodile snare, and the crocs consumed it. Thereafter Bousfield shot hyenas for bait, and says that the crocs fancy it above any other he has ever tried.

It is from Bousfield, who has been in on the killing of some 45,000 crocodiles for the market in the last thirteen years, that I have much of my crocodile information. Bousfield, operating at Lake Rukwa, employs three other shooters and a native staff of about thirty men to work with nooses, nets, and harpoons and as skinners and boatmen.

Jack says that two-thirds of what you hear about crocodiles is myth; for a start, they do not like rotten food if they can find a meal small enough to swallow while it's fresh. Hyenas, he says, are about the right size for a big croc.

The size of crocodiles has been subject to much distortion. The biggest Bousfield ever killed was a bit over eighteen feet, and a big mature croc will run thirteen or fourteen feet. They are deceptively heavy. Average weight may be about 1000 pounds, with a very old, very big croc possibly weighing close to a ton. Body structure is divided into rough thirds – head, torso, and tail – and the croc is enormously heavy in the shoulders. His fantastic strength comes from even weight distribution, powerful shoulders, and tremendous leverage from the long, heavy tail.

Crocodiles mate at night, and lay their eggs in August and September. The egg is about the size of a sea turtle egg; like the sea turtle, the croc parents dig a two-foot hole in the sand, close to water. The eggs are laid in a perfect pyramid of layers, each carefully covered with sand. A clutch can be as small as thirty eggs; 120 is an extremely large setting. Average is somewhere from forty to seventy. One lusty male can service forty or fifty cow crocs. Bousfield says he can generally identify the male by size; he refrains from shooting it, since the cows are prone to hang around the area when the bull is standing at stud.

A female croc in egg is never less than eight feet long, with the exception of the pygmy croc of Uganda. Once pregnant, she eats at night and sleeps all day. As hatching time approaches, the expectant mother goes into a coma and is relatively easy to hunt. The sun does the incubating and the mother rouses herself just before hatching time – December – and usually uncovers the babies. If she isn't there to sweep the sand off her scaly chicks, they scratch out of the shell and claw up to the surface.

They are around seven or eight inches long when born, and they see first light with a full set of teeth. Once they are hatched, the old lady shows no further active interest beyond curiosity, but Papa takes a definitely nonpaternal view of his kiddies. He loves nothing better than a fresh meal of his own progeny. As a matter of fact, the baby croc has a pretty thin time, both before and after birth. The big monitor lizards dote on the eggs, and hyenas, jackals, and marabou storks scratch up the nests. After birth, big catfish, meerkats, and fish eagles haunt the shallow water in which they live. Bousfield reckons that no more than five percent make it from egg to maturity.

The baby croc eats insects during his first year, then changes over to rats, mice, and birds. He has grown rapidly; at a year he's about eighteen inches long. He keeps growing at an average rate of nine inches a year, sometimes as much as eighteen and as little as five, until he reaches seven feet. Then the growth slows down from almost nothing a year to about two inches. Growth varies considerably with the individual croc.

Somewhere in his second year Junior switches his hunger to larger game, such as rabbits, and in his third he graduates to fish and any carrion he can locate. He doesn't start hanging out with the big fellows until he has achieved a length of about four feet.

During the first couple of years the baby crocs are scared stiff of everything, particularly Papa. They stick together in packs, and if the band becomes scattered they call each other like a bunch of noisy kids. Bousfield can imitate the call of a young croc, which is a kind of piggish, grunting squeal, and has had considerable success in attracting adults to his gun. The mothers come, he says, from a sort of idle maternal curiosity, the old boys are looking for a meal, and younger crocs are seeking companionship. Bousfield swears that after a season of calling some of the crocs get to recognize his voice and won't heed his siren song any longer.

Chameleonlike, young crocs change color according to environment. On a sandy beach they tend to yellow. They adapt to the greenish-brown-black of sudd, the floating thick skim of vegetation that is so frequently seen on slow African waters. But they are never marked in black, as are the older fellows.

As to hibernation, Bousfield says crocs will live in sealed holes if a lake dries. He sometimes hunts hibernating crocs by crawling into such holes with gun and light (ugh!) and says that the tunnel runs about eighteen feet with a dome at the end. He once came upon four sleeping adult crocodiles at the end of a tunnel on a lake that had been completely dry for nearly two years, and reckons that the four beasts had been snoozing for a minimum of eighteen months. Crocs hibernate beneath water level, too, which bespeaks some sort of strange conversion of the unconscious breathing apparatus.

There is no possible way of estimating the life expectancy of a wild crocodile, but Bousfield says that he is certain they reach an age of several hundred years. In any case, he adds, neither he nor anyone he knows has ever seen a crocodile that might conceivably have died of senility.

Growth being almost imperceptible after a critter reaches seven feet, it stands to reason that bull crocodile of fourteen or fifteen feet has been around for quite a spell. The largest that Bousfield has ever taped was eighteen feet, three inches, and the biggest cow about thirteen feet.

Professional crocodile hunting on a large scale is a risky business, expensive to organize, and frighteningly dependent on the caprice of fashion. Bousfield reckons that his fleet of boats, motors, skinning-and-packing facilities, plus house and quarters for the natives, needed an original investment of about $25,000. The hides are sold by belly-width, and must be free of "buttons," or calcium deposits in the hide. There are nine different grades of skin, and prime croc today (subject to market whim) is worth about $12, as opposed to its peak of $20 in 1954. The net profit on a prime hide is from $2 to $2.50.

Bousfield shoots crocodiles from a flatboat at night in the dark of the moon, aiming between the eyes, which are picked up by an electric torch. He shoots at close range, and the native boys make a mad dash to slip a noose on the beast while it still thrashes wildly before swimming off and sinking. Noosing traps are also used as well as heavy nets rigged around stockades of poles. Jack's record catch for one netting was fifty-two crocodiles, and it took twenty-two boys to haul in the nets. Netted and noosed crocs are killed by the boys, who use blunt pickaxes to bash out their brains.

Our vulgar friend is amazingly at home on land, and can travel like a streak on his short, bowed lizard's legs. He does *not* crawl or slide on his belly, but runs with daylight showing between him and the ground. Whether he can smell I cannot say for sure, but he has magnificent eyesight and excellent hearing equipment. Certainly the croc feels no compunction about crossing dry land to come to a camp where meat is hanging, which leads me to believe that he can smell. Also, they've been known to drag carcasses of their fellows several hundred yards to get them into the water, no doubt intending to store them in a cave until sufficiently rotten to be mangled into edible portions.

Because they eat each other, crocs fight continually among themselves. Lyell relates that in Uganda a smaller crocodile was chased out of the water by a larger one onto a small pier. It was so frightened that it refused to go back into the water, even when it was attacked by natives who eventually killed it.

The menace of the crocodile is one aspect that has never been overexaggerated. The rapidity with which that innocent log turns into a monster when he is coursing food is amazing to see; a convoy of crocodiles logging knots as they speed through the water leaves a definite speedboat wake, and the nose, as Bousfield has said, does create a beautiful bow wave. A croc is not so nimble on land as in water, but a scared one heading for the deep travels amazingly fast. He does not waddle or slink; he scurries. And his approach from water to a victim on land, or his attack on one in the water, is fantastically swift, silent, and conclusive. Perhaps you may frighten a croc with a splash or commotion, but while you're doing it a cousin will likely take you by the leg.

I can understand the natives' fearful reverence of old *mamba*, god of the river. The unblinking eyes, the silence of his greasy slide through the water, the utter inexorability of his single-minded purpose, the finality of that steel-trap grip of massive jaw, and the ultimate horror of being drowned and taken to that stinking cave in a mudbank to await the monster's hungry pleasure... No, thank you very much. I prefer to play tag with cow elephants accompanied by calves and old gentlemen rhino in the breeding season.

The crocodile, even as the hyena, writes his own epitaph. The hyena's laugh is mirthless and can achieve the shriek of a damned soul. The crocodile smiles, but the smile is sardonic and is only fit for an aiming point, because the croc is smiling at his ultimate unmourned end. For if the aim is good, any killer of the croc who professes either sorrow or sympathy for the deceased could well be accused of shedding crocodile tears.

With few exceptions, Ruark visited East Africa at least once each year from 1951 until the early '60s. During the later years, he came to think of himself as a "semiprofessional" hunter, although he never held any official status and therefore never was authorized to guide clients solely on his own. He had, however, learned enough of the ways of African game to be a reasonably competent guide, and he sometimes accompanied friends on safari as an unofficial assistant to the professional hunter in charge.

In the stories that came from these trips, we can see some of the internal changes that Africa wrought upon Robert Ruark, and in none is the change more clearly described than in "The Baby Sitting Was Fine Last Season," published as his Old Man column in *Field & Stream*, April 1958.

"As I approach senility," he says, "I find that now *I'm* the Old Man, and I get my kicks out of *not* hunting, but of making it possible for other people." We might take exception with Ruark's view of himself, since forty-two is not an age that fully justifies old-man status, but the sentiment is unquestionably genuine.

Michael McIntosh

CHAPTER SEVENTEEN

THE BABY SITTING WAS FINE LAST SEASON

The Old Man kind of eased up on heavy hunting and fishing in his declining days. He would say, "I think I'll send a boy to do a man's work," and run me off to the fields or waters while he snugged himself with a dram in front of the fire. When the boy would return, half frozen or as wet as a drowned rat, the Old Man would smile benignly and say something cynical like, "Old and creaky as I am, I get my fun out of thinking about you freezing to death in the rain, missing those birds right and left, and wondering why I took so much trouble to teach you to hunt."

I have kept a careful check, and I have not found that the beloved old buzzard was ever wrong. As I approach senility I find that now *I'm* the Old Man, and I get my kicks out of *not* hunting, but of making it possible for other people. Not that I sit by the fire, but I still receive more satisfaction in watching other people, new to the business, enjoy themselves – and incidentally make all the mistakes that I once made.

"The best thing about hunting and fishing," the Old Man said, "is that you don't have to actually do it to enjoy it. You can go to bed every night thinking how much fun you had twenty years ago, and it all comes back as clear as moonlight.

"You can listen to somebody bragging about the fish he caught or the deer he shot or the day he fell in the duck pond, and it is a kind of immortality, because you're doing it yourself all over again. In the meantime – and I don't mean to sound like a Pollyanna – you actually *do* feel that it's better to give than to get. Also, a little healthy sermon on game conservation creeps in here, because if you've done it once, and done it twice, and done it three times, then what's wrong with knocking off and leaving some of the raw material for the other feller?"

The old gent's sentiments kept coming back loud and clear last year, when I took some tenderfect to Africa. Apart from taking necessary camp meat and doing a little bird shooting, I never fired a shot. Bob and Jane Low, from Madrid, were the guests, and if you take a poll on Low I think he will sound off strong for the safari business. As for the blonde and beautiful Jane, a lady you'd more expect to see in a slim black dress at the Twenty-One Club, well, you never saw a woman fall more speedily and permanently in love with African bush. Bugs, dust, rain, stuck vehicles and all, the elegant Tia Juana never mouthed a complaint that I heard.

Her husband was a daily delight. Nobody else had ever been to Africa before. He discovered elephants and lions and leopards. He was the first living man to see a green plain dotted with a million antelope and gazelle. Nobody else had ever laid eyes on a buffalo. Such a small thing as the taste of an orange squash became more potent than champagne. He was nearly incoherent for a week after he killed his leopard under rather unusual conditions. The leopard, it appears, went into a piece of bush in broad daylight, and Low and the gunbearers dived in after it. Then the leopard began to track Low (later found its footprints atop Low's big pug marks). They beat the bush three times, and finally the leopard tore out into the open – with the gunbearers just ahead of him.

The boys turned right at flank speed, and the leopard turned left, also flat out. Low executed a snappy shoulder shot, and was back in camp by 11 A.M. with his Land Rover full of lovely spotted cat. I had about five other toms feeding from trees, but this one had been reaped by Bwana Mkubwa Sana Kabisa Low on his own, and he was fit to bust. He broke out in a rash of babble, and I was looking over his shoulder to see how big the slain *chui* was.

Low grabbed me by the collar and shook me violently. "You're not listening to me!" he screeched. "You're not listening to me! And then the boys went back in for the last time and fired some shotguns and the cat came …" And so forth.

At the end of a conversationally leopard week the girls and I came to a solemn conclusion – that we wished the leopard had shot Low. But you must consider that while Low was having this high adventure, which has traveled verbally from Africa to Spain to America to London to Paris, I had more fun listening to it than if I'd committed it, having just shot a difficult *chui* myself the month before Bob arrived. I plain didn't *need* any more leopard for myself. It still pleased me to know that if Bob hadn't shot his cat on his own I knew enough about baits and the right trees to drape 'em in to have had four or five big ones coming earlier and earlier every day, so drunk with power over that reeking big pig were they.

I found that cutting down a stinking, maggoty, half-eaten wart hog can be fun. I knew that nobody else would poach on my tree, and that the leopard would be saved for another year.

Possibly I inherited a malicious sense of humor from the Old Man, but I never laughed so hard in my life as I did on Bob Low's hunting debut in Africa. I had sent the truck and jeeps on ahead, and we flew in to a makeshift airstrip whose boundaries were marked by strips of toilet paper, held down by rocks, and the wind direction indicated for the pilot by a green-wood smudge-fire. Bob and Jane literally flew from starkest civilization into darkest Tanganyika bush country.

The camp was made and ready on a beautiful new site I'd found a month before, and all the boys said, *"Jambo, bwana, jambo, memsaab."* Low had on his new bush clothes from Ahamed Brothers and my floppy Texas Stetson with the leopard-tail hatband, and he looked exactly like a white hunter as played by Stewart Granger with a mustache. The tables were set up in the mess tent with an array of bright bottles, and the refrigerators were humming happily, and the bantam chickens we used as alarm clocks – Rubi and Rosa – had already settled in and Rosa had deposited another egg behind the refrigerator. The Grummetti River chuckled happily, and trees were green, and the fresh-mowed grass was a velvet carpet in front of the tents.

Low was fairly panting to try out his – or rather, my – weapons; so we exposed him to a topi and a Tommie, and after the usual trial and error he was blooded. He came back to cool drinks and dinner, convinced that somebody had made a mistake – that we had blundered into the Waldorf, which had suddenly been moved to the Bronx Zoo.

The first serious hunting day was miraculous. We picked up fourteen lone buffalo bulls, all shootable. They galloped into a small piece of bush. Low went in after them like a little man, and he could not know that in that patch of bush were a couple of lions, a herd of buffalo and a cobra. He also could not know that the bullets for my .450-400 double had gotten confused with the bullets from Don Bousfield's .450-400, and that our guns were chambered differently. Low was forced to wait until one of the boys hared back to my vehicle for fresh asparagus, so to speak, leaving Low more or less naked in the presence of many large, hoofed, horned, fanged, toothy things – now wondering to himself if Africa was always this way.

Eventually organization triumphed and Low shot a buffalo on literally his first day in the timber. But I shall never forget, as an innocent bystander, the picture of Low, all the buffalo, all the lions, and the cobra, suddenly spouting from the clump of bush.

I must say, in behalf of Low, he quailed not and neither did he flee. He was a touch ashen at the end, but that sweet .450-400 spake happily, and Low managed to collect a better buff on his first day than it took me two safaris and six months and about 1000 miles of unpleasant walking and crawling to find. He was no good at all for anything the rest of the day, when the enormity of his achievement dawned.

I do not know many of the details, except secondhand, of the good Bwana's achievements in the veld, as I was chief baby sitter for two girls, and it seems all I did was pour gin-and-tonics, explain whistling thorns and why they whistle, and whomp up birthday parties. Mrs. Low passed another milestone – I believe 21 is the accepted age for all ladies – and I laid on a flock of ex-cannibals to do her honor.

It was quite a birthday party. First I had to explain the basic ingredients of "Happy Birthday to You" in Swahili to Matisia, the Low's personal boy, who is a Wakamba. Matisia then retired to the bush to retranslate the ditty into Kamba and emerged, beaming, with a series of grunts which ended: "Dear Janey to you."

Meantime, while the birthday toasts – martinis, very dry – were being hoisted I managed to smuggle seventy-five Wa-Ikoma warriors into a patch of bush nearby without the knowledge of Memsaab Low. This is a very difficult feat, for the gentlemen had been painting themselves for three days past, wore lion-mane headdresses, had iron rattles bound to their legs, carried knives and spears, and were all slightly drunk and in a most festive mood.

Double Rifle

They erupted as a Masai war party descending on the Kikuyu, and for the first and only time in my life I saw the cool Madame Low shaken out of her calm. Seventy-five war-painted Ikoma lads in full fighting regalia is not a sight to sneer at, especially when it erupts into your lap. I suppose a birthday party in Tanganyika is as much a part of hunting as a fish fry or a picnic, as the lion Low did *not* shoot is a part of hunting.

We had special permission on some lions for Bob, but after he made friends with a few of my leonine friends he flatly refused to shoot one. This suddenly raised him in the community concept from tenderfoot to a member of the old gentlemen's club.

We had been more or less shaking hands daily with a couple dozen of the gracious, lazy, blasé beasts, including two youngsters that were the most beautiful things I have every seen on four feet – one so dark he was almost blue, and the other blond as Marilyn Monroe.

"My God," Low said, "how can anybody shoot one of these lovely things? Be like shooting your best friend. No, thank you very much, no lions for me."

To see a man go from gun-happy to conservationist in a week is quite a thrill. The average first-timer says something like: "How *many* of *what* can I shoot today?" and the professionals look at the gunbearer and shrug slightly. I couldn't have been prouder as the father of twins than I was when Low turned down the easy lions. The atmosphere of the camp changed so that you could almost taste it.

It changed some more when John Sutton, a professional, took Low on what John called a "reccy-run" to see what had happened to the elephant concentration that had been disrupted and widely scattered by unseasonable rains. Fifty miles over no track is a long journey in a Land Rover. Sutton, a serious hunter, took Low on a jaunt of over *six hundred* miles with no camp and no sleep. If Sutton was a basket case when he veered the jeep into camp, Low was an uncomplaining corpse. I felt fine. I had been bird shooting with the ladies, and Rosa had laid another egg.

But Low returned from the dead and got onto his shaky feet and took off next day with the other hunter, Don Bousfield. Living under a poncho on short rations, he didn't come back until he had a beautiful pair of tusks. This was the diploma. We packed up and went to Mombasa and then to Malindi and simply went fishing.

Low's safari gave me more satisfaction than any of my own. He shot out the license in both Kenya and Tanganyika inside four weeks, and did not acquire an inferior trophy. He never shot once to hear the gun go off. As with ships, safaris can be difficult tests of friendship, and in the month we six white adults – me, Mama, Jane, Bob, Don and John – were together, there wasn't a cross word. And I have known fast friends of years to cease speaking after three days in the bush.

My most serious hunting throughout all this was a private vendetta with Rubi, the bantam cock. Rubi and I hated each other on sight. He would leap onto my camp chair, crow and deposit droppings. Then he would crow sneeringly and swagger off to peck Rosa on the head. I armed myself with a syphon bottle and stalked him relentlessly. I may not have collected anything for the wall, but there is one bantam rooster that knows when he's met a better man. I got him one day in full flight, using a duck-length lead with the soda bottle, and shot him down in extremely moist flames. All he needed was a slap of Scotch to be a walking Scotch-and-soda.

I intend, in the best tradition of the Old Man, to test my luck further in the next twelve months. January will find me baby sitting again, and this time it will be with four children. The eldest child is my friend Ricardo Sicré of Madrid, the father of Ricardo Junior, aged twelve and Emilio Sicré, aged approximately ten. The elder statesman of the group will be one Timothy Matson of Greenwich, Connecticut, aged thirteen, but wise beyond his years, because of being the spawn of my agent, Harold Matson. In true agent fashion, I have ten percent of Timmy.

How this adventure will finish, I have no idea. But as I have a personal knowledge of the Sicré kids and young Master Matson as a team, I say let everybody beware. The entire group spent one summer with me in Spain, and everybody remarked that I had gone suddenly gray, and for cause. It is entirely possible that my next safari – not the guided missile – will conquer the world.

R uark describes "Karamojo Safari," published in *Field & Stream* in August 1961, as a "sentimental journey." This was the second official safari in nearly fifty years to hunt the Karamojong area of Uganda – the same country that conferred Walter Dalrymple Maitland Bell's nickname. Bell hunted there from 1902 to 1907. By the time he died in 1951, Bell owned an enormous, though unfortunately somewhat misleading, reputation for shooting elephant with small-bore rifles, and Ruark had bought the last of these, a Rigby .275.

Hunting the Karamojong with Bell's rifle is a concept almost guaranteed to produce a first-class story. So it does – but not the story one might expect. The theme here is the Karamojong revisited, not Karamojo Bell recreated. What makes the difference is the maturity of Ruark's vision. By then, hunting had taken him beyond the exuberance of shooting game and brought him to a quieter place where he could take an equally keen delight in watching someone else discover the thrill he remembered so well.

"Karamojo Safari" is therefore about change, but it's the sort of change described in the fine old French aphorism that says the more things change, the more they remain the same. Ruark found the Karamojong much as it must have been in Bell's time, and in Buz Robinson he found a hunter much as Ruark himself had been in earlier years.

Michael McIntosh

CHAPTER EIGHTEEN

KARAMOJO SAFARI

This was the wild, savage part of Africa made famous by Karamojo Bell. Now I was on a sentimental journey – retracing his footsteps, carrying his rifle.

The kongoni looked up curiously as the power wagon growled and jounced through the grass. It took the animals some time to make up their minds about the iron monster. Then they jolted off stiff-leggedly, bouncing on hidden springs, their hides shining yellow in the sun. They stopped, turned again, and looked with great stupid eyes under the cocked ears that seemed like a second set of horns on their silly long faces.

Selby killed the engine. *"Nyama,"* he said. "Bust the oldest, ugliest one with the worst horns – if such a thing as worst horns on a kongoni is possible."

I have noticed that, after a dozen years of hunting with Harry Selby, he no longer gives me the client conversation. "Meat," says he. "Bust it." Not "Please, bwana, kill this lovely trophy kongoni." Actually, there is no such thing as a trophy kongoni, any more than there is a trophy wildebeest. Some are just bigger and uglier and dumber than others. I got out and automatically reached up to the back seat for a rifle. My gunbearer, Metheke, smacked me in the hand with a battered Remington .30-06.

"Hapana," said I in my faultless Swahili. "Gimme the Bell *bundouki."*

"Hi lisase solid-i tu," the gunbearer said reproachfully.

"I know it," I said. "Karamojo never used anything but solids. This is a sentimental journey. Kongoni or not, gimme the .275. I'm pretending he's an elephant."

Metheke put the Remington back and handed me a Rigby .275. I made a halfhearted stalk over to an anthill, looked between the rabbit-ear rear sight at the shoulder of the closest bull kongoni, and squeezed. He collapsed, kicked a couple of times, and lay still.

"The old gun's still got talent," Selby said as we collected the dead kongoni, which we needed in our business. We needed quite a few kongoni in our business, since we had to feed over thirty black safari hands and nine white faces, two of which were firmly fixed for lion and leopard. Lions and leopard call for baits these days in Africa.

"It should have talent," I said. "It only belonged to the best there was." Then I spoke to the rifle. "Well, gun," I said, "at least I brought you home again. We'll just have to pretend that kongoni was a bull elephant with hundred-pound teeth."

"Karamojo Bell's last gun," Harry said softly. "And here is where he shot all that stuff in the days when it was all wild, and all free for a man to go and come when he wanted."

"Let's go string this poor, bloody kongoni up a tree," I said.

Karamojo Bell – W. D. M. Bell – was the first white man to take a light-calibered, high-powered rifle to East Africa for the express purpose of killing elephants, and he was the first white man to really explore the dangerous Karamojo country of northwestern Uganda, where he found unbelievable numbers of big-toothed elephants and big, ugly, naked, murderous natives who killed each other and the neighboring Suk and Turkana for fun. That was some sixty years ago.

Bell is dead now, and with him his record of more than 2000 heavy-tusked elephants, mostly bulls, killed for salable ivory. He was a fantastic hunter, a fantastic athlete, a fantastic shot who commonly used a .275 caliber rifle as a heavy weapon and who claimed he could follow a bullet in flight with his naked eye. He also knew anatomy – animal and, it is suspected, human. One did not go into the Karamojo in those days without shooting his way through surly suspicion and opposition. Bell was a great one for placing his shots correctly.

I retraced some of the old hunter's steps in the Karamojo not very long ago and can assure his memory that the elephants are still there and that the natives are just as ugly, just as naked, just as surly, and just as ferocious. Fortunately I did not have to shoot either elephants or natives, but we did come upon one of the finest prides of lions I

Africa's Finest

have ever seen; one, at least, is as fine as any lion ever shot. I can brag on this lion because it wasn't I that shot it. I merely helped find it.

The country was just opening to licensed hunting when we went in, the second proper safari on modern wheels to see the area. The first had been in a month or so before and had taken a fine lion but had not disturbed the country. The previous safari of record, apart from some lonely hunters and some elephant-control people, had been in 1911.

What made our expedition particularly sentimental was that I had the Bell rifle with me – a little Rigby .275 in perfect condition that I had bought secondhand in London. It had a slot carved into its stock – presumably to fit the haft of a long-dead gunbearer's spear for easier carrying – and its barrel had never been polluted by a soft-nosed bullet, as its former owner had so often proclaimed. On its trigger-guard steel were the initials "W.D.M.B." It was Karamojo Bell's last elephant killer, and it still shoots straight, if not so consistently straight for me as for him.

All I knew about the Karamojo was that it lies west of northern Kenya and Lake Rudolph, southeast of Ethiopia, and so close to the southern Sudan that you can bounce a rock off the border from atop a tall hill. It is volcano country, dangerously potholed with concealed caverns, and is dry and dusty and overgrazed. You come down sharply from the Great Rift escarpment and drop from eight or nine thousand feet to about 4000, onto a dusty, dreary plain.

It is haunted country. The lonely peaks and carelessly strewn boulders look much as if God had tossed the rubble of Creation into Karamojo. Even the rolling seas of yellow grass look sinister.

The road from Kitale in northwestern Kenya was pleasant enough until we got to Moroto, and not so terribly bad from Moroto to Kaabong. But from Kaabong we were on our own. The Uganda Game Department was pleasant enough too, but not of much help; I suspect that its people did not, at the time, know very much about the area. The natives weren't much help either, since very few of them speak the usual Swahili. They know very little about hunting and don't care to impart much information about the location of waterholes.

Numerically we were almost as big a safari as Karamojo Bell ever mounted, and he traveled in the old foot-safari days with an entourage of about fifty boys, including porters. We traveled on two big lorries, one Dodge power wagon, and a couple of husky Land Rovers, whereas Bell had shanked it. On the white side we were William (Buz) Robinson and Harry Cabot, first-time hunters; Darlene Robinson, Collie Cabot, and Virginia Ruark, our spouses; Harry Selby, John Sutton, and Jack Bousfield, professional hunters, and me – a sort of disreputable whipping boy. We had six gunbearers and about twenty-five assorted cooks, boss boys, assistant boss boys, porters, and kitchen *mtotos*. Old Bell would have turned over in his tomb at the sight of two mess tents, two iceboxes, two showers, two toilet tents, and a stanch regiment of assorted portables.

The luxuries ended there. Once outside the camp it was a straight Bell safari. It turned out that the Uganda game warden didn't know any more about our area than we did, so it took us, among other minor difficulties in scouting, four days to locate the waterholes. The warden had lent us a scout, but he had never been in this country before and he spoke no Karamojong. We had to have waterholes, because Harry Cabot and Buz Robinson were particularly keen on getting leopard and lion, and there is very little use hunting either unless you find a place with enough water to support the animals on which big cats feed.

It took us just a few days to discover that, besides unlimited kongoni, the Karamojo was rich in lions – lions in the bush, lions in the swamp, lions in camp, lions on the leopard kills, lions in your hair. And this was at a time when they hadn't officially reopened a good bit of Tanganyika to lion hunting, and so much of the Masai was closed in Kenya that the old sure spots for lion were few and very far apart.

At first, this new place didn't look liony either. But after we'd found some spotty water and scouted the country, we started stringing up baits and building blinds and dragging dead kongoni around in places where we found pugmarks in the mud or road dust as evidence of lion.

Our No. 1 blind we called the Amphitheater. It overlooked a kind of sunken bowl the size of a football field, with a big dead log for a bait tree. It had a lot of untidy bush piled around it, and thick bush covered the steep banks. The blind was pitched so high above the kill tree that we felt safe about smoking in it.

We roped a kill to the fallen tree and came back next day to check. There had been a decent leopard on the carcass that night, but a big bull rhino had come and driven him off his supper. The rhino's hoofprints and the leopard's pugmarks were intermingled in the soft turf, and the rhino had kicked up great piles of fresh, strawy dung to show his distaste for cats. There had evidently been quite an argument.

We baited with another kongoni, hoping for the best. Next day, more or less on a whim, white hunter John Sutton took Harry Cabot to a morning session in the Amphitheater as a last-minute switch from a blind that John had constructed himself.

About 7:30 A.M., as we were sitting down to breakfast, there was a great horn-blowing and shooting-off of guns outside camp. Sutton and Cabot (who naturally comes from Boston) arrived with a flourish in front of the dying campfire and dumped a large, black-maned corpse on the ground. This was as big a black-maned lion as ever I'd seen, alive or dead.

"We were sitting and shivering in the Amphitheater in the dark," Cabot sputtered, "and all of the sudden there was a lot of growling and tearing of flesh and cracking of bones. And then the dawn came and John said, 'I say, that black one out there *is* a jolly nice lion. I suggest you shoot it.' So I shot it – and it died. Right there. It died. The other went away."

He looked at Sutton with worship, and Sutton looked modestly away into the middle distance. It was a magnificent lion, full-shoulder-maned, as black as ink – big prime, and unscarred by fang, claw, or thorn. All it had in it was a hole where Cabot had socked it with a .300 magnum. Selby reckoned he was as good as the Old Man of the Douma, a legendary black-maned chap with a head of hair it could step on.

I went out that morning and saw what appeared to be seven lions – two males as large as Cabot's, if not so heavily maned, and another whose head was hidden by high grass; the others I judged to be big females.

We had an abortive day otherwise. Robinson, the Denver delegate, went to sit in another blind, also designed for leopard, with the bait hung high in the mizzen of a slant-boled tree overlooking a well-bushed ravine. There were leopards about, all right, but they seemed to be hunting Robinson. One came close by and sneered at him, passing on a side of the blind where Robinson couldn't see to shoot, then strolled off into the grass. That night some lionesses and young lions came and climbed straight up and hijacked the kill. They ate most of it before the vultures relived them and polished off the rest.

We had strung another bait high on a horizontal limb of a completely vertical acacia standing alone on a plain near some high grass. The defunct kongoni's hoofs hung a good twenty feet off the ground. No leopard had fed on it; so I took the Robinsons around to the Amphitheater again, figuring maybe the leopards had dispossessed the rhino and the lions. We were sitting and quietly reading an edifying British tabloid when Selby rattled up, making no pretense at caution.

"There's the biggest lion you ever saw in your life sitting *under* that high leopard kill!" Selby said. "He's waiting for that bait to get ripe and fall in his lap. We'd best go and terminate his troubles for him."

A lion was there, all right, lying like a big dog beneath the flat-topped umbrella tree, looking hopefully up to the heavens in what appeared to be supplication. Selby piled out of the car and maneuvered the excited Robinson up to and into the blind, only to discover, once inside, that the lion had shifted to the other side of the tree. Although my Westley Richards .318, which Robinson was wearing, is a potential weapon, it does not customarily shoot soft-nosed bullets through tree trunks. There was nothing to do but try a flat-bellied stalk to another point of aim. In the midst of this noble effort the lion yawned and said the hell with it. He switched his tail and sauntered off into the tall grass.

Next morning Selby spilled Robinson out of his cot and took him back to the hopeful tree. The black melted and the dawn pinkened up the sky, and there, happily asleep in spitting distance of the blind, were two lionesses and a very nicely maned youngish male. But it wasn't the big chap of the evening before. The plenitude of lions now constituted a bloody nuisance. It's the choice you must make once in a while: Do we shoot the dead cert and hate ourselves if the Big Casino shows up, or do we gamble, let the cinch slide, and hope for the jackpot, knowing we'll hate ourselves if we waste the easy one and the big one doesn't show?

About fifteen minutes after clear dawn, Selby hit Robinson a lick in the ribs and pointed to where the high grass scabbed out at the edges. *The* lion was standing there, stern to, but the light was not good and all Robinson could see was the back of its neck. With a relatively strange gun, it was a dicey shot. If Robinson didn't belt it precisely in the back of that neck – if he hit it in the pants – it was off and away wounded in that grass.

They waited an hour for the lion to move; then he melted into the twelve-foot grass jungle again. Robinson and Selby left the blind quietly and decided to come back for another whack at it that evening.

Two hunters and a native in one blind are plenty; so I stayed on the hilltop with a detective story when the hunters went back to work about 4:30. After I'd sorted out the murderer I went exploring one of those underground villages the hyenas make, and at 6:55, with the light all but gone, I started the car to go and collect the hunters.

I reckoned that poor old Robinson, whose luck had been more than streaky, would be ready to quit. Then I heard my old .318 make its spitting *karawang*, followed by gobs of meaningful, baleful silence. I grabbed my own gun and tore down the hill, figuring that at this hour, if the lion was wounded and got out the back way, maybe I could slow him down before he got into the grass. Halfway down I heard the .318 go again, and then a heartfelt belch from Selby's cut-down .375. Some more silence, and when I raced into the picture they were standing over what appeared to be a black haystack.

It seems that when they stalked up to the blind there was still *another* big male sleeping in front of it. He let out a growl and whipped into the grass. They waited awhile, and then the correct gentleman of their previous planning emerged from the grass and strolled over to the kill. Robinson belted him between neck and shoulder and he went over, looking very done for. But the 250-grain bullet didn't keep him down, and he produced a frightful succession of roars, then started to get up, which accounted for the other commotion with the guns.

All the bullets went into the mane, but the lion still needed the final quieter with a .243 in the nape of the neck, for he was still kicking when I puffed up on the scene. I looked at him with a measure of awe. This was possibly the fourth eminently shootable male to appear since we'd come on the first one sitting under the kill yesterday afternoon – which seemed a year ago. You can't tell about manes, much, when lions are in grass or lying down or facing away, but there had been at least three males of different sizes and coloration. And the whole collection was in that grass!

We didn't actually know what we had until we got the lion back to camp and straightened him out in the white glare of the pressure lamps. With our first good look at him, you could hear the hiss of the sighs, suddenly expelled, drowning the noise the lamps were making.

He was a completely prime lion, about the same size and in the same state of unscarred perfection as Cabot's big black chap. But this one had a mane that measured thirty-eight inches from where it started to where it stopped halfway down his back! He was bright tawny chestnut on top, grading to coal-black as the hair continued. Great tufts of hair grew from his groin and along his belly to join the bush of mane.

John Sutton said that if we'd given that lion another year he'd have been hairy clean down to and around his hips. Muema, forty-two years a skinner and gunbearer, reckoned he had never seen a simba like this in all his years. Selby said he had never seen one to approach it either, including Cabot's, which he estimated to be one of the five best he'd ever seen dead. And I know that I have never seen anything like it, in or out of a zoo.

It was an expensive lion. We handed an edict to Robinson to the effect that nobody should ever walk on this noble beast; that the lion was a proper *Bwana Mkubwa* that should be mounted whole. Robinson's a Scot, like Karamojo Bell, but he was good-natured about his monster. Robinson had to build a new wing on his home in order to make room for his huge black-maned boarder.

And still the lions came. Once, while Selby and I were shooting birds in a grassy gully, I heard a loud roar from the direction of the power wagon, which has no sides. In the power wagon was my spouse, turned to a pillar of salt, and outside were two lionesses with cubs. One mama seemed about to pull Virginia out of the wagon. We were able to drive the more aggressive old lady away without shooting, which was providential, since my armament consisted of a very nice little 20-gauge shotgun.

Another lioness came into camp and treed Mrs. Robinson and Mrs. Ruark in the mess tent. We used the power wagon to chase this one out of camp. Lions also came and stalked around the retiring rooms and the shower tents. Once, when one of the ladies' stomachs rumbled, everybody jumped a foot.

Harry Cabot and John Sutton finally came in with a nice tom-leopard, just before we left. You guessed it – Cabot shot it on a lion bait. A very large leopard picketed our camp, but we couldn't con him into a tree.

Just before we left I got out the Bell gun again and went for a stroll. There was a big buck rabbit sitting on a hillock, and I drilled it neatly with the gun that had once slain elephants. It was the closest thing to a trophy I collected on this sentimental journey, unless you count kongoni, and after living off a steady diet of kongoni – boiled, broiled, stewed, and hashed – for three weeks I prefer not to count kongoni any more. I rather imagine that the late famous wizard, Karamojo Bell, very often must have felt the same way.

"The Lady And The Leopard" also comes from the Karamojong Safari, and it reads with the sparkle and ring of Ruark at his best. Its only flaw stems from his long-standing difficulty in writing about people, especially women. No doubt he intended his characterization of Darlene Robinson to be affectionate and flattering, but the warmth hardly shows; instead, he comes almost offensively close to making her seem by turns, a caustic virago or a petulant airhead.

This is by no means an uncommon weakness in Ruark's work, but "The Lady And The Leopard" is otherwise a fine story, tightly unified and skillfully shaped. If the lady comes off as clumsily treated, the leopard does not. The piece appeared in *Field & Stream* November 1961.

Michael McIntosh

CHAPTER NINETEEN

THE LADY AND THE LEOPARD

I had often heard the phrase "Never underestimate the power of a woman," but this was the first time I'd seen it demonstrated in the leopard-hunting business. It had all started as a joke – a joke that became deadly serious. If you've read much about leopards, you probably know that this lovely, great spotted cat is one of the most fascinating things in the world to hunt. Not the odd leopard you run onto by accident in the open, but the cat that you start to work on before you've met him, or even know that he exists at all.

The fascination of the leopard, magically seduced into coming to a tree in daylight so that he may legally be shot, lies in the fact that he is a nocturnal animal that does not range widely from cover and rarely kills or feeds by bright day. He haunts the thick bush and caves and rocky *kopjes*. You can hear his dry, sawing cough as he hunts up and down a riverbed, and you can trace his progress by the screeching of birds and the outraged cursing of the monkeys and baboons that hate him as a natural enemy. Your aim is to force the leopard to change his habits, if not his spots – to literally drive him into a daylight command appearance.

There is no such thing as a standardized reaction from the leopard; that's what makes him fascinating. He can be bolder or spookier, braver or more cowardly, smarter or stupider than any animal I have ever hunted – his inconsistency is consistent. There is only one thing you can depend on: He will always react in some way, almost as if he were a chess opponent. If you offer, he will counter-offer. And the battle is always personal. You may never see him, let alone shoot him, but you know he's there, thinking. And he knows you're there, too, if only intuitively.

Until about fifteen years ago leopards were not hunted methodically, which means paying close attention to tree location, placement of bait, blind construction, blind approach, and waiting procedure. They were shot more or less off the cuff – sneaking around a camp intent on pilferage, spotted snoozing (rarely) in the open, or being driven from a small piece of bush. And, of course, being blinded by a torch and shot illegally over a bait at night.

The safari firms might guarantee you a lion, a buffalo, a rhino, an elephant, but they would always insist that the leopard was a dicey bet, and they couldn't promise results. One safari had been trying for eleven years, they would assure you truthfully, and still no leopard. All a matter of *shauri a Mungu* – God's will.

That's not true any longer. I know two dozen hunters who will guarantee you at least a shot at a leopard in a couple of weeks' time, barring absolute freakish bad luck, and I know at least ten who have developed tricks in building blinds and baiting that are almost tantamount to smearing the tree with catnip. But the best of these chaps are sometimes outfoxed, especially when the leopard is mating and not quite normal in the head. In the case we have under examination here, five pros and one semi-pro spent nearly two months to collect a leopard for one man – and his wife.

It might be said that this particular hunt began in Denver, Colorado, where I was visiting with Buz Robinson and his wife, Darlene, a tall blonde lady. Casually, Darlene announced that she and her husband were coming on safari with me and the Henry Cabots of Boston.

"All we want to do," Darlene said breezily, "is to take some pictures and perhaps Buz will shoot some birds. Oh, yes – I have decided that I'm the type of girl who would look very nice on a leopard skin in front of the fireplace. Buz thinks this has great possibilities, so he'll take a little time off from his birds and pictures, and shoot me a leopard."

Perhaps it was Darlene's excellent martinis; anyway I received this news with complete aplomb. Reaching for another martini, I said that if the everloving was willing to invest in a full license, plus the special one for leopard shooting, plus his piece of the safari costs, I was prepared to offer my services and the expert services of John Sutton and Harry Selby, two seasoned pros who have accounted for

In the Shade - Leopard

a rough 170 or 180 leopards between them. Possibly I smirked a little; the previous season Sutton and I had shot a sort of bewitched camp leopard that everybody had been making passes at for a couple of years.

Now, Darlene is a very pretty, soft-spoken girl, but behind this most attractive facade is a solid slab of Scandinavian hard-headedness and a whim of purest chilled steel. We hadn't left the hotel in Kitale for our first leg of activity in Uganda when she started working on the leopard. She greeted the dawn with, "And today Buz will shoot my leopard," and she signed off at night with "Well, tomorrow Buz will shoot my leopard." She was conducting an experiment in very heavy positive thinking.

Old Buz seemed to be snakebit from the first. The Karamojo country of Uganda, which was freshly opened and almost virgin to organized hunting, was leaping with lions and aquiver with leopards, but Buz's leopard luck was out. Lions chased leopards off his kills. So did rhino. When we left Uganda, after three weeks, Buz had shot a lion – more or less accidentally, because it came unbidden to a leopard bait – but a large number of nonsmoking, nonscratching, nonsneezing, almost-nonbreathing sessions in leopard blinds paid off a double zero. When it looked as if Robinson would collect his *chui* and take a little of the strain off the camp, something unforeseen would happen, such as a leopard stalking him, instead of the other way round. Then another doleful carload of weary hunters would roll into camp without the gunshots and horn-blowing that herald a triumphant entry.

Finally the area played out. One of the things you know if you hunt Africa enough is exactly when an acre has had it. A hunt builds to a climax, and if the climax is unpunctuated by a gunshot, *kuisha* – finish. It's intangible, but somehow there is an air of defeat; the Africans are morose, the common game is spooked by too much wheeled activity, the guinea fowl and francolin disappear, the big stuff moves on, and leopards lose interest in kills. Darlene's positive thinking had intensified into a sort of voodoo, but the prospective leopard upon which she was casting her whammy was apparently doing some very strong negative thinking....

It is a mean, hard haul from camp to Kaabong and Moroto in Uganda, to Kitale in Kenya, then down the long hill until you come to a place called Kijabe, which means "place of the winds." If you turn right onto the lava track leading off Kijabe you will hit something called Narok, and if you keep right on going for a hundred bumpy miles you will eventually come to an escarpment standing bluffy over the Mara River, with the Trans Mara plateau sweeping west. It is as beautiful as the Karamojo country of Uganda is ugly.

This year it was especially lovely. There had been the first light scatter of rains, and everything was tender green. The migrating European storks were circling in vast vortexes of hundreds of thousands. The tsetse fly area of the southern Masai was seething with game, including one herd of ornery elephants that must have numbered 150. The southern Masai "tame" lions – almost personal pets of the game warden, Major Evelyn Temple-Boreham – were still rolling and tumbling around for the photographers. And to the southwest the Mara Triangle, which is National Parks now, was absolutely stiff with game – buffalo in the open on the velvety green glades, and vaster herds of common stuff than ever I saw. I felt sentimental and a little sad about all this closed country. I had hunted it seriously when it was open to shooting a dozen years ago.

We made a proper camp now, tucked into the green embrace of a folded hill just under the lip of the escarpment, and with the Mara River chuckling boisterously almost at our feet. There was a hippo trail with fresh tracks on it, and at night, when the fire leaped and snapped, the lions roared on the plains, the hyenas sang, and you could hear the leopards hunting up and down the Mara's banks.

"Now," said Mrs. Darlene Robinson, "Buz will get his leopard and I will have it for our eighth anniversary next week. *Won't I, darling?*" she said to her mate, and it was not a question.

"Yes," said her mate, who had just invested in another license – a full Kenya ticket with a leopard permit on top. At these prices he could have bought her a mink wall-to-wall. We went to work, hanging kills, building blinds. There were leopards up on top of the plateau, the natives told us, as well as plenty of impala and topi and waterbuck and a lot of water. It looked as though the big rains would be early this year, and the mornings were biting cold and wet at the bottom of the scarp. You didn't start to thaw until you hit the top and the sun sliced through the low clouds and misting rain.

Harry Selby and I were off doing most of the scouting. Harry Cabot was hunting buffalo with John Sutton, and Robinson was checking his leopard blinds with Jack Bousfield, the third pro, who was long on crocodiles but a little short on leopards. The country was pretty, all right, and we gave it a week's hard college try, but our leopard luck stayed sour.

Darlene had displayed very ladylike patience through all this, but now her Norse spirit began to emerge. One night she told us that she'd go along personally next morning to see if she couldn't speed up the process. As a further measure I cast a reasonably impressive witch doctor's spell, using an old human skull somebody had found. With Selby pitching petrol into the flames, we had quite a gaudy ceremony in the dark of the moon. Something had to give. We hoped it wouldn't be us.

Next morning Buz and Darlene accompanied by Bousfield and Muema, the seasoned-in-stone Wakamba gunbearer, went up the mountain in the dirty black before dawn to sit and shiver over one of the kills. They were a little late arriving in the Land Rover, and in the early gray light Muema saw a leopard jump down out of the bait tree and sneak off into a clump of bush. Bousfield jammed on the brakes and everyone got out. It was a very nice patch of bush – small, compact, isolated in the open. And it contained one very large male leopard.

Muema handed Robinson the .318 Westley Richards that had killed Robinson's big lion a couple of weeks before. Bousfield and Robinson went out in the clear, to one side of the bush, and Muema pulled the trick that comes only to the lucky. It's simple: If a leopard is occasionally dumb enough to run off and hide in a little piece of bush that is open on all sides, you throw sticks and stones at this bush. The leopard will depart and head for less noisy surroundings. So Muema threw sticks and stones.

The barrage evoked much snarling and growling inside, and when a particularly hefty stone hit the bush, the leopard fetched another angry growl and suddenly came out. He didn't fly out or burst out. He just came out and cantered across Robinson's bow, broad on, at a distance of less than fifty feet. He looked as big as a spotted horse, and as her spouse drew down on him Mrs. Darlene Robinson, watching from a safe seat in the Land Rover, mentally chose an effective costume for rug-sitting.

Then Buz drew down and squeezed, and the leopard kept moving, and Buz squeezed again and the leopard kept moving, and Buz yanked and the leopard went permanently away from there. Darlene had her eighth anniversary, but the rug was gone, the fire was out, and she was sitting lonely on the cold, cold floor.

The reason was quite simple. My .318, which Buz had been using, had no safety catch on it, for it had been fitted with a low-mounted scope, and the flip-up safety had to come off. The way you kept it "safe" was to leave the bolt half up. When you wanted to shoot, you hit the bolt handle with the heel of your hand and you were cocked and ready.

Robinson, in the almost paralyzing excitement of seeing a leopard boil out of a bush after the tedium of a month of blind-sitting, had somehow blundered. Perhaps the gunbearer had given him the gun with the bolt at half-mast and he'd forgotten to lock it home when the time came to shoot. Or – and this is more likely – he had been handed the gun with the bolt handle in firing position, had moved it up to safety, and when the leopard appeared, had forgotten to shove it down. It was the kind of thing that happens to all of us occasionally.

Happy anniversary, Mrs. Robinson! Buz was pale when he came to camp. And so was Darlene. They both held up pretty well, though. Nobody said much that night and everybody went to bed early, and the next day we gave it one more look and said to hell with it, we would go to the southern Masai and pitch a camp in a place near Ol Donya Rash, a favorite spot of mine where I had always found many respectable leopards.

We pitched our camp in the backyard of the Masai game warden, Major Temple-Boreham. It was a good location; being close to a main road you could get out if the rains fulfilled their ominously clouded threat. There were always leopards aplenty around its rock-strewn river, and over one way was Majimoto and Narrasura and leopards, and the other way, off the Loliondo forks, was a big Masai *manyatta* with great herds – and more leopards. Back to work we went, and now we enlisted the Major; he knows every animal in the Masai by a pet name, and most of the grass by the blade. All of us – three white hunters, me, scouts – got heavily into the leopard business.

A variety of things happened. Selby and I were working on an enormous cat which was breeding and which I almost, but not quite, shot three times. This one broke all the rules – feeding at 10 A.M. but not at dawn, coming back at noon but not at 5 P.M., not eating at night but waiting until we left at midday, and frustrating us to a point where Selby, in a fit of shrill exasperation, declared indignantly that, "This bloody leopard is behaving in a *most* unleopardlike manner." Two more leopards, male and female, were taunting us a mile away from the big Masai manyatta. The vultures we needed in our business wouldn't settle on an extra kill. Vultures we didn't need came and robbed baits we wanted to stay intact.

Temple-Boreham's pet lioness bit Darlene gently on the behind, a sort of affectionate gesture. Jack Bousfield's wife was having a baby in Tanganyika, so he had to leave and was replaced by a big Irish ex-Kenya police reservist named Liam Lynn, naturally known as Paddy. John Sutton had to go to Rhodesia, and the Cabots had to go to Boston. Virginia Ruark got dramatically sick – probably from leopard nerves – and had to be flown to Nairobi. Among other catastrophes, a tornado came and blew the camp down, and it poured endlessly with rain, washing out a bridge we'd have to cross.

And no leopard; the rains knocked off the feeding. The vehicles got stuck every time you moved them, and the loss of the Cabots and Sutton and Bousfield made a hole in our spirits. I flew Virginia into Nairobi and saw she was going to be all right. By that time the washed-out bridge had been repaired, and Selby came to collect me in a Land Rover. We drove back to the Masai campsite – and found it nearly flat again.

"Don't tell me we had another tornado," I said. "I can stand one. Two is too many. Where the hell *is* everybody?"

Juma, the headman, came up and rattled some very fast Coastal Swahili.

"He says they've taken a fly outfit, left us the camp, and gone off the Narrasura. They've got a big leopard feeding over there that the Major's game scouts say has been molesting the native women when they go to water. Also some *shauri a machawi* – witch doctor business. I don't quite understand."

"It's *all* witch doctor business," I grumbled. "Let's go see what's happening to the bottom kills."

It figured. The two cats feeding from the same tree had finished the bait animal, and I resolved then and there to kill my old gunbearer Metheke for not taking time to replace the kill before he went romping off to Narrasura. The other leopard – the enormous one I almost had a shot at three times – was still keeping his weird hours. Also it was pouring again. We went back to camp and crawled into bed in the soggy mess tent. I was sick of safari, and especially sick of leopards.

The troop came back next morning, bringing the sun with them. Buz Robinson had grown a solid five feet since I'd last seen him. Major Temple-Boreham's mustache was shooting sparks, and Paddy Lynn looked like a cartoon of Ireland triumphant. Darlene Robinson wore an I-told-you-so look. And they spilled seven feet, six inches of leopard skin out of the back of the Land Rover. A story went with it – a harrowing tale.

It seems that Paddy Lynn had encountered a witch doctor who told the piteous tale of a leopard so large that only a squad of Masai with six-foot spears could keep it from eating the native ladies when they went daily to the only waterhole in the area. The witch doctor had brewed up some magic and produced a miracle – Robinson, Lynn and Company, which now included the gallant Major. Having earned his fee, the witch doctor left the rest up to the majesty of law and order, in the person of the Major.

Now, as often as not, this sort of thing can be washed out as the product of an inflamed imagination. But Liam, Buz, Darlene, and the Major went to the waterhole, and lo, there were indeed the pugs of a very large male and the smaller tracks of his lady fair. Somebody shot a bait animal, then strung it into a tree and built a blind near the waterhole.

But meanwhile the witch doctor must have been brewing a little extra medicine. The leopard fed during the night and then spent the night in the blind! When the party made a morning approach to the bait they found fresh claw marks and coughed-up balls of impala hair. This evidently was a city-slicker leopard, one that had grown used to people and their habitation. As a result he could be as painfully easy or as painfully difficult to shoot as any maneater, depending on any whim he took. After leaving the blind, the natives reported, he had again driven the women from the waterhole. He and Darlene Robinson shared one thing – determination.

At noon Metheke went for a stroll and found that the leopard was watching his kill the easy way – by taking a light snooze in another tree about a hundred yards distant. Through the glasses you could see him sprawled on a limb high in the foliage, all four feet dangling and his long tail curved into a limp question mark. This was a wise guy. He could see a mile in all directions.

At about four that afternoon the unquenchable hunters stalked carefully into the blind. They sat silently for an hour, and then Metheke pinched Robinson's leg. The leopard was sitting in the blind behind them, gazing calmly at the inmates. They had stalked the blind carefully; the cat had just as carefully stalked them.

The leopard licked a whisker and bounded off into the bush before anybody could turn and shoot him. Paddy Lynn decided on the Irish gambit – talk loud and walk bold. The inmates of the blind began to gabble and strode bravely away in full view of the big puss in the bush. After all, he might as well get used to white people too.

Next morning the leopard was crunching happily away on a chunk of the impala that he had gnawed off and carried to the foot of the tree. He fed until daylight; then, just before shooting time, he lugged his full belly back into the bush, to lie there and sneer between belches.

Since the Masai have a nasty habit of stealing bait animals, this one had been strung in the tree with barbed wire. At 5:30 P.M. the hunters were in the blind again, and suddenly the leopard's big face and shoulders appeared in the fork near the kill. Buz was settling on him, ready to shoot as he reached out and gnawed at the kill. But then the cat ran afoul of some of the barbed wire, snarled, and leaped down to the ground out of sight A few minutes later he did a tightrope teeter up a wrist-thick liana, made a fast pass at the kill, ripping off a chunk, and leaped to the ground. He crouched in the grass and commenced to munch, again out of sight. All you could hear was *crunch*.

Then he made a mistake – sat up like a dog to look around and glare at the world. Robinson remembered this time to tuck the bolt handle into its cradle. The old .318 is an obedient gun and generally shoots where it's pointed. Robinson held on the leopard's shoulder, and Darlene finally had her rug. The Masai lugged the carcass back to the village, with the witch doctor holding its tail – politicians never do the tough work – and I believe the *pombe* flowed all that night.

Civilization was saved.

Today, in Denver, two beautiful little girls and one tiny boy romp on a seven-foot, six-inch leopard-skin rug with a head that grins malevolently in front of the fireplace. Darlene, their mother, looks on lovingly. For herself she now thinks that a large polar-bear rug of a certain blue-white tone might be more suitable. She looks speculatively at Buz, but what Buz is thinking, I have no idea.

"Grouse On The Dot" is Ruark's last and certainly his best piece on African bird-shooting. If his interest in big-game hunting was on the wane, as these later stories suggest, his love for hunting birds was not. As an inveterate bird shooter myself, I cannot read this story without some wistfulness and a wish to have a taste of it. I felt the same way the first time I read it, in *Field & Stream* November 1962. In writing as in other things, timelessness is a virtue.

Michael McIntosh

CHAPTER TWENTY

GROUSE ON THE DOT

T he only birds in the world who bother about time were prompt, as usual. We couldn't see them yet, but off in the clean-washed African sky there was a lazy, distant chuckle, which grew in volume. Now we could see the flight, like long strings of tiny ink dots spattered against the blue blotter of the sky.

The fellow with me looked at his watch. He shook his head and clucked appreciatively. "Nine o'clock. Right bang on the nose," he said. "They never miss unless it's overcast, and I suppose you've had your share of transportation trouble in bad weather, too. Man the artillery, chum – here they come!"

A birdy roar rose from who knows how many thousand thirsty throats as the flocks swarmed toward the tiny spot of water in this heat-smitten desert wasteland. Punctual to the point of suicide, the grouse that are not grouse at all had arrived for their morning drink.

The sand grouse – so-called because they are found in arid, open areas – are an offshoot of the stock that produced pigeons. There are sixteen known species, the smallest the size of a park pigeon and the largest as big as a ruffed grouse. They live in southern Europe, Asia, and Africa, and recently the U. S. Fish & Wildlife Service collected some of the birds from Southeast Asia for experimental release in parts of the United States with similar climate and terrain.

The birds are feathered like grouse: Their legs are furry clear to the toes and they are downy under their sleek feathers. Their coloring is mottled: quiet, tweedy combinations of buff, brown, black, chestnut, yellow, and off-white. They have long, pigeonlike wings and are strong fliers, but they hate trees poisonously and will neither perch nor roost in one. Neither will they drink on close-forested rivers.

During most of the day sand grouse are on the ground eating grass seeds and roots. The flights come in the morning and in some cases the evening, when, with their famous dependability, the birds head for their favorite waterholes. Their fidelity to time and place is an extraordinary virtue – but it may be more rewarding for the hunter than the grouse.

If you are shooting for the pot, and are murderously inclined, you can slay bushels of these birds just by waiting until a cloud of them swirls up over a watering place, either coming in to drink or arising afterward. But the sporting way is to take them by twos and fours and sixes, standing up in full view to scare them off the waterhole. When you put them up this way, they'll zoom away faster than a dove or wood pigeon in a hurry. Under these conditions the best wingshot will miss considerably more than he kills.

I've eaten sand grouse cooked about every way, and it's as tasty as any bird I know. The breast meat shades from russet red to white, with delicious red finger-sized fillets at the side. Each half breast of the little sand grouse that you find in cloudlike quantities in the more fiercely arid land is about the size of a whole quail breast. Four of these are enough to make a hungry man happy. Other species vary in size, of course, so you dish them out accordingly.

Apart from its attention to time, very little is known about the habits of the bird. Nobody knows exactly how far they fly daily to water. They have the back-raked wings which make flight easy on themselves, and can climb like jets, glide, swoop like a bee swarm, or stiffen their primary pinions and make a whistling dive like a Stuka.

Once, during a period of extreme drought in Tanganyika I found a waterhole by following flights of sand grouse from as far as I could see behind me to as far as I could see before me before I lost them. The waterhole was the only one in an area of more than a hundred square miles, and the birds got there every morning at a quarter to eight. (I got there at 7:30.)

In the years I have been going to Africa, the sand grouse has given me more shooting pleasure than any other creature, furred or feathered. He is dependable in the size of his flocks: No amount of shooting or trapping seems to thin his numbers or make him shy, and the varmints that get him on the ground don't seem to make much of

a dent in his numbers. This in itself is rare. The sand grouse is supposed to mate for life, and the hen usually lays a clutch of only three eggs, nestling in a shallow hole scratched out of the rocky ground. You would expect chicks born under such circumstances to be more speedily adaptable than most birds. They are not.

One African authority who has attempted to raise them says they are much more stupid than other game birds he has reared successfully. They are covered at birth by their mother's down, against the sudden decline of desert temperature at nightfall. The parents take endless trouble to feed them, and the mothers even go so far as to fan out their wings to shelter the babies from the broiling sun. The man, who tried to feed the chicks such dainties as white ants and grass seeds, says they are hopeless and die after a week or so. The natural supposition is that in the wild state only the hardiest survive.

The sand grouse is purely terrestrial and will perch for protection on nothing, although some species have a fully developed back toe. They flutter out a little shallow dent in the dust or sand and turn in for the night, easy meat for the roving jackal or bat-eared fox. They can be netted at the water's edge, as the Japanese net ducks, and a few times I have seen them get their feet stuck in gluey mud as they drink, miring themselves hopelessly as they fought the air in a blur of wingbeats. Still, their numbers do not seem to diminish.

Nobody has ever proved that the same birds drink twice a day, although it's pretty definitely known that the majority of the sixteen species drinks in the morning. The tiny Lichtenstein, the four-banded, and the double-banded grouse drink from late afternoon through dusk and sometimes into the dark, which makes for tricky shooting against the skyline as they drop in like darting silhouettes of snipe.

I have never heard an explanation of their attachment to one particular waterhole, which they will repeatedly fly to under normal dry conditions, ignoring another stretch of terrain close by even though the drinking conditions are similar. You can repeatedly scare them off a favored spot and they will not bother to change places – even to save their lives.

Another characteristic I have noted is the habit of some species to travel in groups of three. I have often watched these threesomes either flying high, crouched down in the desert sand, or coming in to water. Invariably they arrive and leave together, and I can only conclude that the Third Man is either a friend of the family who's lost its mate, an unmarried member of the last clutch, or just a schemer waiting a chance to bust up the happy home.

If much is inexplicable about the sand grouse, you can at least be sure that they will be around – probably always – in tremendous numbers. The only times they are not reliable is during the wet season, when the plains are dotted with potholes, the *lugas* – dry river beds – are in flood, and every waterhole is brimming.

It is very difficult to say where the shooting is finest in Kenya, Tanganyika, and Uganda – the Africa with which I am most familiar. I'd say there are probably more sand grouse to be had around a place called Lysamis or Lasames, a dry river bed in northern Kenya, than any other place in the world, although I had some incredible shooting at another *luga* at Porr. And it's hard to leave out a dam near Ikoma or a place on the Great Ruaha River in Tanganyika; a certain sandy stretch around Lake Rudolf, on the Kenya-Ethiopia border; a place called Ol Donya Rash, on the Loita plains of the southern Masai in Kenya – or, for that matter, wherever it's dry enough to command the epithet "camel country."

But perhaps the fullest shooting day of my life, if it's mixed-bag gunning you fancy, revolved around the sand grouse of Ikoma. On the vast, short-grassed plains of the Ikoma area we had come on occasional patches of squatting grouse and walked up a few birds, shooting them going away. This was tricky, for the sand grouse seems to have an uncanny ability to judge the power of your shot, and manages to take off just far enough out of killing range to tempt you into a shot that usually results in nothing more edible than a vapor trail of tailfeathers.

I am accorded to be a little nuts by the natives, who scorn any bird smaller than a spur-wing goose. They tap their heads and smile pityingly, calling me *"Bwana Ndege"* – the bird man. But crazy or not, I wanted to find where those grouse drank, so one morning I sent the serious hunters off to worry with leopards, lions, and buffalo, while I stayed put about thirty miles from camp with a gunbearer and a Land Rover. The grouse *had* to be drinking somewhere. I aimed to wait for the big flight and follow it as fast as I could shove that Rover over the pig holes and sharp rocks that hide under the knee-high grasses.

Along about 7:30 I heard a far-off *chuckle-chuckle*, and soon the sky started to speck with long strings of the water-bent birds. They were high in the pale blue, gaining altitude as flock joined flock. Then they formed a pattern and headed for water. With very little regard to life, limb, or tires, the boy and I took off after the flight.

I shaped a rough path in their general direction, and when they finally disappeared I kept on in as straight a line as I could, considering that African plains are strewn with hills, lonely mountains, old thorn orchards, and occasional patches of unlikely forest. The farther I went, the more game I saw – zebra and wildebeest, Thomson's and Grant's gazelle, a herd of fourteen buffalo bulls, and two of the finest twin male lions I have ever seen.

"Simba, bwana," the gunbearer said, pointing, and I said "Damn Simba – I'm looking for birds." The lions would have to wait for another day. The mad bwana was looking for little birds.

The last grouse were just leaving when I found their waterhole, and I felt like Balboa getting his first glimpse of the Pacific. This area had been closed during the Mau Mau emergency, and I hadn't hunted it since 1951. In that interval they had built a big dam to accommodate the increase of cattle as the Wa-Ikoma tribes pressed deeper into the game country. That dam held a dozen acres of water. It had nice sandy lips, and a fine, unobstructed plain all around. We had been hunting off in another direction, and hadn't run across it before.

The plain was seething with animals and vast flocks of grazing Egyptian geese. The water itself was dotted with birds – wood ducks, tree ducks, knob-billed geese, black mallards, whistling teal, and brown-and-gray nondescripts I'd never seen before. These ducks had no place else to go, and seemed never to have heard a shotgun or investigated its dangerous potential. Most important, the sandy shore was scarred with a million sand-grouse tracks.

It was too late for the grouse, but I had the gunbearer take his *panga* and build me a shoddy thornbush blind about fifty yards from the tracks. A high, turfed ridge that formed a protecting wall for the dam would make an admirable progressive series of additional shooting butts; I merely had to hide on its far side, away from the water. I did not shoot then, but the next morning I was back early with our light aluminum boat, and we were open for business.

It is difficult to describe that day. Perhaps 100,000 sand grouse began to come in – groups of big yellow-throats settling on the prairie before taking their walks to the water, blackfaces coming straight in to drink in smaller groups. As they swirled and swooped they achieved the thickness of the rolling banks of weaverbirds, which appear to be a tornado, so thick is their flight.

Crouched behind my sketchy little boma of thorn branches, sitting on an old ammo box, I unlimbered a pair of shotguns. There was no necessity to brown the bunch, although I had about thirty mouths to feed, and an African consumes small birds in a bite, like peanuts. In the first big flocks, even if you picked a bird at the edges, your shot trail was apt to down half a dozen, and if you shot in the middle, the sky would fall.

After a moment I got out of the blind and stood erect. The first shots broke up the big packs, and also raised the squatting yellow-throats, the big boys. And then the fun began. They came over crossways, straight-away, angling, high, low – every skeet possibility was repeatedly present. The only bother was picking out the pairs, the trios, the sixes, and eights, to avoid killing a cartload with each barrel.

A really big series of flights will give a serious shooter enough variety of shots to turn his shoulder blue and his ears deaf. I quit on a rough hundred, figuring that three birds apiece were plenty for the hors d'oeuvres. Besides, there were those ducks and geese, which would go well for a main course.

I had a beer while we picked up and moved away to let the birds drink and to collect our game. There was no difficulty on the pickup. The boys had become like trained bird dogs, and one of the more endearing traits of a sand grouse is that he does not run when wounded. He sits, and while the camouflage is so perfect I've stepped on birds without seeing them, my bunch of hawk-eyed Africans rarely left anything edible on the ground.

The ducks and geese had roused from the water but were returning to light again, as they had no other place to go. We launched the little boat to pick up cripples and keep the ducks moving, and I sent one of the boys out to circle the Egyptian goose pastureland in the jeep to stir up the hordes.

Now it was all pass-shooting as the ducks and geese arose, flew out over land, circled, and came back to water again. They came in quantity, not so thickly massed as the grouse, of course, but thick enough and frequent enough to smother you in waterfowl – shooting undreamed of outside a private preserve.

I would feel apologetic about taking thirty or forty ducks and geese except that I had long been conscious of the African appetite and knew that everything but the bills and feet would be eaten. Even so, half-a-lorry load of waterfowl bruised my conscience as well as my biceps, and although I had made less than a tiny dent in the multiple thousands, I wouldn't do it again. Next day I gave my serious hunters one big shoot, and then imposed a limit of a couple of dozen each per day. It was really more fun to watch the aerobatics, and occasionally try a long, semi-impossible shot and marvel when a bird actually tumbled out of the blue fifty or sixty yards away.

For mixed-bag shooting that spot really was tops. But there was another day on a dry riverbed called Porr, in Kenya's scorching Northern Frontier District, that was even more memorable.

It was very hot, even as early as 9 o'clock in the morning. We were shooting in shorts and shoes at the grouse as they slanted down to drink amongst the herds of Turkana and Samburu camels and goats that were sharing the little water that was there. One side of the *luga* was rimmed by mighty rocks, and we leaned against these, snap-shooting swiftly at birds that were on us before a man could raise a gun, providing climbing, going away, and crossing shots. Up and down the twisty *luga* came big blue pigeons in pairs, flushed from the palms by the fusillade. Once I saw a peregrine falcon powerdive after a high-falling grouse, and I would swear the hawk was logging 200 miles an hour when he screamed out of the sky after that plummeting bird. His outstretched talons caught the grouse no more than ten feet off the ground, and he braked, turned, and climbed in as beautiful a demonstration of controlled speed as I will ever see.

I may remember that time so well because I made the longest on-purpose passing shot of my life (I must have led that grouse twenty yards). But maybe it was just being on the *luga* in the peace of the morning, knowing that whatever happened in the rest of the day, it had gotten off to as good a start as possible.

There may be sportier shooting, which I doubt, but I never knew another grouse or a duck that cared what time he arrived, or was faithful to a patch of wood or water, or showed up in such hordes to offer such a variety of shooting. The sand grouse may not be a grouse at all, but for my money he's as fine a target as any pedigreed bird you can name.